THE LAST OF
THE WAR HORSES

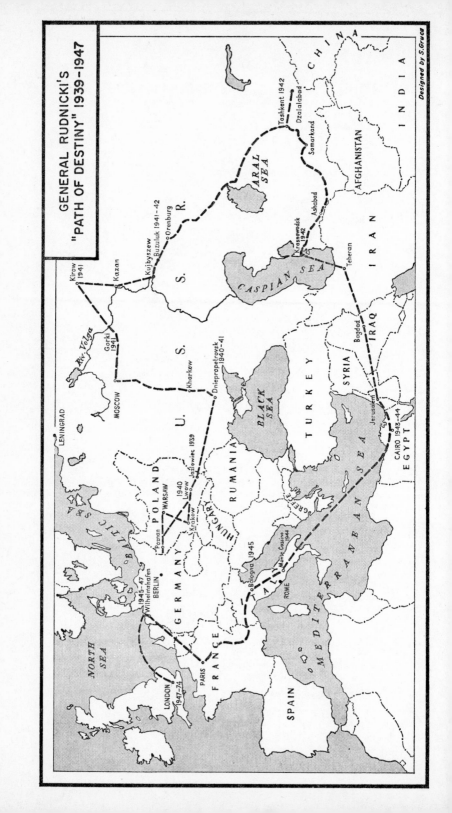

GENERAL RUDNICKI'S
"PATH OF DESTINY" 1939-1947

Designed by S.Gruca

The Last of
The War Horses

by
K. S. RUDNICKI, DSO

Illustrated with maps and
with eight pages of photographs

BACHMAN & TURNER

LONDON

© K. S. Rudnicki 1974
First published 1974
by Bachman & Turner
45 Calthorpe Street WC1X 0HH

ISBN 0 85974 013 7

Printed by
The Barleyman Press, Bristol
and bound at the Pitman Press, Bath

Contents

7

LIST OF ILLUSTRATIONS

ACKNOWLEDGEMENT

My thanks are due to Mr W. K. Geringer d'Oedenberg
for his kind help in preparing my manuscript in the
English language.

CHAPTER 1

The Path

I SET OUT on the path at Jazlowiec on 6th August, 1939. Naturally I did not realise it; I did not even know then that there was a path. Today I am quite sure of it.

It was the traditional path trodden by our Polish ancestors for many generations.

On this path were reminders of the battles fought on our native soil, of conspiracies, and of deportations to Siberia, with the long Gehenna of prisoners and with the modern *kibitki* (police vans). It stretched out long ago to strange countries at the foot of the Pamir mountains, where a legend of a far-away Poland was still vividly pulsating; then to Persia, Irak of the Thousand-and-One-Nights tales; to Palestine and the Holy Land; and to the Pyramids, erected by the Pharaohs; it was followed by our Italian campaign, where one could still almost perceive the marks of the marching of Dabrowski's legions, who fought there in the Napoleonic campaign; and finally it reached Germany, reviving echoes of problems with which Kniazie-wicz was faced as Commander of Napoleon's Polish Rhine Legion.

A path glowing with life, storms, blood, people and striking events. A truly traditional Polish path, and endless, not yet leading back to Jazlowiec.

How odd that we should have set out on it with the customary ritual, according to the best old traditions, yet completely sub-consciously. Perhaps it was an atavistic impulse that prompted us, the 9th Lancers from Malopolska (South-Eastern Poland), while on manoeuvres near Buczacz, to knock at the gates of the Convent of the Sisters of the Immaculate Conception and crave leave to offer an *ex-voto* to Our Lady in Jazlowiec.

Who first thought of it? It really does not matter. It was a common

11

impulse, full of cavalry tradition, reminiscent of the romanticism of Sienkiewicz's historic novels, pulsating in our hearts through the influence of our natural surroundings.

How, by Jove, escape sentimentalism when 600 horses are stamping behind you on a Podolian track—passing by canyons glittering with silver dew on green hazelnut trees, blackberries and weeds, and crossing stubble as far as your eye can reach, where innumerable straddled stooks rest, their loose sheaves bent over to the ground by the weight of the heavy wheat crop!

How escape an incorrigible romanticism when, after passing the town of Jazlowiec and having reached the plateau, you see in front the canyon of the Jazlowczyk river, feel your sabre under the saddle panel, and perceive on the right the ruins of the old castle of the Princes Jazlowiecki, at its feet the monastery, covered with shingle, grey with age!

And what shall we say about the charming Sisters? Their blue-and-white gowns almost form part of the surrounding landscape. And what about their strange, unique qualities? They are like Vestals, filled with chivalrous virtues, who have stubbornly established themselves on this old Tartarian track, used by Eastern hordes from time immemorial as an approach to the frontiers of the Polish Commonwealth. Once, when there were no longer strong walls, or even any guns to mount on them, they decided to replace the walls—romantic souls! From faraway lands they brought a white statue of Our Lady, dressed, like themselves, in a blue gown, and gave her the name of "Our Miraculous Lady of Jazlowiec". Like knights of old they stopped there, protecting her, on the track—the last bastion of chivalry! And they always watched over the Podolian Lancer regiments—especially the 14th Lancers of Jazlowiec, which had founded its fame, and their own, in 1919 during an attack on the fields of Jazlowiec. No wonder these nuns seem to live in a spiritual community unlike any known elsewhere.

We were of the same blood as they, the same as Podolia, as the Tartarian track; we realised our duties in the same way.

It seemed to us quite natural, at the time, when a heavy thunderstorm was gathering momentum on the outskirts of our country, to ask Our Lady at Jazlowiec to guide our steps and take us under her protection. And so we did, on this early August morning.

The ceremony itself was short, but nevertheless impressive, thanks to the special request of one of the nuns. Sister Lauretta, the gatekeeper, told us that our heavy machine-guns should be placed in position in the watch-tower of the old castle, and should, at the appropriate time, fire several salvoes. Our suggestion that the roar of machine-guns would not befit the quiet of the Convent, did not prevail. "There must be loud bangs," she said; and so there were!

The Regiment formed up in a hollow square, the squadrons in double rank, the regimental Colours and the trumpeters on the right flank. The Mother Superior took the salute, and then I made a short speech. I begged pardon for the Lancers coming to Our Lady covered in dust, for they had had a long ride, and they felt they were not coming to strangers but to their own folk. Besides, Our Lady was used to trumpets, drums and battles. Since time immemorial she had accompanied the Polish cavalry into battle and they had her image, even that day, on their Colours: she could not refuse to protect them. We handed over our *ex-voto* to the roar of our machine-guns, and continued our round in Podolia.

An urgent recall of the Regiment to our peace-time quarters in Trembowla then reached us in the Miodobory Hills. From this time onwards, events moved with lightning speed, and the path carried us on with all its power of seduction.

On the 27th August, 1939, at 5 p.m., we received a telegram ordering the mobilisation of the Regiment. It was brought by the usual postman, riding his bicycle. We received a telephone warning by the postmaster that in a few minutes we should get news of "top importance". Everybody in the small town, from the Town Clerk to the postmaster, knew what was brewing, but we tried to appear casual: mobilisation is a secret matter.

The duty officer, Lieut. Zelenski, was, as chance would have it, walking in front of the gate of our barracks. Major Z. Elsner, the officer responsible for the mobilisation of the Regiment, had for several months been working at the complicated details, and these were already filed in pigeon-holes and locked up in iron cases. He was now sitting quietly at his desk. In the barracks one could hear the jingling of chains by which the horses were attached to posts for their ritual grooming.

To facilitate complete fulfilment of the routine regarding the mystery of mobilisation, I was waiting in my flat for the expected telegram which the duty officer had to hand over to me, as was laid down in the "Plan", from which none of us would dare to deviate.

I could not deprive the duty officer of the pleasure of carrying out that rarest of his duties, studied and practised so often during war games: the mobilisation of the Regiment.

13

At last the dice were cast. The telegram giving the code word read as follows:—

Readiness—yellow—ordered.

We knew this order very well from the files in the iron cabinets. It meant that the Regiment should stand by at 36 hours' notice to entrain.

During this time we were supposed to receive several hundred recruits from our reserve, and as many horses; we had to issue completely new equipment from store, or to complete the equipment already issued and reckoned to be part of our field equipment; to organise our regimental transport; and to carry out many of the "one-minute" duties foreseen by our thirty-six hours' continuous turmoil.

I began with an officers' meeting. I ordered that "A" hour should be at 6 p.m., and I finished my address by the phrase, traditional in our Regiment, which everybody expected to hear: "You are responsible for the honour of our Regimental Colours." This was a repetition of the words uttered in 1920 by Lieut.-Col. Dunin Borkowski, the then Commanding Officer of the Regiment, when dying on the battlefield by the river Horyn.

Mobilisation went smoothly. The first reserve lancers joined the Regiment in the second hour and were followed by many others. The atmosphere was splendid. Everything went according to plan, with the exception of obtaining the extra horses, for the commissions for them were behind schedule and could not keep pace with the time-table. A few quick orders restored the situation, and soon the squadrons, increased to their war strength, left the barracks, one after the other, to take up their quarters in neighbouring villages. The recently-issued armour-piercing rifles, two to a platoon, were a novelty to us. They looked formidable, and were very heavy and difficult to strap to saddles.

At last the final parade was over and we began to entrain, railway transports leaving one after the other. Only the men's families remained in Trembowla—poor, frightened, families, herded together, and filled with a presentiment of what would soon happen to them.

Our transports went through Cracow-Czestochowa to the west. We started to detain on the 1st September near Nekla, already exposed to enemy air attacks. The officer in charge of the detrainment of the Podolian brigade told us that the war had already begun and that we formed a part of General Kutrzeba's "Poznan" Army.

Our concentration was confined to the woods in the area Wagowo-

Czachniki, near Gniezno. We had to reach it immediately. Full of confidence, we started going up to the line.

To begin with, something occurred which, perhaps, to most people would be completely meaningless—but how sweet it was, and how much in line with the tradition of Podolian romantics with sabres under the panels of their saddles! I could not possibly omit this story.

After we had detrained and were riding through the forests towards Gniezno, I decided to drive ahead in our regimental jeep with Captain Juszczak, my A.D.C. It was a beautiful morning. We were full of youth and buoyancy. A brisk breeze blew over our heads, erasing the memory of the troubles we had experienced in the barracks with the mobilisation and other peace-time nuisances. We were ready to forget Podolia, Jazlowiec, and all the rest of our "yesterday"— looking forward with all the eagerness of our lancer mentality to the "tomorrow".

We had but one thought—that we would not disappoint our commanders—we, the 9th Lancers from Malopolska. But our past— Podolia, Jazlowiec—was brought back to our attention in no time.

Just as we were passing through the terrified Nekla, we suddenly realised how hungry we were, remembering that for the last few days we had had no time for food. We stopped our jeep at the first café encountered, and all three of us, including our driver, Cpl. Jakiello, strolled in.

I went first. As I entered the door, the sound of our regimental march came from the loudspeaker of the wireless set—as in days of old, when the commanding officer was met by his trumpeters sounding the regimental march! Obviously it was a recording of regimental marches by the Warsaw wireless station, played to stimulate the fighting spirit of the country on this first day of war. But what a coincidence! That they should play the 9th Lancers' March just at the very moment when members of the Regiment, with their Colonel, entered the door of a café—entered by chance on the first day of their mission to fulfil the first duty assigned to them in the battle!

No wonder we stood speechless from emotion. From sheer habit we stood to attention until the last notes of our march faded away. Silently we looked at each other, amazed. Jakiello spoke first:

"Sir, it is Our Lady of Jazlowiec who sends us this message. She takes us under her protection. Hurrah!"

I did not say a word, but our Podolia came back to my mind, and I thought that Jakiello was not such a stupid boy if thus quickly he could find a key to the mystery. Also, he convinced us: we felt released from our worries, and, after a plentiful meal, we drove cheerfully ahead.

On our way we stopped in Gniezno, where the Army Headquarters were billeted. It was something I felt I must do.

Many times during the last few years, I had helped General Kutrzeba in organising and conducting war games in Gniezno for the General Staff, when he was getting ready to assume his actual responsibilities and command; so I felt I had to see him again.

In those days I had been a lecturer in the Staff College, and thus a close colleague of the General's. Today, as a regimental commander, I was only a little cog in his strategic Army machine, and very little concerned with the command on such a high level; but my incorrigible curiosity took the upper hand. I wanted to grasp the situation and the organisation, which so vividly occupied my mind. I thought that one glimpse of my expert eye would reveal many secrets to me, which eventually might be of some use.

We easily found the Army H.Q. in a school building on the outskirts of the town. When far off I spotted the General's figure. He was walking in the school yard, as usual smiling and apparently calm, but I could detect the deep anxiety which overpowered him— he could not conceal it from me who knew him so well. It did not surprise me. This profoundly intelligent and able officer, being one of the best informed generals as to our situation, realised only too well the real limitations of our resources. How pleased I was then that I was in command on such a low level!

General Kutrzeba was obviously pleased to see me. He enquired about the journey and the state of our preparations. He told me that our Brigade had originally been intended to join General J. Rommel's Army "Lodz", and that he was very pleased with the change. He told me: "I need some cavalry. You will take over the duties of covering the manoeuvre; you will go as far as Miedzychod." Then he called me aside and, with deep anxiety, said: "You know the general plan of action of my Army: it is very similar to the one we have so often discussed in our war games. You realise that we have to retreat, and to retreat deep into our country. It won't be an easy manoeuvre in the conditions now prevailing. We need really good soldiers. Will you do it?"

This question was in fact the answer to what I wanted to know, and it was fundamental and dramatic. I did not dare to reply, for a reply could only have been non-committal and trivial. It was not a question addressed to the C.O. of the 9th Lancers, or any other unit of his Army—we knew what they were like. It was thrown into the face of Fate by a man full of anxiety, but highly conscious of the situation.

The General knew well what the already prevailing conditions were, and he realised what they would soon be.

The concentration and regrouping of the Army were still progressing when the enemy started offensive activities, which meant he took the initiative before we were ready. This would necessitate improvisation, which, in view of the enemy's air superiority, would undoubtedly end in chaos. Should we be able to go through with it—successfully covering our retreat, and carrying out the defensive manoeuvre to the end, so that somewhere about the lakes of Mogilno or Znin our counterblow could come into being?

We were facing a defensive manoeuvre under continuous air attacks, with short supplies of food and munitions, and with indifferent liaison. Was it really feasible? But the achievements of the Army were dependent on it.

Such seemed to me to be the General's train of thought, prompted by the anxiety implied in the tragic question "Will you do it?"

I was not surprised that the General asked it; it was characteristic of him. He had always had an unusual capacity for getting at the core of a subject while others were still talking round it. In such grave situations every question seems to be of equal importance, but there is always the most critical one, on which final decision must depend. It is often difficult, however, to spot which *is* the most important. In soldiering, this capacity is called "a gift".

The question I heard was sufficient answer for me, more than satisfying my curiosity. I could not discover anything further at Army H.Q. I took my leave of the General and drove into the forest to join my Regiment.

The morale of the Regiment was splendid. They told me about a German 'plane shot down over their heads by a Polish fighter, and asked me when we should start our offensive. The atmosphere was as it should be.

Deep anxiety may gnaw at the Army Commander, but to us in the Regiment everything must appear simple and clear-cut.

We started energetically to repair any last apparent shortcomings. At first, with farmers of German origin, brought to this area during Prussian occupation from the west of Germany, we exchanged a few of our horses for taller and stronger ones. Some of our conscripted Podolian farm-horses were too small, and they died under the weight

17

of the saddles. We had time to adjust the harness issued after the mobilisation, which previously we had not had time to do, and soon we were ready for what was to come. Then we received orders from the Brigade H.Q.

CHAPTER 2

The Enemy Invisible

WE MOVED on the 3rd September at dusk. We formed a part of the Brigade under the command of Colonel Strzelecki, consisting also of the 6th and 14th Lancers and the 6th Battery of Horse Artillery. We were supposed to release the 14th Infantry Division, which was still west of Poznan, executing her covering manoeuvre. Our 9th Lancers were ordered to release a battalion of the National Defence Force near Wysogotow (nine miles north-west of Poznan) and to reconnoitre towards Szamotuly, Zbaszyn and Miedzychod.

We passed Poznan before dawn. The streets were deserted, although nobody was asleep. Many people peered through slightly opened doors and windows, lured by the clatter of hooves of the horses on the pavements. No lights were to be seen. If anybody asked a question, it was in a whisper—probably in order not to attract the enemy air force! The town was obviously terrified by yesterday's air-raid, and evidently the people were anxious to know in which direction the troops were moving—to the west or to the east. Everything depended on this, and the town endeavoured to believe it would not be surrendered. The Regiment, therefore, was met with subdued applause: we were riding to the west!

We reached Wysogotow at dawn. Luckily the ground was enveloped in a slight mist, thus covering us and the released battalion.

This was very useful, because overhead we could hear the incessant droning. Flight after flight they flew to the east. Shortly after, we heard gloomy sounds of nearby explosions, thunderously falling, or the indistinct bubbling of the faraway ones.

Soon, "conditions expected to come into being" began to materialise.

Immediately after our arrival, as ordered, we sent out reconnais-

MAP OF POLAND IN 1939 AND POLISH FIRST LINE DEFENCE ARMIES

THE GERMANS STRUCK ON THE 1st SEPTEMBER
THE RUSSIANS ON THE 17th SEPTEMBER

LATVIA

LITHUANIA

WILNO

Riv. Niemen

GERMANY

DANZIG

EAST PRUSSIA

"POMORZE" A.

BYDGOSZCZ

"NAREW" GR.

BARANOWICZE

BIALYSTOK

"MODLIN" A.

Riv. Narew

POZNAN

GNIEZNO

Nekla

"POZNAŃ" A.

Riv. Warta

Modlin

Molkinia

WARSAW

BRZESC

PINSK

Riv. Prypec

U.S.S.R.

KALISZ

LODZ

"ŁÓDŹ" A.

P O L A N D

Riv. Visfula

Riv. San

Riv. Bug

"KRAKÓW" A.

KRAKOW

PRZEMYSL

LWOW

TREMBOWLA

CZECHO

"KARPATY" A.

Jazlowiec

- S L O V A K I A

SCALE

0   50   100   150   200 km

H U N G A R Y

R U M A N I A

Designed by S.Gruca

sances towards Zbaszyn, Miedzychod and Szamotuly. They were supposed to reach the frontier and find out the position. It was a heavy duty entrusted to them. In the fulfilment of this task they would have to ride over ninety miles without a break. When could we expect the first report from them? Again, the horse was their only means of liaison. It did not look very promising.

Nevertheless, the reconnaissances carried our their duties. The first reports arrived about noon—by the car transporting police officers, by private motor-cycle, even by telephone, for the postal telephone lines were still in use.

In the evening we had quite a clear picture of the situation. It appeared that in our sector, from Zbaszyn to the north, as far as the river Notec, there were no important movements. Rather, the refugees maintained that heavy motorised columns drove north of the Notec, from the west to the east, apparently in the direction of the Tuchola Forest and of Bydgoszcz. It looked as if the enemy had by-passed the "Poznan" Army and directed his attack against the Pomeranian Army, outflanking us from the north. We did not know what was happening south of us.

We thought we could not do very much in our present situation, and new orders arriving on the 5th at dawn were met with "full understanding" and even with relief.

But we were ordered to recall our reconnaissances immediately, and to march by day back towards Gniezno. And we were not very pleased with this.

There were difficulties in assembling our reconnaissances, and we envisaged the tremendous effort of such a long ride. We did not like the idea of marching in day-time, and were not in the least pleased to pass Poznan in bright daylight. Not only would we be exposed to attacks by the German air force, still buzzing over our heads, but, obviously, we should not be warmly acclaimed by the local population. Marching to the east would denote we were retreating. The order to blow up the bridge on the Warta completely stunned us, as it was in the very centre of the town: we felt that this would cause us to lose face in Poznan and that after the war no 9th Lancer would dare to show his face there.

In spite of our doubts, we carried out the orders received precisely, and before dusk we were back in the forests surrounding Gniezno.

But the surrounding landscape by then had been completely changed. Masses of refugees from Poznan thronged the main roads and lanes; in the evening they were so dense that they formed an uninterrupted chain. They drove in carts and carriages; they walked, drawing hand-carts and barrows loaded with bundles.

Separated units of the 14th Infantry Division, groups of police officers, frontier guards, Customs officers, etc., could only with difficulty find their way through the stream of refugees.

We were witnessing a gigantic exodus of the population. All the inhabitants of the western part of the Poznan province were escaping to the east. If the stream of refugees did not stop, and the same haunting fear obsessed the eastern part of the province, then the situation would become threatening, and all movements of forces or supplies would be endangered.

We tried to persuade them to stop, but always received the same answer—they were escaping because of orders issued by the Warsaw wireless station. We were unable then to ascertain whether these orders were *bona fide* or only a German hoax: but even had we known the truth it would not have mattered.

How could one dream of influencing refugees when the mob was on the verge of panicking? One could not blame them. Round about one could see the glare of fires caused by bombardment: Gniezno was in flames. The perpetual droning of 'planes carrying their loads of bombs, or returning empty, was devastating. From time to time, unexpectedly, a German fighter released a burst from his machine-gun, sowing bullets along the roads. After dusk one could hear single rifle shots or short bursts of fire from sub-machine guns. This time, perhaps, it was the activity of the fifth column.

In this confusion it was difficult to grasp the situation: so many contradictory reports and rumours—about treason, landed parachutists, Germans disguised as civilians, etc.—were whispered; even the stoutest heart could be affected by them.

New orders now reached us. Together with our Brigade, we had to return further to the east towards Sepolno, covering from the west the regrouping of units of the Army.

We were ordered to burn on our way all stacks and barns with crops, and to drive the cattle to the east. Only a deserted and devastated country was to be left to the Germans.

I do not know who issued this order, in imitation of Kutuzov's famous scorched-earth policy. But we immediately recognised red tape in it. The order was probably prompted by extreme nervousness, and it was definitely impossible to carry out. It was quite unfeasible to drive herds of cattle along overcrowded roads. I think only a few stacks were burned on our way, and in my opinion it was wrong to do even that.

We moved the same night of the 5th/6th September, and by dawn we were hidden in forests near Strzelno. During the next night we passed Mogilno and Kleszczow, and on the early morning of the 7th we stopped near Sempolno.

What we saw during these three consecutive days' march seemed to corroborate the "conditions expected to come into being", as predicted by our Army Commander.

The population of the eastern part of the Poznan province had begun its trek amid bombardment and conflagrations, jamming roads and interrupting Army units and transports.

Somehow we managed to go ahead, as we mostly rode across country. No supplies were delivered to us, so we had to live off the land. Our transport and stores had stuck somewhere on their way. We had no field-cookers. It was quite impossible to form a rear-guard, and there was no necessity for it, as the enemy did not follow us, nor had we contact with him.

Though our horses and lancers were exhausted, we were raging with the frustration of impotence. We knew something was collapsing —something had gone wrong, and we could not help it. It dawned upon us that the same thing might be happening all over the country; if so, what would be our fate?

Placed thus, we would have preferred to plunge into a deadly battle, but that was impossible—there was nobody to fight! We had no contact with the enemy.

At last, however, some feeble shadows began to loom on the horizon.

CHAPTER 3

Enemy Encounters

IT WAS ON the 8th September that I was ordered to attend a meeting with General S. Grzmot Skotnicki, C.O. of the Pomeranian Cavalry Brigade.

We were told that his Brigade was transferred from the Pomeranian Army to the strength of our Army: it was no more a full-strength Brigade. What remained was barely a combined regiment commanded by Col. Jastrzebski, consisting of remnants from all the other regiments. The Brigade had sustained colossal losses in battles, north of the Notec, with German forces, of which we had heard from our reconnaissances while still in the Poznan area. It was clear that the war was a war to the death.

General Skotnicki did not show signs of depression, although he had lost almost his whole Brigade. He was in good form and composed.

I also met there our Brigadier, Col. Liszko from the 6th Lancers, Col. Godlewski from the 14th Lancers, and the C.O. from the 6th Horse Artillery; together with a few officers from the Brigade and Army staff.

The General intimated to us the intention of starting an offensive. During the night of 9th/10th September, two infantry divisions were to execute a surprise attack, striking from the area of Leczyca, southbound towards Ozorkow, on the flank and rear of German forces, to stop any movement towards Warsaw. Two cavalry brigades would take part in this manoeuvre—the Wielkopolska (Poznan) Brigade of General R. Abraham on the left flank of this Infantry Group, and our Podolian Brigade, reinforced by the remnants of the Pomeranian Brigade, under General Skotnicki, on the right flank.

The basis of the activities of our Brigade was the river Ner near

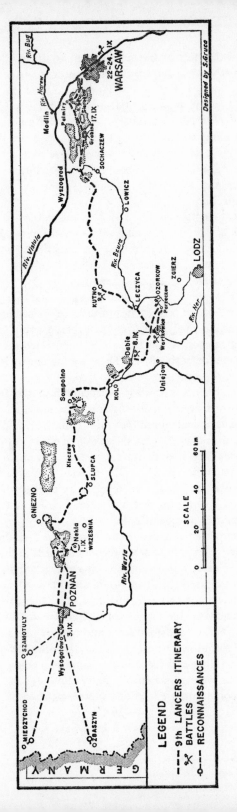

Designed by S.Gruca

GERMANY

MIEDZYCHOD ○ ○ SZAMOTULY
○ Wysogotow
3.IX
POZNAN
○ ZBASZYN

GNIEZNO ○
○ Nekla
1.IX ○ WRZESNIA
Kleczew
Rw. Warta
SLUPCA ○

Sompolno

KOLO ○
Dabie
8.IX
Uniejow ○

KUTNO
LECZYCA
OZORKOW ○
Wartkowice Parzeczew
ZGIERZ ○
Rw. Ner.
LODZ

Rv. Bzura
LOWICZ ○

SOCHACZEW ○
Grabno 17.IX
Palmiry
Modlin Rw. Narew
Wyszogrod
Rv. Vistula

Rw. Bug
WARSAW
22-24.IX

SCALE
0   20   40   60 km

LEGEND
9th LANCERS ITINERARY
✗ BATTLES
○ RECONNAISSANCES

Dabie. Until the start of the action—that is, during the day of 9th September—it was the duty of the 9th Lancers to establish a defence line on the river in Dabie. The remaining units of the Brigade were concentrated in forests north of Dabie. The Brigade's Artillery was to support the 9th Lancers. After dusk the 6th Lancers would strike from Dabie along the main road to Uniejow on the Warta, take it during the night, and then destroy the bridge over the Warta, thus securing our right flank. They would be followed immediately by the 14th Lancers and by the 9th Lancers after it had abandoned the defence of the Ner.

The two regiments would bypass Uniejow to the west and, having deployed on a wide front, would attack in the general direction of Ozorkow and Lodz, the rear of German units tied in a fight with our Infantry Divisions. The meeting was then dismissed; we were glad that at last we were to have some real work to do.

I returned to my Regiment and took it to Dabie. After a short reconnaissance of the possibilities of defence, I occupied Dabie and the bridge on the river with two squadrons, leaving the remaining squadrons in reserve. At the same time I contacted the artillery and we agreed about defensive firing. There was no enemy in sight on the other bank of the river.

I sent our platoon of cyclists to reconnoitre the forefront. The platoon returned at noon, having lost its commander, Lieut. Sieminski, and a few men. About four miles from Dabie, in the direction of Uniejow, they came across German armoured cars, and after a short skirmish they had to retreat. About 3 p.m., some German motor-cyclists appeared near Dabie; they proceeded cautiously, avoiding ambushes. They were repelled by artillery fire. Mounted patrols were sent out immediately afterwards but found no Germans within a perimeter of several miles.

No changes occurred in our situation until the evening. The enemy limited his activities only to small reconnaissances in the direction of Ner, and was quietly proceeding eastwards. We thought that our surprise action during the night would stand a good chance.

At dusk, General Skotnicki came to Dabie. Immediately, the 6th Lancers advanced on the main road to Uniejow, followed closely by the 14th Lancers, and then we relinquished our defence lines and linked up to the 14th. The night was so dark that it was difficult to see the lancer riding in front, and it would be easy to lose the track. The squadrons were riding in file, and regular reports reached the head of the column that everything was all right.

26

Having ridden a few miles towards Uniejow, we turned left, to a road leading south-east. We then heard a violent battle raging in the direction of Uniejow. There was the sound of explosions and heavy machine-gun fire, and we saw on the dark sky flashes of artillery and many Verey-lights—probably shot up by the startled, surprised and frightened Germans.

We pushed ahead, availing ourselves of the prevailing confusion to go as far as possible to the rear of the German forces between Uniejow and Lodz.

Before dawn we halted for a short rest, but soon pushed ahead. We realised that we were now at the rear of the enemy. We met more and more small German army-units, which we annihilated. We caught up German cars with Staff officers, and also German supplies, from which our lancers delighted in "supplying" themselves with cigars, tinned food, bread, and other provisions.

In the meantime, the 6th Lancers, after a violent battle, captured Uniejow and linked up with us. They repelled the Germans and destroyed the bridge.

We had no news about the battle fought by our Infantry Group advancing from Leczyca. Nevertheless, we thought that we must have caused considerable havoc behind the enemy lines by breaking into a gap and upsetting his organisation, thus relieving our infantry.

Up to then we had not met with any considerable enemy forces, but at dawn on the 11th our Brigade got involved in a more serious battle near Parzeczew. The 6th and 14th Lancers were attacking from the south, our 9th Lancers from the west.

At last, from the hills near Parzeczew, we could watch the battle near Ozorkow, and see our two divisions advancing from the north towards this town.

The enemy's resistance was visibly stiffening. German artillery was taking part in the battle with increasing intensity.

In the afternoon, after a part of the Regiment had entered Parzeczew from the west, we received new orders.

We were immediately to retire from the battle and to move back to the west in the direction of Uniejow, there to stop any advancing enemy forces and thus cover further activities by our Group from the west.

The enemy was probably badly shaken by our roaming about in his rear and by the threats to his left flank by the activities of our Combat Group. He had recovered from the initial surprise and probably he was assembling forces from all sides to restore his position. According to information received from the Brigade H.Q., he had already managed to repair the bridge near Uniejow, had crossed the Warta, and was advancing directly against us.

By about 5 p.m. the Regiment, with the attached Battery, was on the move towards Uniejow. At dusk, our patrols met enemy infantry advancing from the west, about half-way between Uniejow and Parzeczew.

Our vanguard came into contact with this body while they were engaged in crossing the river Ner. After a short fight we saw clearly how German detachments, which already had crossed the river, retreated speedily to the west bank. We then took some prisoners. From their statements we learnt that we were facing a battalion of the *Landwehr*, who, being without artillery, had been suddenly alarmed and were ordered to go *via* Uniejow in the direction of Lodz, "where there was a break through the front line". They were exhausted by their march and very frightened. We did not find indications of any prevailing fighting spirit in the representatives of the battalion, and we felt certain they would not dare during the night to relinquish the bushes where they had taken shelter.

In spite of our terrible exhaustion, we organised a small sally during the night to wear down the enemy's morale, and postponed further activities until dawn.

At daybreak the whole Regiment crossed the river Ner near Wartkowice, and we developed our attack, trying to outflank the enemy from the south and cut off his rear.

Our plans were impetuous, but we realised that only a very weak detachment of infantry would have been alarmed by our attack. In a dismounted action we represented a very feeble force compared with a battalion of infantry deployed in the terrain.

The frontal attack was led by Major S. Tomaszewski. He had with him the 2nd and 4th squadrons, with eight heavy machine-guns and one battery of artillery.

The 3rd Squadron was deployed to attack the enemy from the rear. I watched the advance for some time, but soon they had to dismount, probably encountering resistance. It was thus that Capt. E. Ksyk led his lancers in an attempt to "outflank" the German battalion.

As reserve and cover for the Artillery, I left the 1st squadron, which was this day guarding our Colours. They were to be used for action only in case of extreme emergency, being only 50 lancers strong; and anyway, such a force, at least, had to be left as cover for the battery and the horseholders, because of the possibility that our rear might be endangered by new enemy forces, probably approaching speedily from various directions.

Our movements provoked a violent infantry fire. We answered it, but the enemy had superior fire-power—machine-guns, submachine-guns and rifles—and our battery had difficulties with observation. The observer, not finding a good observation post, went into the first line and was killed. The battery had to change its emplacement, as they were too near the enemy and had trouble in firing from such a close range.

The battle became stationary, and we had no chance of removing the enemy from positions on the river. Anyway, we were convinced that the enemy felt no willingness to advance as he still had no artillery. He would therefore develop his defence on a wide perimeter.

There were no changes till 5 p.m., when the enemy received two self-propelled guns, which were kept in the rear, but which very often sallied to the front to fire over open sights. They were cautious and avoided being caught by fire from our anti-tank guns. They did no harm to us, and our horses were well under cover.

At about 6 p.m. we received new orders from our Brigade H.Q. to desist from the fight and to retreat towards Leczyca, as the rearguard of our Brigade. An officer from the Brigade H.Q., who brought this order, told us that our infantry had met strong enemy forces near Ozorkov, but had had to disengage and were retreating towards Kutno. Our Brigade was to form the rearguard of the whole Group.

We immediately obeyed our orders, covered by the 2nd Squadron, which remained in position until dark and then managed to disengage from the enemy, step by step. We were extremely tired and hungry, having been for the last ten days on the move and for the last three days and nights engaged in battle.

I felt great admiration for our horses, who stood up to it all, unsaddled for such a long time, and only occasionally fed by hand by our lancers.

It was still light when the Regiment mounted on horseback and stretched out, like a long snake, towards the east. In the middle rode our battery with the wounded on farm-carts. The 2nd Squadron was still behind. It was as warm as a July night; the air was completely calm, and even the leaves did not rustle.

I stopped beside the road and watched the march, amazed at how well it all looked! Horses snorted, the lancers chatted happily and carelessly, the sergeant-majors followed up their squadrons closely with the field-cookers.

Passing squadron commanders rode up to me and reported their losses; they were less than anticipated. They had even managed to order a dish-out of dinner before mounting on horseback. Horses had been fed by horseholders, who had stood idle the whole day. It was splendid! Much better than I had expected; and, above all, the men were in good spirits and confident.

The Regiment marched by. I stopped on the road again, waiting for the 2nd Squadron. We dismounted; my staff nearby loosened the girths, and the horses, jingling their bits, began to feed on clover growing in a nearby field. We were really happy.

Slowly it was getting dark; a light mist rose, spreading in streaks from the river Ner, and settling down on the fields, which appeared to grow longer and looked almost like a steppe. Podolia, Jazlowiec, our *ex-voto*, again became vivid in our minds.

Had Jakiello been right, in Nekla, in that roadside café? We were beginning to feel that he had been right.

We heard the 2nd Squadron approach through the mist; we heard the clattering of stirrups hitting each other, and the jingling of bits. We could hear no trampling of horses: they were on soft soil.

The Squadron was led by its commander, Capt. Antek Bielecki. I valued and liked this officer very much: hard on himself, but just to his men, he was a born soldier and commander. The lancers loved him; they would willingly have given their lives for him, although he kept them well in hand. He did not allow any tricks and he was often uncompromising. I waylaid him. The Squadron had suffered hardly any losses: he had managed to feed both lancers and horses, and was ready to proceed. The Germans were not moving, and probably would not attempt to do so during the night.

Capt. Bielecki asked me to detach from his command one of his officers who appeared to be useless; he had first noticed him in Parzeczew, and now, after the last battle, he was convinced of it. The officer's nerves were overstrained and he was spoiling his platoon. Obviously I had to exchange the officer; and already I had a substitute in my mind—Kazio Rostworowski, my adjutant. In this capacity he was useless: instead of his waking me, I had to pull *him* from his couch, and he liked being well looked after. This disqualified him as an adjutant, but he was eager to lead patrols and to take part in real fighting, and would therefore be suitable to work under Antek Bielecki.

The Captain and I rode for a time together, then I left the squadron and galloped to reach the leading squadron.

We continued acting as rearguard during the 13th and 14th September. We passed Leczyca going towards Kutno—always in contact with the enemy and putting up resistance.

On the 15th we rode through the bombed and still smouldering Kutno. We passed by the units of our Army, to become the point troop. General Skotnicki stayed with the rest of his Brigade as cover for the Army. We had to join the Wielkepolska Brigade and form a Cavalry Group under General R. Abraham, to clear the road for the Army through the Kampinow Forest to Warsaw.

Only then did we hear that Warsaw, encircled from all sides, had been putting up resistance. We were now in a swarm of German forces, and were faced with having to hack our way through to our metropolis to strengthen her defences. The menace and sinister implications of the general situation became clear to us.

During the day of the 16th September we could hardly move along the road to Sochaczew, which was jammed with transport and Army units. Bypassing the whole Army, we could take good stock of her, seeing clearly what had been concealed from us while forming the rearguard.

It was not yet a collapsing Army, but the prevailing condition of roads jammed by thousands of army vehicles deprived it of real freedom of movement and forced it to the edge of catastrophe. In this chaos it was impossible to organise supplies or to exercise skilful command.

Late in the evening we reached the outskirts of the Kampinow Forest on the Bzura, leaving Sochaczew on our right.

We found General Abraham in the forest, on the river side. He was organising a crossing as there was no bridge, only a deep ford. The opposite bank of the river was steep, accessible only by mounted lancers.

I reported to General Abraham, who gave me an overall survey of the situation.

Warsaw was beleaguered on all sides. It appeared that German forces were weaker between Modlin and Warsaw, in the area of the Kampinow Forest, and we must therefore try to hack our way through from this side.

The Cavalry Group's task was to seize the whole Kampinow Forest by repelling the enemy, and to secure for the whole Army bases on the perimeter of the forest for a strike towards Warsaw. The Army was successively supposed to cross the Bzura and to regroup in the forest.

The Kampinow Forest stretched its two 12-mile-long arms from the Bzura to the Modlin-Warsaw main road. The two arms were separated by a two-mile-wide stretch of marshy meadow with a few dykes connecting both sides. It gave excellent cover from the air force, and probably from enemy tanks, and secured appropriate conditions for the approach movement to Warsaw.

The majority of the Cavalry Group forces had already forded the Bzura and moved along the northern arm of the forest. The 15th Lancers from Poznan remained in the southern arm, to cover our right flank. There was no news from regiments moving in the forest.

The General was especially anxious about his right flank, as the main German forces were concentrated in its direction. The 9th Lancers were accordingly entrusted with the task of reinforcing cover from the south. Therefore we had immediately to ford the Bzura and, by moving along the southern arm of the forest, to seize and secure bases for an approach to Warsaw *via* Blonie.

It was pitch dark when we began to ford the river. The squadrons marched closely, one after the other. The water reached as high as the panels, and the tired horses climbed up the opposite bank with difficulty. Our vehicles and field-cookers could not possibly attempt the fording, so we left them on the spot, hoping that by next day we should be able to find an easier ford or to cross the bridge in Sochaczew, if the enemy would let us do so. I suggested to Jackiello to abandon the jeep—anyhow, we had no more petrol for it—and to take a seat in a machine-gun carrier. He was most indignant, and said:

"Sir, you may be assured I shall come to Warsaw with this jeep."

In view of his determined attitude I could do no less than bid him goodbye and wish him good luck, although I did not expect ever to see him again.

We concentrated on fording our anti-tank guns and machine-gun carriers, pulling them out of the water with ropes.

At last, having worked very hard for an hour and a half, we were all on the other bank, though without our B. échelon transport, and we entered the forest, aiming at its southern arm.

It was so dark that we could not ride, especially as we were liable to meet the enemy at any moment.

I dismounted the 4th Squadron, and ordered them to fix bayonets and to form the vanguard, myself going with them. The remaining squadrons followed, leading the horses. I ordered Capt. G. Poborow-

The 9th Lancers on a church parade in their garrison at Trembowla in 1939

The Regiment's machine-guns

The nunnery of the Immaculate Conception at Jazlowiec

The ceremony in Jazlowiec, 6 August, 1939

ski, O.C. 4th Squadron, to move as noiselessly as possible and, if he came upon any Germans, to kill them all with bayonets and hand-grenades, thus keeping the road clear. We did not expect to meet a strong force in the forest.

After we had started our march, Capt. G. Poborowski approached me and, visibly in despair, confessed that he had left the hand-grenades in vehicles on the Bzura.

I reprimanded him in a few, very sharp, words, and added, worst of all: "How is it that I can no longer rely on you? Or is it, perhaps, that you and your squadron are so tired you don't want to fight any more? Had I suspected this, I would have chosen another squadron for the job."

I must admit that these words, in view of our appalling tiredness, were somewhat harsh and inhuman. Poborowski only murmuerd that he would try to reassure me that I could rely upon him. Three days later he was killed in a similar situation. Alas! he *had* convinced me.

We went on slowly and cautiously, stopping now and then, listening in the dark night. Our only chance was to approach the potential enemy unnoticed, at point-blank distance, and to strangle him before he could realise what had happened.

Soon it became obvious that all this was completely unreal. Our bodies simply could not keep pace with our spirit. Everyone was overcome by unsurmountable fatigue. After the strain of the last few days, and now after this march on sandy soil in the forest, our lancers, when halted to listen attentively, fell asleep like stones on to the soil.

Could anyone dream of hand-to-hand fighting under such con-ditions?

Capt. Poborowski rushed from one lancer to another, trying in the darkness to touch the inert bodies, tragically attempting to pull them up and force them to proceed, although unable to see whether they were all marching, and knowing well that these very somnolent lancers could not fulfil their duty as the vanguard. My hair rose on end as I realised that the same thing might happen to our horse-holders and to the remaining squadrons leading their horses. Per-haps a few would drag along, spurred on by will-power and by the force of a few of the more dutiful and more seasoned officers, even if the remaining part of the Regiment was overtaken by sleep, stretching along the long forest ride which we had just traversed. . . .

There was nothing for it but to close the Regiment and halt some-where to rest. We only had to enter deeper into the arm of the forest

—if possible in its wildest part, where there was less chance of meeting the enemy and where it would be easier to find shelter.

After a short walk we found such a place, and, putting guards all around, we fell on the ground to rest.

It was dawning when the whole Regiment reached the selected spot. With daylight the tiredness seemed to diminish, and sergeant-majors were foraging around to find at least some hay for the horses. Soon a haystack found in the forest was divided fairly, and the lancers removed the bits from their bridles and fed the horses. Somebody discovered a field-cooker left behind by the 15th Lancers, with some food. We dished it out equally, and everybody had his share; it was the only food we could supply for our lancers.

CHAPTER 4

Into a Trap

SUDDENLY, at 8 a.m., we were alarmed by hearing single rifle shots north and south—*i.e.*, on both outskirts of our arm of the forest. In a few moments reports came in from our patrols: in the north, in the glade between our arm of the forest and the northern one, which was crossed by the remaining regiments of our Cavalry Group, small groups of German infantry had been spotted moving towards the forest. From the south, German tanks and infantry were moving along a narrow forest ride straight towards us. At the same time we were attacked by machine-gun fire from an airplane almost touching the tops of the trees; it was so close that we fired at it with our rifles and pistols—I think successfully, too, because after the second attack it did not return any more. Perhaps we had managed to shoot it down, no one could tell—it was flying so low and disappeared behind the trees. We had several wounded.

In the meantime, our anti-tank gun was ambushed in the narrow ride down which the tanks were arriving. I stood close to the gun and saw clearly what was happening. The gunlayer, his eye close to the range-finder, aimed at a point of the ride, no more than eighty yards away: it was the very brim of our horizon; a sand-dune prevented us from seeing any further. The gun was badly camouflaged, but there was no time to rectify this. The issue of this duel must depend on whoever spotted the enemy first.

We heard the roar of approaching tanks; they came nearer and nearer. At last an iron turret protruded from behind the dune. Shots were fired from both sides simultaneously. I clearly saw holes made in the turret and the tank disappeared behind the dune. The enemy fired short; the missile exploded in front of the gun, only a splinter hitting the leg of the gunlayer. A few seconds later everything was

35

over; we heard the tanks withdraw and we were left in peace. Fresh good news arrived from the south, from Bielecki's squadron: he had expelled the Germans from the forest into open fields where they deployed and opened fire.

We did not risk a second attack; besides, we had to fulfil our task. We therefore mounted our horses, aiming towards the east. Our wounded, dressed by Dr. Paczkowski, our M.O., were left in the forester's house under the care of his wife. Unfortunately we could do no more for them.

Capt. A. Bielecki then led our vanguard straight to the outlet of the road to Blonie; we had still about ten miles to traverse to Blonie.

Capt. G. Poborowski was in command of the rearguard. The 1st Squadron sent out patrols along rides to the outskirts of the arm of the forest.

Soon it became obvious that we were marching, as it were, into the sleeve of a trap. There were many Germans all around the southern border of the forest. Probably they had stretched themselves out as far as Warsaw, having taken the lead well before us. North—in the glade between the two arms of the forest—were Germans, too, but not very numerous and looking rather bewildered; probably they were remnants of detachments driven out from the northern arm by the main forces of our Cavalry Group and were attempting to hack their way through to the south, to their own forces. As they found the southern arm occupied by us, they remained in the meadows, not risking an entrance into the forest.

It was much worse in our rear. Capt. G. Poborowski now had to repel a much stronger attack by tanks. He scored direct hits on two of them, but lost one of his own anti-tank guns, which was simply run over by a tank after its crew had been machine-gunned. Only with difficulty could he disengage himself from the enemy and try to link up with us, firing back all the time.

The situation was by no means amusing. To cap it all, a few bombers came in our direction. They flew in flight formation, at 300 yards above the trees, and soon we heard the bombs fall. Luckily none of them hit the road or the narrow-gauge railway track over which we rode. They fell somewhere in the forest, or perhaps on the meadows; and some failed to explode.

We still had to advance deeper into this bottle-neck—there was no other choice.

About 5 p.m., Capt. Bielecki reported that he had reached the border of the forest in the direction of Blonie and that all the exits were closed. He tried to strike at the enemy.

The situation was exceedingly grave. We were in a trap! Our only chance was to hack our way through ahead, and to do it quickly before we were overrun from the rear.

I myself galloped to Capt. Bielecki with Capt. E. Ksyk's 3rd Squadron as reinforcement. The remainder of the Regiment, under Major S. Tomaszoewski, had, together with Capt. G. Poborowski, to stop the enemy and cover our action from the rear.

I met Capt. A. Bielecki on the border of the forest. The whole squadron was fighting a dismounted action with the enemy, who occupied all the surrounding dunes and sandy brush land, covering with strong machine-gun and mortar fire all the exits from the forest. . . . Bullets buzzed like wasps; the artillery began to respond; it was quite impossible to emerge from the forest.

With Bielecki I fully appreciated the seriousness of the situation and came to the conclusion that it was beyond our power to pierce the German ring towards Blonie. What would be the use, as no other Polish forces were left behind us and we were pursued by strong enemy detachments with tanks?

We were clearly in a trap, and there was no way out from the front or the rear.

I decided to do everything possible to remain and hold out as we were for the time being, and after dark to disengage from the enemy, to leave the roads and to drop out in the forest, then rest a little and, before dawn, to cross the northern arm of the forest and link up with the main forces of the Cavalry Group.

In the meantime, the enemy began to exhibit further activity. From our right flank and from the rear we heard the buzzing of German machine-gun bullets. Two German tanks drove into the forest—in a part where the trees were sparse—between ourselves and the remaining part of the Regiment, and from a distance of about a hundred yards they covered us with bullets and we had to take shelter behind trees.

The situation had become extremely grave and called for immediate reaction. Unfortunately, the crew of our anti-tank gun could not see the tanks as they were behind a screen. Capt. Bielecki sent an orderly, and a few moments later we could see Staff-Sergeant Kolodziejczyk galloping with the gun to a new position. We did not know whether they would destroy him or whether he would be able to take up a new position: it all happened at close range, under cover of the trees alone.

37

At the same time I ordered Capt. Ksyk to attack with bayonets—or, rather, with a roar: perhaps it would frighten the Germans!

Events followed with lightning speed. Capt. Ksyk's squadron ran with loud shouts straight towards the tanks, Kolodziejczyk's gun fired several rounds, the tanks retreated, and we realised after they had moved that there were more than we had thought. Two of them were in flames; others disappeared behind the horizon.

The crisis was over; peace would be ours till dusk; the Germans would not risk a new attack.

When it became completely dark, we left our position as noiselessly as possible, joined the remaining squadrons and rode deep into the forest, leaving the roads completely free. They might look for us if they liked. Capt. Poborowski linked up with us, so we were again all together, squeezed into a square of 100 yards—safe, and sure that that night nobody would roam about among the bushes and discover us.

At about 9 p.m., the Germans, realising that we had disappeared, began to direct their artillery and mortar fire against the forest, trying at random to hit us. But we suffered no losses. Besides, everybody was so terribly tired that the lancers did not care: they simply collapsed on the ground and fell asleep like stones. I called the squadron commanders to consult on what to do and to issue orders, whispering only. Poborowski's squadron suffered the worst losses; it was a good squadron, but had definitely had bad luck. Others had only slight losses. Ksyk lost only two men while attacking the tanks with bayonets and was very proud of his lancers. He remained as in a trance, which usually happens after a successful charge.

I decided we would sleep until 3 a.m., when all must be ready for the march. We would attempt to hack our way through to the north and join the main force of our Cavalry Group. Capt. Bielecki would form the point troop. A patrol, consisting of volunteers, must find the way and reconnoitre the northern outskirt of our arm of the forest, and they were to leave immediately.

Cadet-Officer Rosciszewski and three lancers volunteered. I gave them instructions myself and went to sleep. Dr. Paczowski told us he was not tired so he would watch. He was a brave and honest man; he assumed the duties of the duty officer and was the only scout in the Regiment. I told him to call me and the squadron commanders at 2.30 a.m., and instantly I fell asleep. . . .

Somebody pulled at my arm to waken me. I regained consciousness with difficulty. It was Capt. Kowalski, O.C. our Signals platoon.

He whispered that he had a very important message. Half-conscious, I looked at my watch: it was only 11 p.m.

He told me he had just received by our wireless receiver a communiqué. Moscow wireless had reported that on this day, in the morning, Russian troops had entered Poland and had occupied Tarnopol and Trembowla. He was shaking all over. I tried to be understanding: he had left a young and beautiful wife in Trembowla, as many of our families were left there. Only then did I regain complete consciousness. I realised what this really meant. I was not thinking about general repercussions: it was a direct blow for our Regiment, and especially now, in this very tragic situation, when we needed such steady and strong nerves. Now we had reached the very depths of misery.

My God, but there was nothing we could do about it! I told Kowalski to go to sleep and not to awaken anybody: we would tell our men later on, when we were out of this situation.

I lay down again on the moss; but I neither slept nor watched: I was wandering in mind. I was not here . . . I was riding across the Zascianek forest, close to the canyon of the river Seret. My thoroughbred filly Jesien coquetted, walking like a dainty maiden. Both of us lowered our heads to avoid low-hanging branches; and then the unforgettable view—Podolia! Podolia. . . . And the three sweet rosy faces of my little daughters twinkled at me. . . . Then followed a terrible nightmare. . . . Suddenly I rose to my feet. It seemed to me that the dawn was breaking. . . . Three a.m., and everybody asleep! Paczkowski had failed me: he had not awakened us! The day was breaking; we should not be able to get out. . . .

I tugged at men, but I could not rouse them. I rushed across to Paczkowski, who was sitting, leaning against a tree.

"What have you done?! Why didn't you wake us? It is 3 a.m.!"

Paczkowski looked at his watch, then at me. It was 11.30 p.m. I verified by my watch—he was right. I recovered consciousness. The doctor bade me lie down next to him and covered me with a greatcoat. I fell asleep.

The Road to Warsaw

At 3 a.m. we mounted our horses and rode ahead, led by Rosciszewski's patrol—but without *him*. Rosciszewski had been killed during the night.

There was a narrow ride leading north. After the incident with Rosciszewski the Germans had probably retreated, for we did not encounter any.

It was now almost full daylight; only a fleecy mist still spun, like cobwebs, over our heads when we emerged from the forest and rode into a small hamlet, Kolonia-Roztoka. We had to water our horses quickly—they had had no water since we had forded the Bzura.

As soon as the squadrons dispersed among the farmyards, as the water-cranes began to shriek, an airplane appeared with a loud roar over the hamlet looking for us. Perhaps they would not spot us, because of the mist. . . .? But no! in less than ten minutes a short but sharp artillery burst came over us—two bursts, one after the other.

I could never have believed it would be possible to leave the hamlet so rapidly, with the Regiment dispersed in scattered farms; but in a very few minutes we had all met outside the village and were walking in orderly file ahead. We again lost an anti-tank gun: the Germans had scored a direct hit in the middle of the team of horses, just when it was leaving a farmyard; this left us with only two.

Having ridden another few miles, we met the 15th Lancers and Capt. Choloniewski from General Abraham's Staff. We were to link up with the main forces in the Palmiry forest, where the battle for the entrance to Warsaw was raging.

On 18th September, in the afternoon, we entered Palmiry. The whole Group of General Abraham was there—6th, 14th, 15th, 17th and our 9th Lancers, the 7th Mounted Rifles, and other units belonging to the Brigades. There were also various infantry units and single infantry men from units previously disintegrated.

Attempts, on the 18th, to hack our way through to Warsaw along the Modlin main road were a failure. We had to execute our real attack at dawn on 19th September *via* Sierakow and Laski.

During the night of 18th/19th, the whole Cavalry Group was re-organised and directed to new bases, *via* the forester's house, "Pociecha".

On the 19th September, before the sun rose, the 17th Lancers and a part of the 7th Mounted Rifles, who formed our leading troop, broke into Sierakow, occupied by enemy armour. A furious battle—a sort of improvisation—followed.

Straight from our march-column, under the fire of enemy machine-guns—whose tracer bullets formed a canopy over our heads—we went to fight a dismounted action.

Our 9th Lancers went straight along the main road through the village, and the 14th Lancers down a glade and through trees.

It was not a planned attack, but from the start an assault on an enemy taken by surprise.

Poborowski went along the main road of the village, Bielecki across some fences on his right. The 1st and 3rd Squadrons, who had been left behind, did not arrive in time to take part in this assault.

In spite of heavy machine-gun fire, both squadrons attacked in a series of rushes. Several tanks and cars left behind by the enemy were captured, and small groups of Germans were quickly annihilated. After a few minutes the whole village had been occupied. But we suffered heavy losses. Capt. G. Poborowski, Lieut. J. Rylski, and several lancers, had been killed, while Lieut. Dabrowiecki, Lieut. K. Rostworowski, Lieut. Longchamps, and about twenty valiant N.C.O's and lancers, were dangerously wounded.

The attack was continued across the forest towards Laski. The attackers were reinforced by the 6th and 17th Lancers and the 7th Mounted Rifles, all dismounted. Colonel Kowalczewski, of the 17th Lancers, was in command.

In the meantime, a counter-attack by about sixteen enemy tanks came from the south-west from the direction of Truskawy, towards Sierakow. Both the rear of the attacking troops and the horse-holders were threatened by it. There were two anti-tank guns in Sierakow—I do not remember from which Regiment—which saved the situation. The gunlayers mastered their nerves and opened fire at point-blank range. Three tanks immediately burst into flames and the others disappeared behind cover. The attack was repelled in a few minutes' time. I watched it myself, standing on the border of the forest, and I was full of admiration for the brave crews. I stood there with Capt. Kowalski, his Signals platoon, and the Regimental Colours.

We were indeed left alone. Bielecki and the remnants of the 4th Squadron, without an officer (for J. Rylski was in Poborowski's squadron), joined the attack, led by Col. Kowalczewski. The remaining squadrons were probably with the horseholders, and there was obviously a danger of being entirely cut off. I could not risk the safety of the Regimental Colours: I was afraid of the possibility of an accident during another surprise attack. The staff was too heavy and cumbersome to be carried, so I ordered Kowalski to remove the Colours with the silver eagle and the nail from the staff and to put them in the leather case and strap it to his belt. From this time onwards Kowalski was personally responsible for the Colours, and had orders to keep always close to me. It was a grave decision to make, but we afterwards felt much relieved and walked towards Laski.

The situation was serious. The Institution of the Blind's building provided the enemy with a strong point of resistance, enabling him to slow down our attack.

Losses caused by enemy fire were considerable. The attack slowly died down, and in the afternoon we were able to weigh up the situation—*viz.* that it would be quite impossible to hack our way through to Warsaw in the appointed direction of Laski; at the same time we could not remain where we were, because, sooner or later, it would mean the complete annihilation of our units.

General Abraham decided on a fresh plan.

We were to interrupt the attack against Laski, to disengage from the enemy before dusk, to join the horseholders, and re-group in the forest near Sierakow, and, under cover of the night, to strike through Wolka-Weglowa and Mlociny towards Bielany in Warsaw. General Abraham probably considered that the all-day continuous battle for Laski had drawn the whole attention of the enemy to this sector and would thus increase the chances of an imperceptible passage through the terrain a little north of it. The Group closed at about 6 p.m. near Sierakow—the whole Cavalry, artillery, Signals, and vehicles, together with the wounded on carts. Besides our units, there were many hangers-on and loose infantry groups that had become separated from their own divisions, moving towards Warsaw. They were creating confusion and increased our vulnerability in the event of a new attack by the enemy. Major Z. Elsner, with the 1st and 3rd Squadrons, which did not take part in the battle, took over the watch.

Before dusk, General Abraham assembled all regimental commanders and issued orders.

It looked very unpleasant. We all had to dismount, leaving the horses to our horseholders. Everyone, including the Brigadier, had to take a rifle, fix the bayonet, and, under cover of night, steal through to Warsaw. Local guides would lead us across country. The horses, the wounded and the guns must be left with only minimum cover. If they could manage to do so, they were to follow us on the roads at dawn the next morning.

It was a dreadful order, smelling of "*sauve qui peut*". And it definitely ordered us to relinquish our horses and equipment without any real hope of ever seeing them again. One had to be a member of the Regiment to realise the implications of that, and of the fact that the wounded were to be left behind, though this might be prompted by concern for their welfare—that is, if they would be cared for.

I do not know if this is the proper interpretation of General Abraham's order; he may have had some other information which prompted him to come to such a decision; anyhow, we were all very critical of his instructions and they were not completely carried out in detail.

To leave ten horses with one lancer gave but a faint hope of bringing them to Warsaw, so was tantamount to relinquishing them altogether. We dismounted in the normal way, and I ordered Lieut. Romanowski, who was in charge of the horseholders, under no pretext whatever to jettison the horses but to follow us as long as was possible. I saw that similar instructions were given to the Artillery Battery, whose guns were not jettisoned. We then took our rifles in our hands, and, at dusk, moved across the forest, passing by Wolka Weglowa from the south. We marched the whole night across rough tracks and through valleys. Several times, rather by accident than design, we came across fire from German mortars or machine-guns (using tracer bullets), but on the whole our course was uninterrupted: the enemy stuck, more or less, to inhabited areas, leaving spaces between them open. Kowalski marched all the time close to me.

At dawn we reached Bielany, where we encountered patrols of Warsaw's defenders, and the Regiment camped in the woods surrounding the Central Institute of Physical Culture.

About noon, to our great joy, Lieut. Romanowski linked up with all our horses, the wounded on carts, anti-tank guns and machine-gun carriers. Amazingly, he had not lost anything or anybody! He was followed by horseholders from other regiments, by transport, equipment for signals, and artillery.

He told us that at dawn they had moved on to the main road and encountered resistance in the first village, but the artillery took position and opened fire, sending a few accurate volleys, and the various marauders who were about simply moved ahead, which caused the enemy alarm and made him desert the field. After this incident, they were unmolested till they reached Bielany.

We were overcome with joy, especially as Lieut. Romanowski had also brought with him some war booty—two jettisoned field-cookers, "collected" by him.

We began to check up and call over nominal rolls, to groom and water our horses, and to feed them with grass. We found some food for the cookers and were only short of bread.

In the evening we accounted for about 350 mounted lancers and

43

about half that number of dismounted ones, from whom I formed a dismounted squadron under Lieut. Kolat; up to then he had been our anti-tank gun platoon commander.

We still had six machine-guns and one anti-tank gun.

Throughout the night men were coming in: hundreds of infantrymen from various units, and transports moving on through Bielany. Not belonging to us, they by-passed us quickly and sped towards the centre of the town, as to a port of safety, there becoming a serious embarrassment to the Defence Command.

Finally, Cpl. Jakiello arrived with his jeep! How he succeeded in this I do not know. He had fulfilled his promise, behaving valiantly, and we gave him a hearty welcome.

There were many missing, however: Major Z. Elsner, Capt. Palka from the 1st Squadron, Capt. Ciepiela from the machine-gun squadron, Lieut. Malachowski, and many others—killed or wounded, we knew not.

Apart from the difficulty of obtaining food, our greatest difficulty was finding adequate shelter. The park and the woods round the Central Institute of Physical Culture were overcrowded with both horses and men: use had been made of every bit of cover to avoid observation from the air; nevertheless, it would be easy to discover us.

Our Regiment was in the worst position. All the most sheltered places were occupied by others, only a few groups of old fir or pine trees being left for us. These provided but poor cover, and we could be easily detected. In comparison with the other regiments and detachments, who had adequate shelter, we were in a precarious situation. We were wondering what we could do about it when some aircraft came over and attacked. Bombs were dropped over the whole area, but luckily we were not hit. Major Beck's Signals Squadron of the Podolian Brigade and other units were, however, badly affected —bombs exploding in the centre of their groupings. Losses were severe. We certainly were lucky: not even a horse had been scratched.

Some time later, Capt. Juszczak, the A.D.C., came to me and reported whispered comments among the lancers. They maintained that the reason we had not suffered so heavily in spite of our bad situation was that "before the war the Colonel took us to Jazlowiec". Juszczak also was of this opinion. I explained to him that good or bad cover did not influence the accuracy of the bombing: bombs were released over the fields, and the airmen had not aimed especially at us; but I did not convince him. He concurred in the general opinion.

The lancers then made a further interesting discovery. They found that all decisive moments in the Regiment's destiny always happened on a *Sunday*, beginning with the mobilisation, which was ordered on Sunday, the 27th August.

For curiosity's sake, we began to check up on it. Lieut. Lewek Sapieha excelled at this, his extraordinary memory enabling him readily to recall dates. There seemed, indeed, to be something in it. We counted up the Sundays.

We had received the telegram ordering mobilisation on Sunday, 27th August; on Sunday, 3rd September, we left the forests of Wagowo for our first encounter; on Sunday, the 10th September, we fought our first battle in the offensive launched from Dabie; and on Sunday, 17th September, we went through the most formidable of our war experiences, when we had been trapped in the Kampinow Forest, near Grabina, and our families had fallen into the hands of the Bolsheviks. How amazing were all these dates of decisive importance to the Regiment!

"Look here, boys," I asked them, "don't you remember when we offered the *ex-voto* in Jazlowiec?"

"Of course!—on a Sunday, the 6th August," they answered.

Rumour thus spread in the Regiment of strange mystical connections, and the lancers looked to it for comfort and hope for the future.

I did not pooh-pooh their beliefs: anything that could raise morale was decidedly to our advantage and to the good of the men. As our physical stamina dwindled, the more our morale needed boosting; so I let the men find what consolation they could in these coincidences.

CHAPTER 5

The Defence of Warsaw

AFTER all our previous experiences, our lucky entry into Warsaw had especial significance for us. We felt like shipwrecked sailors who, after weeks of gales and unexpected events, had safely reached port.

We were fed up with forest warfare—with unco-ordinated battles, with hacking our way through, with continual changes in the tasks entrusted to us and, above all, with the retreats.

If the general situation was so bad that chaos had to overcome it, thus annihilating the outcome of our efforts—well, now at least we had a clear and unalterable aim before us: to defend Warsaw.

We were fully aware that it would be no rest, and we envisaged strenuous battles; but there was a tangible and concrete aim—no longer weary and hopeless retreating, which had no effect on future decisions even though it demanded much heroism.

We were convinced that Warsaw's Defence H.Q. would be delighted to receive an invigorating injection in the form of seasoned and tested soldiers who, with our reputation, might be entrusted with special tasks in Warsaw.

Everything, however, turned out to be *vice versa*.

I heard, in our Brigade H.Q., that General J. Rommel, O.C. Warsaw's Defence, was greatly annoyed by our arrival: he did not want us. He had enough forces for the defence of Warsaw, and he had no food for us or our horses; we should only be living at his expense and become a liability. We should have by-passed the metropolis and carried on the struggle in the open country—there was no room for cavalry in a besieged town. We had committed an unpardonable mistake by piercing the defence ring of Warsaw; instead of strengthening, we had only weakened his defence potential.

Theoretically, General Rommel was probably right; but where, by hell, had we to go. . . .?

As a result of his views, we received fresh orders, passed on to me by Col. Strzelecki, our Brigadier. The Cavalry Group were immediately to leave the town and regain the open country, to join up with some Polish Army groups and co-operate with them. The sally should be achieved to the south, through Wilanow, after the piercing of the perimeter of the beleaguering forces.

The cavalry would, accordingly, re-group on the 23rd September in the area of Belweder, to prepare for our new task by reconnoitring and selecting the best place for our action. The break-through would be effected by the 25th Infantry Division, which was just entering Warsaw from the area of the Palmiry woods.

We were simply thrown out of the town. It seemed that in our whole group there was not one officer or lancer who liked this order. Nevertheless, it had to be obeyed; the order was unconditional.

It took us the whole day of 23rd September to traverse Warsaw from north to south. Two squadrons of the 6th Lancers, under Capt. Duszacki, joined our Regiment. Because of its decimated strength and the indisposition of its C.O., the remnants of that Regiment had been divided between the 9th and 14th Lancers while the Brigade was being re-grouped.

Warsaw appeared to us to be depopulated. There were no trams running. Just an occasional Army car. Everywhere we saw small groups of armed people, often in civilian clothes, mounting guard at various barricades and strategic points. The town looked orderly and the morale seemed high.

The Regiment stopped in the Aleja Szucha, where the horses were put under the cover of trees planted along the pavements, and the Regimental H.Q. was established in the Garrison Officers' Mess. The Brigade H.Q. occupied the cellars of the General Staff building in the Aleje Ujazdowskie, almost next door to us.

We did not see many ruins in the town. Many shops were still open; even restaurants served vegetable soup, though without bread; telephones and water supplies were in working order. The town seemed accustomed to warfare and had adapted itself to prevailing conditions.

We were terribly sorry for our horses. We watered them, but they were very hungry and gnawed at the trees. They stamped their hooves on the asphalted pavement, and had soon devoured the grass in the squares.

47

At dusk the situation improved a little. The Brigade's Quartermaster supplied us with some oats for our horses, but warned us that we must definitely not expect further supplies. This was issue "for the road", and that was all.

At any time we expected our orders for the march; however, there was some delay. I heard in the Brigade H.Q. that the promised units of the 25th Infantry Division had not arrived.

At last we were ordered to reach our exit bases by dawn on the 24th September. One battalion of Col. Rawicz' Regiment was apparently on its way to join us. They represented the force which till now was called "Units of the 25th Infantry Division".

We left the Aleja Szucha, and before dawn on the 24th September we halted in Park Street, along the high wall of Lazienki Park. Other regiments were in the Podchorazych Str. and in the park itself.

We waited. We doubted whether we would ever leave Warsaw at all. It would have been feasible if the garrison of Warsaw could have afforded a deep sally carried out by considerable forces to defeat the enemy in the direction of Wilanow, thus enabling our Cavalry Group to occupy the created gap, without the necessity of getting tied up and involved in a battle just outside the metropolis.

When it became apparent that the 25th Infantry Division—remnants from the battle on the Bzura—was a myth, and the promised battalion would never link up with us, we became convinced we would never leave the town; on the contrary, events might well throw us into the task of defending the city.

Our forebodings were soon confirmed.

The enemy's activity in the Wilanow sector increased to such an extent (it was probably a general feature of the whole forefront), that that same day we were compelled to reinforce the defence.

The Regiment went into the first defence line and occupied the exit of Gorska Str., opposite the Sielec wood, and by an outguard the Dabrowski Fort.

At the same time, the enemy increased his activities with his airforce and artillery.

We were so absorbed in our duties and with current events that news of a German ultimatum, demanding our capitulation and threatening to demolish the town in case of refusal, passed unnoticed.

Finally came the two most tragic days for Warsaw, the 25th and 26th September. Air raids and artillery bombardment raged uninterruptedly, day and night. Besides furious masses of explosives and the terrific blasts resulting therefrom, incendiary bombs were dropped in profusion, landing on roofs, roads and squares, and either igniting or else melting them. We were encircled from all sides by conflagrations; the town was falling into ruins, and was burning helplessly.

My Regimental H.Q. was established in the ground-floor flat of a many-storeyed house in Parkowa Str. Bielecki was in Gorska Str., opposite the Sielec wood; Ksyk in Dabrowski Fort. I had no liaison with them, telephones being already out of action.

The night of 25th/26th September was macabre. It was an incessant roar of explosions, piercing through a crackle of flames, the crash of houses falling into ruins, mixed with—or so it appeared to us—stifled human screams. Women and children crowded in the cellar of our house; everybody took shelter there, thinking it would be safer in a regimental H.Q. What an illusion!

Red, glittering flames illuminated our horses standing quiet and immobile along the walls of the Lazienki Park, resembling saddled skeletons. A few of them were lying dead; some were bleeding, exposing huge torn wounds. We went among them with Kowalski, deploring our helplessness. Kowalski's horse Cenzor was still alive, lying with its bowels ripped out. Not so long ago he had won the Army's Challenge Cup in Tarnopol. He had been our pride. A shot in the ear, however, shortened his sufferings. The next day, probably, somebody needing to still his own hunger would cut out a joint from his loins.

In spite of the surrounding fires and the masses of projectiles being hurled over our heads like a hailstorm, the defence was still alive. From the Lazienki Park, Belweder, Mokotowska Str., tracer bullets from our A.A. guns climbed laboriously into the skies in search of airplanes.

Suddenly, close behind the wall in the Lazienki Park, there started a hellish rifle and machine-gun fire. We thought the Germans had probably forced our first defence lines and broken into our rear.

The alarm was given. The devoted and reliable Lieut. Klaczynski rushed with a patrol to reconnoitre: we must have information where to counter-attack.

He returned after a while: nothing had happened: a grenade had hit a small cart filled with small arms ammunition which was now exploding.

In the morning I received news from Ksyk: he had been thrown out from the Dabrowski Fort. I took a squadron from the 2nd Chevaux Légers, under Capt. Wieniawski, sent to me by the Brigade H.Q., and led them along the Pelczynska Str. to counter-attack. In the middle of the Pelczynska Str. I gave Wieniawski a general direction: he was to draw near the Fort, establish liaison with Ksyk who must be somewhere thereabouts, and counter-attack. I could not give more precise instructions because of no support. Wieniawski was in perfect form: I did not notice even a moment of hesitation or of lingering. He briskly replied, "Yes, Sir," and quickly marched his men along the edge of the street, close to the houses. For a while I heard his voice raised energetically to his men, who crouched after every nearby explosion and hugged the walls:

"Forward! Don't lag behind there!"

Finally I lost sight of him and, as it proved afterwards, I lost him for ever—Antek Wieniawski, my dear friend, a reserve officer, a brave gentleman-farmer from the Grodzisk area, and the father of two beautiful children. He did not reach the fort: he was caught on his way by terrific gunfire, which riddled his body and completely wrecked and dispersed his squadron.

The Germans remained in the fort.

The 26th September was for us the most strenuous day of the defence.

After our loss of the Dabrowski Fort, the enemy closed in on our main defence line. Bielecki was fighting at point-blank range, and probably the same was happening elsewhere.

We could expect a general attack at any moment, especially as the activity of the air-force and artillery was still increasing and looked like a preparation for some fresh onslaught.

Another long night kept us keyed up to terrific tension.

During that night I received an order to recommend three soldiers from my Regiment for the Virtuti Military Cross and 25 for the Military Cross; they were to be decorated in the morning in Brigade H.Q. We did not think the order well timed. Was something approaching its end? Had new decisions been reached? Or, maybe, even negotiations? But we abandoned this last possibility.

The choice of men to be recommended for decoration was very difficult to make; so many deserved it!

Finally I decided. For the Virtuti Military Cross would be recommended: Major S. Tomaszewski, Capt. A. Bielecki and Capt. E. Ksyk. Twenty-one Military Crosses I allocated for distribution to the squadrons, and I recommended four soldiers from my Staff in the following sequence: Lieut. Klaczynski, Lieut. Dr. Paczkowski, M.O., Capt. Kowalski and Cpl. Jakiello.

On the morning of 27th September the gunfire seemed to be less intense. I drove to the Brigade H.Q. with Major Tomaszewski to collect his decoration; Bielecki and Ksyk, however, remained in their sectors, as I would myself collect their Crosses for them.

I was told at Brigade H.Q. that there were talks with the Germans then proceeding about our capitulation. On our side they were conducted, on behalf of General J. Rommel, by General Kutrzeba. Both ammunition and food were exhausted; the civilians, left without water supplies and jammed in cellars, were living under appalling conditions; there were vast numbers of wounded, and many people were buried under the ruins of houses. Further continuation of the defence would lead to a complete annihilation of the population and give no satisfactory result.

From Brigade H.Q. we drove in our jeep to the Hospital of the Holy Spirit in the Elektoralna Str., where we had left our wounded from Sierakow. We managed to get there by circuitous routes with difficulty and were horrified to find that the hospital no longer existed: it had been burned down and had fallen in ruins, burying hundreds of the wounded.

Details of this tragedy were given us by the local population. They said that when the hospital began to burn, all who could use their legs crept out of the building and got shelter in the neighbourhood, as people took them into their homes. The hospital staff, in spite of heavy gunfire and bombardment, gave proof of their high devotion to duty by evacuating the dangerously wounded and carrying them to cellars in the vicinity. They worked without respite until the building collapsed. Almost all the wounded from the passages and wards on the ground floor had been evacuated, but the others died. We remembered that our lancers were on the ground floor and prayed that they were safe.

Feverishly we began to search for them in the cellars. It was only then, while doing so, that we fully realised the hell that had been endured by the population, the unbelievable sufferings of wounded women and children; of families—many mothers searching for their missing children; but at the same time there were no complaints or even a shade of reproach directed against the defenders. We ceased our investigations on being assured by one of the hospital sisters that all the wounded from the ground floor had been rescued; there was, therefore, more than a possibility that our lancers did not perish under the ruins: perhaps they were in some other part of the town. . . .

51

We returned to our emplacement. On the way we stopped in the Army H.Q., in the basement of the Post Office Savings Bank, on the corner of the Swietokrzyska Str.

Just at that time there was an officers' meeting for consultation. There I saw the Generals Rommel, Kutrzeba, Tokarzewski, Knoll and Czuma. I exchanged a few words with Col. Praglowski, General Rommel's Chief of Staff. Yes, the capitulation had just been decided; talks about the conditions were continuing; soon we might expect a cease-fire order; it was useless to continue.

We did not feel happy there. Miserably, we hurried back to our own sector, to the Regiment.

There we found no change in the situation. The normal exchange of shots continued. But how much pleasanter this was than the atmosphere at the H.Q.!

Across holes made in walls and newly-trodden footpaths I speedily went to the Sielec wood to decorate Capt. Bielecki with the Virtuti Military Cross, which he so well deserved. There I could once more breathe refreshing air and was comforted by the signs of the squadron's morale. No sign of despondency there, although they were barely twenty yards from the enemy. They had cut loopholes in the walls of houses and made observation posts and trenches in the streets. At the slightest movement they fired and were proud of having pinned the Germans down to the ground.

They had organised the defence, jointly with a small infantry detachment from Warsaw's Defence Forces, very well. A rota of relief was adopted, enabling them to take an occasional rest.

Without a word I decorated Antek Bielecki with the Cross and embraced him heartily.

"Our country be praised," he said simply . . . and it was all over.

I did not inform him of the talks regarding the capitulation—I could not.

Before dusk I returned to my H.Q. in Parkowa Str. There I found new orders, received in my absence by Major Tomaszewski. We were to relinquish our positions, close the Regiment in Pius XI Str., and stand by there in the doorways of houses; it was almost an unharmed area and we could easily find shelter there. And I was to report personally to the Brigade H.Q. for further orders.

I drove to the Brigade H.Q.: Tomaszewski closed the Regiment and took it, in small groups, mounted and dismounted, to the new area. I arranged to return later to Pius XI Str.

There was a Commanding Officers' meeting in Brigade H.Q. We

were told the conditions of the capitulation: owing to the soldierly qualities of the defenders it would be an honourable capitulation. German units would enter the town after the defenders had left it. The German Command guaranteed that all other ranks would be released to return to their homes, and they would not be treated as prisoners of war.

Only officers would be taken prisoners, but they would have the right to retain their side-arms as a symbol of surrender, with full honours of war!

The Polish Command would order the collective surrender of all firearms, machine-guns and artillery. The Germans agreed not to watch this humiliation.

The units would march out of the town in columns, at times agreed upon by both Commands.

We listened silently to these grim words; there were no questions or comments. Our minds recognised the inevitability of capitulation, but our feelings could not accept it. It was as if something was locked both before and behind us; we could not be reconciled to it. Was this to be the end? It was as though one had had a heavy blow on the head and was overcome by some mental paralysis. We did not see any way out. But this would surely come later—it *must* mature in us. Our whole desire was reduced to the will to be faithful to the end and not to lose our dignity.

That was all we could do now.

It was late at night when I found the Regiment in Pius XI Str., and immediately I called all the officers to a meeting in an empty flat on the ground floor.

In our very neighbourhood there was a tragedy. In the yard of the same house there was a well—the usual deep-planked well—with water in the bottom. Somebody must have removed the cover, and the horses, sensing water, began to crowd round it and to push their thirsty muzzles into the dark opening. One of them fell into it, as into a grave. We could not see into it. It was so deep, even the beam of a torch did not reach very far. We could only hear the groaning— the muffled, horrifying groan of a faithful companion in arms. . . . It was almost human. We could not rescue it. The horse would not capitulate to the Germans—it had found another solution. . . .

The officers arrived. Somebody managed to procure a candle and I spoke by its dim light. My heart was heavily burdened, although I tried to speak briefly and in a matter-of-fact way.

I read the order regarding the capitulation and the conditions appertaining to it. I explained that the order was issued by the officer entrusted with the command there, General J. Rommel, who had no doubt reached his decision after having exhausted all other possibilities of action, and although it was heartrending, it must be carried out by us in every detail, honestly and in a soldierly manner. That was our duty. Besides, they themselves could appreciate the situation: any further continuation of the battle was, for the civilians' sake, impossible.

The regular officers of our Regiment had to drain this cup of bitterness to the end and, until all N.C.O's and lancers were freed, according to the conditions of the capitulation, they would not be allowed to relinquish the ranks and seek cover in civilian clothes in Warsaw. I gave permission to the reserve officers to do so immediately: they need only say at once, on the spot, whether or not they wished to avail themselves of this opportunity.

There were no applications; nobody wanted to desert the Regiment.

I finished my address with the usual phrase: "Are there any questions?"

I watched their hard-bitten, tired faces. . . . A long and heavy silence reigned. . . . In the end it was interrupted by Capt. E. Ksyk, from the 3rd Squadron: "Sir, will you allow me to speak?"

The little figure of Ksyk stretched to attention, as stiff as only he could, and next to him stood his subalterns—first, second and third, clicking their spurs.

"I report, Sir," said Ksyk, "that I myself, and the whole of my 3rd Squadron"—again the rattling of the spurs—"refuse to obey the order to capitulate. Tomorrow morning we shall attack the Germans so that it can remain the regimental tradition that the 9th Lancers do *not* surrender."

He finished.

Something strangled my throat. It was so fine a gesture, and I knew there was no pose in it: it was typical of the traditions of our Regiment. I thought of our Podolia, of Jazlowiec, of the incorrigible romanticism of "the last of the Mohicans" with their sabres under the panels.

In a long and persuasive speech I tried to explain how silly such a step would be. It might suit fainthearted bankrupts, but not us. We would not be giving up the fight—it was only a break in the Regiment's war activities and existence: one period was closed, but the next would definitely come. They were, however, only convinced by a particular phrase, heard once somewhere by me, which I quoted to them:

". . . Who cannot endure a defeat is not worthy of victory. . . ." This appealed to them, and they gave way.

While I was speaking, however, something happened to me. My mental paralysis receded and again I visualised a way out from behind this locked door—a simple, clear, and positive way, not like the one chosen by the horse in the well.

My thoughts formulated more clearly: a new decision was born. Ksyk brought it about.

CHAPTER 6

Captivity and Escape

ON THE 28th September we were transferred to the barracks of the Chevaux Légers in Lazienki. All the cavalry were concentrated there and all regimental questions were settled before they marched out from Warsaw—or, rather, before the real dissolution of the regiments.

There took place decorations with Military Crosses, promotions of N.C.O's and the bravest lancers; payments on account to O.R's and officers, until the whole cash in the regiment had been exhausted; and above all, arrangements were made for depositing the Regimental Colours in safe custody. The Colours must not go into captivity: they must be hidden, with the greatest secrecy.

On 29th September, my Regiment stood for the last time on parade, in double rank.

All other ranks, with homes to the east of the German-Soviet demarcation line, who expressed the will to return there were supposed to leave Warsaw that night. About one-third of our lancers and the majority of our N.C.O's came from this part. They were returning to Trembowla to their families. Major Tomaszewski, my Second-in-command, accompanied them to the demarcation line, where the Germans had to hand them over to the Soviets.

The remaining other ranks and all the officers and horses remained in Warsaw to march in a column to the west, probably on 30th September.

It was the last opportunity of saying goodbye to the whole Regiment.

The Regiment paraded under Major Tomaszewski. . . . Everyone was impressed by the gravity of the moment. I greeted the Regiment, and for the last time passed in front of it. The A.D.C. read a final regimental order, and I made a speech.

56

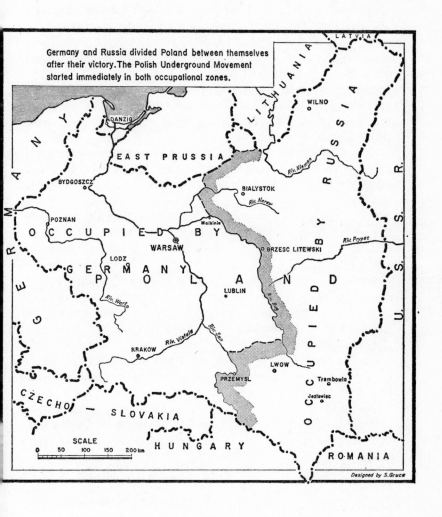

Germany and Russia divided Poland between themselves after their victory. The Polish Underground Movement started immediately in both occupational zones.

LATVIA

LITHUANIA

WILNO

GERMANY

DANZIG

EAST PRUSSIA

BYDGOSZCZ

Riv. Niemen

BIALYSTOK

Riv. Narew

OCCUPIED BY RUSSIA

POZNAN

OCCUPIED BY

Malkinie

WARSAW

LODZ

BRZESC LITEWSKI

Riv. Prypec

GERMANY

POLAND

Riv. Warta

LUBLIN

Riv. Bug

OCCUPIED

U.S.S.R.

KRAKOW

Riv. Vistula

Riv. San

LWOW

PRZEMYSL

Trembowla

CZECHO-

Jazlowiec

SLOVAKIA

SCALE

0   50   100   150   200 km

HUNGARY

ROMANIA

Designed by S.Gruca

I paid homage to our dead companions in arms; I thanked the living for the commendable fulfilment of their duties; I spoke about the necessity of contining the struggle, pointing to France as the place we should each try to reach; and I expressed deep faith in our ultimate victory and trust that our Regiment would soon be reformed.

The farewell was crowned with a hurrah for our country and the usual "*Czolem Ulani*" ("Hail, Lancers!") answered by "*Czolen Panie Pulkowniku*" ("Hail, Sir!"), but sounding this day strangely unlike the usual shout.

One copy of the last regimental order was taken by Capt. Juszczak, who was going to the west, the other by the Regimental Sergeant-Major Semeniuk, who put it in the leg of one of his riding boots, taking it with him to the east.

Thus we closed our regimental affairs, and immediately afterwards I went with Kowalski and Sapieha in our jeep to town, to seek a suitable place in which to hide and preserve our Colours in safe custody.

The decision was very difficult. Finally we chose St. Anthony's Church in Senatorska Str. It was a church which alone had remained undamaged, surrounded by ruined and burned-down houses. It appeared to us the proper place.

At first the old priest was afraid of the great responsibility and was doubtful whether he could take such a valuable deposit. Later on he took us round the outside of the church and, carefully watching his step as he went, showed us in what a miraculous way the church had remained undamaged.

"You notice," he said, "this bomb-crater so close to the church, but the building remained intact. See, all around is burned—even the palace of the Zamoyskis upon which the church leans; but no harm has come to our church. Look at this burned corner of the roof: it took fire from the palace, and there was nobody to put the fire out: St. Anthony extinguished it himself. It burned for a short while, then it went out by itself, miraculously."

He apparently changed his mind about the Colours, for he led us to the altar. When we had knelt down, he put on his stole, told us to take the Colours out of the case, gave each of us a lighted candle to hold, and said prayers over us from his missal; finally, he shook hands with us and took the Colours.

We were confounded and embarrassed by this unexpected ceremony. It seemed as though we were in another world. But we made no protest: probably this was the appropriate rite.

While we were there he put the Colours in the vestry, among other liturgical vestments, and said: "I shan't even tell my curate—it is unnecessary. He might blab. You can be sure you will receive the Colours back yourselves, with Our Lord's help."

We said goodbye to the old man and went back to the Regiment. Sapieha remained in town to collect a few civilian suits of his father's and to leave them with the parents of our officer, Lieut. Neuman: they might be useful to us should we escape from German captivity. The former Foreign Secretary, Eustace Sapieha, was away from Warsaw, and I was sure his wardrobe would promptly be given to serve our country.

The morale of the Regiment was good. They brought us wine from the cellars of the Polish President in the Castle—valuable vintage bottles. It was far better that we should empty them than leave them for the Germans! The wine was excellent, though an amazing assortment: Tokay a hundred years old; then aged Burgundy; again Madeira so thick that one could almost slice it; and again Tokay. . . .

The whole Cavalry Group was ordered to pass the crossroads Ksiazeca Str. and Nowy Swiat on 1st October at 1 a.m. We mounted our horses and walked them: there were sufficient horses for us all. With us we took one field-cooker and a few carts. We wore our Sam Brownes, sabres at side, and did not look too bad: the Germans should see us looking smart until the end.

It was bright daylight when we passed Wola and when our Brigade stretched along the main road to Pruszkow. Outside Wola we were met by German motor-cyclists and armoured cars which led us to a field near Pruszkow, where we stopped to bivouac, adding to the number of thousands of soldiers assembled there from units of Warsaw's defenders.

German tanks surrounded the field—we were prisoners of war. This, the first day our Regiment went into captivity, was, by a strange coincidence, again a Sunday.

For several days we remained there; later we were moved to a similar field, near Grodzisk. The weather became foul: it drizzled and was cold; and we were hungry. No food was supplied either to us or to our horses: we had to live off the fields, on the cabbages and potatoes we found there. We were indebted to the local population for bringing us food in their baskets and bags, which the Germans did not forbid.

Meanwhile we released our lancers in turns, and we handed over our horses. Finally, after ten days' bivouacking near Grodzisk, there

59

were only officers left in the camp. We were then marched to Blonie and shut in the match factory there, thence to be entrained for prisoner-of-war camps in Germany.

There, for the first time, I saw people at their worst; there were horrible displays of crass selfishness. From time to time quarrels arose about a supposedly better place on a straw bed, or about priority in the queues for meals; or about a wretched surplus spoonful of food. Conduct that would be unthinkable in normal life took place in captivity—but, thank God! not too frequently. Nevertheless, it gave one a terrible foretaste of possible experiences in the future.

Some of them were men whose natural empty-headedness or vulgarity was concealed only by a very thin layer of superficial culture; others were simply poor wretches, outcasts from ordinary social life, who were unable to adjust themselves to such a changed environment. They entirely forgot themselves when deprived of responsibility and freed from the critical eyes of their subalterns. Luckily, such cases were rare, and they met with energetic counter-measures from more steady colleagues.

The next day after our imprisonment in Blonie, I summoned the officers of my Regiment to a secret meeting, outside the fences of the factory. I told them that now that the lancers had left it was the duty of every one of us to escape from captivity and to cross to France, where a new Polish Army would be formed to continue the struggle begun by us. We must do it at once, before we were sent to Germany, whence escape would be extremely difficult. I told them that, personally, I had decided to quit the camp: Bielecki was the only officer I had asked to remain, as he was terribly exhausted and ill, and I was afraid he would not stand up to fresh exertions.

Alas! my initiative was met by disapproval from the C.O. of the 17th Lancers, who as senior in rank took the place of our Brigadier, Col. Strzelecki, who had escorted a party of lancers to the east. The C.O. expressed the opinion that it was our duty—especially of high-ranking officers—to remain in the camp.

I did not agree with this, and I notified him officially that I should avail myself of the first opportunity to escape. We parted coolly.

It is possible that, thanks to his point of view, comparatively few officers decided to risk this step. Obviously it was not an easy decision to make. The German Camp Commandant had issued definite orders to shoot at anybody who attempted to escape, and these were promulgated to everyone. Nevertheless, actual conditions for escape were certainly more favourable there than they would be later on in Germany.

Four officers from our Regiment escaped with me, thanks mainly to Dr. Paczkowski's help; he enabled us to pass the gates disguised as medical orderlies carrying seriously ill patients to the hospital in the town. I myself was carried out simulating a dangerous illness, and found myself in the hospital, billeted in a school building in Blonie, where all the wounded soldiers collected from neighbouring battle-fields were assembled by the German authorities.

It was a temporary Polish hospital, with Major Dr. Jacobson in command, the other doctors and staff being recruited by the Germans from the prisoner-of-war camp in Blonie. There were no medicines or dressings in this overcrowded hospital, and seriously wounded soldiers were lying on the ground. Doctors and nurses worked without ceasing, to try and save those poor mutilated bodies.

The parish priest and the local population took over the supply of food.

The hospital was surrounded by German guards, but nevertheless it was an excellent springboard from which to escape from captivity.

I sent a boy on a bicycle to Warsaw, and he brought me back one of Prince Eustace Sapieha's suits previously deposited for us. I also informed Countess Theresa Lubienska of my whereabouts, as I knew that all underground activities in Warsaw would be concentrated in her flat. Mrs. Wieniawska, the wife of Antek who was killed attacking the Dabrowski fort, brought there her husband's fur coat for me.

Finally, on Sunday, the 22nd October—again a Sunday!—messengers arrived from Countess Lubienska; they were Louis Plater Zyberk and my brave cousin, Miss Isabel Czarkowska-Golejewska. They had come to take me away in a car flying a huge Red Cross flag. The flag worked wonders: we could pass without challenge; I had only to change quickly and to walk with them out of the building. We passed the guard at the gates without any difficulty. The engine started with alacrity, and we hastened towards Warsaw. The nightmare of captivity vanished; the road to France, back to our Colours, was open.

CHAPTER 7

Appraisal

I THOUGHT a great deal about the 1939 Campaign after my return to Warsaw—and later during my incarceration in Soviet prisons.

Being for several years a lecturer on general tactics in our Staff College, I had taken an active part in training officers for our field staffs, and had helped to shape the opinions of our Army on tactics and strategy.

Our strategy was based on studies of military classics and compared their values with historical examples and our own experiences in the Campaign of 1920. Our main idea was to obtain a decisive victory in the field of battle. We thought it was possible to achieve this by applying tactical mobility, by economy of force in the choice of a promising direction for the attack, and by the greatest exploitation of the surprise element. We decided that, because of our slow rate of mobilisation in comparison with the readiness of our potential enemy, and our lower war potential, we should aim at results by succeeding stages originating from a counter-offensive. We underlined the necessity for a tactical defence as an element of economy of force and a cover for the future build-up.

As such a doctrine required great strategic flexibility and mobility, we aimed at training suitable flexible and skilful staff officers understanding our strategic principles, and we tried to adapt the organisation of the Army and of the staffs to those demands.

In our theoretical work we took into account the modern battle-field—*i.e.*, intervention in great strength of air power and armoured units—and we tried to adapt to these military developments our classical principles.

The classical strategic and tactical doctrines were well known to our Commander-in-Chief and the Chief of the General Staff and were approved by them. This was confirmed during many inspections of the Staff College and by entrusting us, in the last years before the war, with the organisation and leadership of war games, *i.e.*,Tactical Exercises without Troops, for strategic task forces and their staffs and for generals and staff officers, thus enlarging the activities of the Staff College beyond the ordinary training of their students.

Of course we did not know the actual war plans, but our doctrine was correct and would meet the demands of the plan.

When, after a month of fighting, we had not only lost the war—which was probably inevitable—but had lost it in so short a time, I was forced to reconsider the whole problem. Something was wrong. Either the doctrine itself was bad, or the actual plans failed to match it.

I had to reject the first possibility, even if only because the Germans had a completely identical doctrine and they could hardly complain of it.

There remained the second alternative—that it was not adapted to our own war potential and plans, and, as a result, was bad for us.

The mobility of the Germans in a manoeuvre was 25 miles an hour; we could reach only $2\frac{1}{2}$ miles; thus the German fire-power was at least ten times superior to ours. In view of this disproportion, our determination to seek decisions by operational manoeuvres and tactical concentration of fire was to say the least of it, unwise. Placed as we were, we ought to have had a doctrine more closely adapted to our war potential.

It should have been a doctrine of "endurance"—entirely defensive, at variance with our natural aspirations—and with our military traditions and our hopes of becoming a great Power. At first sight it would appear to be faint-hearted and mean, and a powerful authority would have been necessary to launch us on such a new course without fear of accusation of incapacity and defeatism.

Had the idea of strategic defence, as opposed to offence, been launched at the highest level, however, I think we should have been able to provide it with theoretical arguments, and to arouse sympathetic understanding of it among our soldiers. Then, I think, results would have been entirely different.

It would not have caused any undermining of the principles of war: it would simply have been an adjustment of the means of their application to actual conditions.

I now visualised our future plan and doctrine as follows. We must reject the idea of seeking a decision in a way involving our two powerful enemies, Russia and Germany, without Allied intervention; otherwise we would stand no chance of victory. Accordingly, we must adopt a defensive strategy to enable us to hold out until the effective intervention of our Allies. We must therefore train our Army and prepare the country for defence in depth by detailed attention to all organisational and training factors and by accumulating stores for this one aim.

We must discard as unreal the possibility of achieving a full mobilisation of the so-called "national potential", which in the last war had to be carried out after war had begun. We must also halt all movements of the civilian population as unnecessary. Instead, we should organise, in readiness, a number of large defence centres, located in terrain easy to defend against armoured divisions, and with good air cover and well-stocked stores, to emerge from these fortresses only in exceptional circumstances.

These apparently extreme views were formed in Warsaw in discussion with many of my colleagues.

With such a strategy we thought we should be able to face with confidence any enemy invasion or war imposed upon us.

What would be the likely result? After a thorough discussion, we came to the conclusion that a campaign would probably be protracted through a winter, giving our Western Allies time to organise their forces and keeping enemy forces tied up in Poland.

We thought that our conception was feasible and that it might be prepared and carried out.

Even now I am not sure whether this plan would have been the answer in our particular situation. Nevertheless, one thing is certain: the official strategy with which we went into battle in 1939 was not adjusted to our war potential and was, because of that, wrong. We needed some other conception—probably on the lines I have sketched above.

Our tactical principles, however, as opposed to our strategy, did not seem to need re-thinking.

All the tactical principles and teachings in our manuals, as accepted and propagated in the Army before 1939, were completely reasonable. Anyone disregarding them would be courting disaster: their application, at least, ensured the minimum losses.

But I saw many culpable and deliberate violations of our tactical principles during the September campaign; very often I could not understand why such mistakes had been made.

64

In 1939 the cavalry wore helmets

An artist's impression of a cavalry skirmish in 1939

General Wladyslaw Sikorski

General W. Anders,
Commander of the Polish
forces in Russia, 1941-2

For instance, in spite of the principle that a defence sector of an infantry division should not be extended beyond five miles, since a longer front rendered the defence purely nominal, during the 1939 Campaign there were divisions entrusted with the defence of sectors as wide as *eighteen* miles. This resulted in a complete upsetting of all operational plans, as they were based on an ineffective defence. We could not find any answer as to why it happened.

There was also the tendency to launch ill-mounted attacks without co-ordination of the various arms. This was as disastrous as the over-extension of our defence. People preferred to look back to the year 1920, rather than pay regard to the planned tactical principles which every commander knew well enough.

Perhaps this was due to improvisation resulting from the fact that the original strategy was lacking in reality, coupled with the impetuous nature of Polish soldiers in a hurry to make good their losses and to prop up the organisation which was falling into ruin.

The cavalry question was one of our greatest disillusions.

We entered the war with forty mounted regiments of cavalry and with faith in their fitness and usefulness in the battle-field. After the 1939 Campaign, we had to admit that mounted cavalry had, in the face of modern weapons, become obsolete. Its fire-power was negligible by comparison, and the horses made it very vulnerable when exposed to enemy fire.

This does not go against the principle of mobility as represented by cavalry, but today horses have to be exchanged for cars or tanks, and before the war we cavalrymen were fervent opponents of this modern ideology. Our devotion to horses and ancient cavalry traditions were to some extent a brake on the propagation of the idea of a change of mount, and that was undoubtedly our mistake; nevertheless, our acceptance of mechanisation would not have been helped much, because of our restricted financial and industrial resources, which in any case prevented the introduction of modern weapons and equipment.

In fact, the cavalry did not play an important part in the campaign, except in terrains inaccessible to tanks. The cavalry was never wrecked, but it could never defeat a formidable mechanised enemy.

I had an opportunity of comparing the morale and the training of soldiers in a regiment in 1920 and in 1939. I must admit that the average value of a soldier during the latter campaign was much the higher of the two. The officer and the lancer were better trained and educated in the military sense. They fought most gallantly, with no difference between Poles of undoubted Polish stock and the descendants of other nationalities.

Considering all the facts, one can only find words of highest praise for the soldiers of our regiments.

CHAPTER 8

Conspirator

I WAS back again in Warsaw, wearing Sapieha's suit and Antek Wieniawski's fur-coat.

Going straight to Theresa Lubienska's flat in Zbawiciela Square, I met there Col. Godlewski (now called Suchodolski), Col. Swiecicki and a few other "deserters" like myself. It appeared that Theresa's flat was a centre and meeting-place for such "deserters": there plans were made to rescue men from camps, or from hospitals which would soon be taken over by the Germans; there everyone could find shelter, help, advice, and a plateful of soup from Theresa's larder.

Mr. Witkowski—or Teczynski (he had several names)—a partisan from General F. Kleeberg's Group, as he introduced himself, was the inspirer of our activities. He already had a car, and had contacts with the "Blue" police,* and even with the German police. He was in his element roaming about Warsaw. The town was coming back to life, but was still in great confusion.

We had all taken the same decision: to reach France as soon as possible. We chose as our best route Cracow, Hungary, and Italy. We rejected the alternative route *via* Lithuania and Sweden—it was alien to us and we preferred to keep to countries known to us.

The thoroughfare from Warsaw to Cracow was very difficult because of the bad communications. Railways were still out of order, and, according to Witkowski, would not be ready to resume services for ten days. The general chaos that reigned in the first days of the occupation, and the Germans' lack of knowledge about our affairs, were rather an incitement to us to hurry. Witkowski suggested bicycles, and some of our "deserters" used them. Finally, by chance, he found a firm of haulage contractors who were carrying passengers at greatly increased fares.

* Polish policemen; forcibly taken over by the German occupation authorities.

Godlewski and Swiecicki availed themselves of this opportunity, but I decided to stay on for another few days in Warsaw. I simply wanted to watch the life and to consider the situation more closely.

First, I had to provide myself with an identity card, which meant changing ny name and assuming a civilian identity. I went to the Warsaw Town Hall and received from their Internal Security Department a temporary certificate stating that my name was S. Bogusz, an inhabitant of Warsaw, and that my papers were lost during the fire. The officer who was issuing such certificates knew well that I was somebody quite different, and a long queue of similar customers was waiting for him: of his own free will he was deliberately issuing false papers so as to help people.

Three days later I was informed that for this activity he had been arrested by the Germans, that the certificates issued by him were invalid, and that all holders of them were being arrested.

In the meantime, however, Witkowski had mobilised his own "factory" for identity cards. He was printing new forms and he managed to acquire a lot of original identity cards. From his collection it was easy to choose a document with a description to fit one's personality.

From there I secured the genuine identity card of a Mr. Joseph Ruminski, whose photograph was replaced by mine. The missing part of the impressed round stamp was then artistically drawn in on it.

To this day I still do not know who the real Mr. Joseph Ruminski was. If he should still be alive, I would like to apologise for assuming his name without his permission and using it for almost three years.

Having thus put in order my personal affairs and recovered freedom of movement, I began to explore Warsaw. First, I went to St. Anthony's Church to see if the Regimental Colours were still safe there.

The old priest did not recognise me at once, but later he expressed pleasure at seeing me and showed me where the Colours were hidden. Fearing the Germans might search the church, he had taken the Colours from among the liturgical vestments, put them into the case and hidden it behind an outstanding marble cornice, above the door to the vestry. "There it will await better times," he said, "as only you and I know this hiding-place."

Yes, there let it stay; anyhow, I could not do anything more, so I said goodbye to the worthy priest.

Then I went to visit the hospitals to find our wounded and to learn their fate. I found Rostworowski in the Ujazdowski Hospital, still in a grave state. At the best, he would be a cripple always and have to use crutches; I could be of no help to him: Theresa Lubienska would look after him.

I found Longchamps and Dabrowiecki in the Hospital of the Knights of Malta, now in the Resursa Kupiecka (Merchants' Club) in Senatorska Str. They were both improving and would soon need assistance to escape so as to avoid being sent to a prisoner-of-war camp. I thought that could be done.

Unfortunately I could not trace the remaining wounded: Elsner, Palka, Ciepiela and others—they were probably in hospitals outside Warsaw.

Finally, I rambled around Warsaw itself. The poor city, although in ruins, was still pulsating with life. Food was very difficult to acquire, however. Windows in undemolished houses were usually plugged up with planks or cardboard: it was impossible to procure glass. Everybody was trying to hoard food; everybody was trading. There were plenty of tradesmen in the streets selling goods. Nobody knew to whom these goods belonged or where they had come from: probably they came from bombed shops or those destroyed by fire. Nobody inquired into this, and nobody was surprised. People were buying and selling—some to earn money for a living, others simply motivated by the mania for trading and speculation. It was most difficult to obtain food, as official supplies had not been resumed; but the enterprising spirit of individual tradesmen, or of self-styled "wholesalers", was fabulous—they knew just how to smuggle in goods from the country. In spite of German orders and various misadventures, food was supplied more plentifully (and could be obtained at excessive prices) on the black market. Without it I think Warsaw would have perished of starvation. The frenzy for trading completely took possession of the inhabitants, awakened their ingenuity, and saved the town.

But there were other phenomena haunting our minds.

People were discussing and digesting our defeat. It was not so much that they were looking for culprits—that was left rather to the representatives of political Parties, who had to settle their accounts with the Governmental *Sanacja*—as that they were raging to have their revenge on the enemy. Rumours spread by German propaganda trying to discredit the Polish war effort were, though readily repeated, not believed; and in any case they did not weaken the common will to fight.

From the very first day Warsaw hated the occupiers, and they were jeered at in the streets.

Posters showing Mr. Neville Chamberlain with his umbrella against the burning Poland in the background, with the inscription: "*England, this is your work!*" reaped a quite opposite result to that intended. People had faith in the West and were expecting liberation from there. Any gossip about the bombardment of Gdansk or Allied parachutists dropped in Eastern Prussia—although completely improbable—found a ready following and spread like wildfire.

Roaming about, I visited many cafés. Lourse's and Blikle's were always full—and no Germans went there. They were the haunts of many Polish officers in mufti, who were easy to recognise at a quick glance. At first they did not even attempt to conceal their identity: many of them were lawfully free, especially officers from Modlin, whose conditions of capitulation had been different from ours in Warsaw. General Thommé, O.C. troops encircled in Modlin, had managed to obtain consent from the Germans to free and send home all soldiers, irrespective of their rank; only later did they have to register.

Thanks to these circumstances we felt safe and were able to discuss the past, and to plan for the future. In cafés and in the streets we were listening to the rhythm of life and the currents pervading it.

The main topic of our conversation was how to reach General Sikorski in France. Everyone was well aware that a new Polish Army was being formed there. At the same time, rumours spread about General M. Karaszewicz-Tokarzewski, who was alleged to be hidden in Warsaw and organising a secret resistance.

Personally, I had decided to go to France: I was attracted by Army life, not by conspiracy, and I was determined to quit Warsaw as soon as possible—especially when I noticed harmless-looking German advertisements in the *Goniec Warszawski*, also posters, asking officers to register in the building of the General Staff in Pilsudski Square. Officers were to attend to this duty in alphabetical order on various days named, to facilitate this formality—which, allegedly, would not endanger them at all.

Many hours were spent in cafés discussing the subject. Should we register or not? I was definitely opposed to it and would not do it. I advised everybody who asked me my opinion to change their name and to go abroad—or at least to hide somewhere.

Some, however, did go to register. They were received in the General Staff offices with utmost kindness and were not detained long: they had only to fill up a form of registration, stating their actual address—a sheer formality dictated by German pedantry, they were told.

The number of officers willing to register therefore increased daily—especially those with families who did not want to expose their dearest ones to possible harm. These men were trapped like children. The first registration was followed by a second—a stricter one; and then the Gestapo collected these people from their flats and sent them to prisoner-of-war camps. Posters called upon the missing ones to report on a given day at the railway station, with their luggage—to be transported to prisoner-of-war camps, otherwise they would be declared outlaws. Many obeyed this summons, thus shattering their naïve faith in German benevolence.

However, there were many of us who were not deceived by the Germans. But we could no longer meet in cafés, and we lost our freedom of movement.

Then, secretly, I began meeting the active politicians—cool-headed men like M. Niedzialkowski from the Polish Socialist Party; Mr. A. Debski from the National Democratic Party, and Mr. B. Biega from the Christian Democratic Party, all planning seriously ahead. But there were some "hot-heads", too, collecting arms and burying them for future use, and also organising groups of diversionists to fight the Germans immediately. Witkowski surpassed all the others in this work: he kept everything rolling, sent out people to collect arms in the Kampinow and Palmiry forests, and in Kock, etc., where a lot of equipment had been left uncollected. Even jettisoned airplanes were dismantled and hidden for the future.

It was with pleasure that I noted all these activities—a healthy symptom, proving an invincible spirit to revenge; but I was terrified by the impetuosity and the individualism displayed, which might bring misfortune so easily.

I did not want to be dragged into these activities, as I intended going to France; but my conscience would not let me stand aside.

Before leaving, I decided to assemble all these individualists and, if General Tokarzewski really had some organisation in being, to hand them all over to him so as to co-ordinate their activities under his leadership. Mysterious rumours about Tokarzewski were incessantly circulating, but nobody knew if they were true—nor how, or where, to find him.

Finally, somebody suggested to me the name of Col. Albrecht, C.O. the 1st Chevaux Légers, who was supposed to be co-operating

71

with Tokarzewski. I did not know Tokarzewski well, but Albrecht had been my colleague. I therefore thought I could find him, hand over my contacts to him, and thus recover freedom of movement.

It was not so easy. At last, Witkowski found out that Col. Albrecht's wife was a nurse in the Ujazdowski Hospital. I found her, asked for a private interview, and told her who I was and why I needed her husband's address. She refused to give it, saying she did not know it herself; I persevered in my attempt; she began to hesitate. At last she asked me to visit her again the next day, in her flat, though she did not promise anything. I supposed that she had to ask somebody's advice—perhaps her husband's. I thought I was on the right track.

The next day in her flat I met Capt. Landowski, a former pupil of mine in the Staff College, who knew me well, and he probably had to check up on my identity. Their caution pleased me.

But Landowski was not authorised to disclose the secrets of the organisation, not did I want to know them. I explained straight away that I was going to France, and only wanted to establish contacts between their organisation and my "individualists"—above all, with Witkowski, who, because of his ebulliency might become dangerous.

Landowski listened to all this, and the next day he gave me the address of an engineering firm in Polna Str. which would mediate in establishing contact with the organisation of "Michael"—i.e., Tokarzewski.

It was all I wanted. I passed the address on to my friends and left Warsaw with a clear conscience.

I went to Cracow from the main railway-station, by one of the first trains that were running—needless to say, travelling third class and standing in the corridor: Germans were sitting in the compartments. When I tried to put my suitcase on the shelf in the compartment, the order came, "*Weg damit!*" (Take it away!). I raged inwardly, clenching my fists, but my common sense warned me, "Be patient. . . ."

The train crawled, and it was late in the afternoon before we reached Cracow. One could see German armed guards and many soldiers about; probably from Army transports. Cracow was definitely a station for the occupying Army, and the few "civilians" who alighted from the Warsaw train felt like intruders. Cracow was not for us—it was no longer ours. . . .

Furtively, we slipped away from the station. A railway worker asked me about Warsaw, particularly about the Gornoslaska Str., where some relations of his used to live: for there were not many eye-witnesses of the Warsaw tragedy who came to the Wawel (the castle of the Polish Kings in Cracow). He then warned me that the "police-hour curfew" began at 7.0 p.m.; after this time it was prohibited to move about, and German patrols had the right to shoot if one did. I also read the warning on posters hanging in the railway station.

I looked at my watch: it was 5 p.m.—I had still two hours in which to do something. But what to do I did not know.

As far as I knew, I had no friends here; besides, I did not want to expose anybody to suspicion. I could not go to a hotel—probably they were all occupied by Germans. Therefore I strolled along to the centre of the town. November dusk was already spreading. I passed Basztowa Str., and crossed the Planty (a big park surrounding the city). A few drops of dew fell from the trees on to my collar. It was misty, but the asphalted pavement in front of the Barbakan (the ancient citadel) gleamed as before. I passed the Florianska Gate—and there Cracow stood as always: dear old Cracow. . . .

I walked ahead; everything was so familiar to me, so homely. It was calm and quiet, and I did not see any Germans. There were no ruins or gaps; I became almost buoyant. It was the emotional reaction after Warsaw, where tragedy peeped out of every corner, out of the stumps of trees in squares and parks. It was, if anything, more painful still from a distance. . . . Dear old Cracow! Perhaps they did not dare to touch it: perhaps the majesty of Royalty prevented them.

I entered the market-place and saw the Sukiennice, the "A-B Line". There were lights in Mauricio's café. I walked in. From experience acquired in Warsaw, I knew that in cafés one could often get wind for one's sails; it probably applied to Cracow, too.

I was right! I immediately spotted the long nose of Miss Mary Krzeczunowicz. I could be reassured about my future!

Mary had volunteered at the outbreak of the war as a nurse. She had been in different sectors of the front line: she saw and knew everything—only for fun or excitement, you know. Now, here in Cracow, she was looking after such people as myself—again, only for fun. But this, of course, was untrue. I knew her too well; her gener-ous heart and her splendid character. She was wise, like a rabbi; courageous, like a devil; sweet, dear Mary.*

Immediately she found a night's lodgings for me, and the follow-

* Later she became the Resistance spirit of the Cracow district. Several times she went, as courier, to Budapest and Rome. Finally she was killed, somewhere in the Balkans, during one of her escapades.

ing morning I became a "permanent inhabitant" of Cracow, with all my papers in order—she had connections everywhere, even in the Town Hall—living in 14, Pieracki Str. (where she lived, too) as the subtenant of some friends. She began to introduce me to members of the Cracow "Underground" organisation, which was just then beginning to simmer.

The situation here was similar to the one in Warsaw. Besides wanderers with faked documents like myself, aiming *via* Cracow for the Carpathian Mountains and Hungary, or for Lwow and Rumania, local enthusiasts had started an organisation.

There were quite a few of them. There were the National Democrats under Mr. S. Surzycki's leadership; there was Col. Wolf-Gierzkowski, belonging, as far as I could make out, to the Pilsudskist Governmental Party; and Pakosz, who pretended to be a colonel and was organising the groups of diversionists in and around Cracow. They were all active and exuberant; but they neither knew how to organise nor had any directives from the Polish Government, and they did not even know if General Sikorski had entrusted anybody with the leadership. Any one of them would willingly have accepted this task.

I realised the danger of such spontaneous, unplanned activities—which could lead here, as in Warsaw, to tragic consequences.

Together with Col. Godlewski, whom I found here, we decided that before going on to France (*via* Hungary) we would try to establish contacts between the local spontaneous groups and the Warsaw organisation of "Michael" Tokarzewski, which was beginning to be known in Cracow, although it had rather a bad name. Cracow was following the leadership of the National Democrats, and recoiled from co-operation with "Michael" because he had been a leading personality of the pre-war *régime*, on whom they blamed responsibility for defeat. People said: "Miedzinski?... All the pre-war *régime* people back him."

"You and Godlewski were not politicians or active members of the pre-war *régime*; therefore you have an opportunity of doing something and getting a following. You should stay here."

That was true: we were not the political "colonels" of the pre-war *régime*; we had never been politicians—only soldiers, who knew that it was the Germans who were responsible for our defeat, not our pre-war Government. But we wanted, as soon as possible, to join a real army; we were not suited to conspiracy.

In view of the situation, however, we came to the conclusion that it was impossible to quit Cracow, and that we had to help to iron things out. Thus we got involved in "politics" with the zealous youth of Cracow.

From my cousin, Miss Zaba, a doctor in the Bonifratres Hospital, I knew that Col. Thaddeus Komorowski,* from whom I had taken over the command of the 9th Lancers in 1938, was hidden in the hospital. I had known him for years, and had always kept him in high esteem. He was an excellent soldier, of crystal-clear character, who had a gift for social activities—as I fully grasped later when taking over from him the chairmanship of the Co-ordinating Committee of the Polish Welfare Organisation in south-eastern Podolia.

He was obviously the right man for the job. We must thrust *him* into the resistance activities in Cracow and recover our freedom.

I paid him a visit in the hospital, and he at once accepted the task. He had no documents, but already possessed a civilian suit. I asked him what name he would assume for his new identity.

"Call me Korczak," he said.

In three days Mr. "Korczak" left the Bonifratres Hospital to take lodgings in Pieracki Str., under Mary's wing. In the meantime, I became his Second-in-command and his Chief of Staff. Godlewski went to Chrobrze to stay with Zygmunt Wielopolski, an officer from his regiment. He was left there as reserve, in case we should be caught. We were becoming cautious.

Komorowski soon became known to active people in Cracow and established many local contacts. But we experienced grave difficulties, being without money and not having established liaison with the Polish Government in Paris: this was extremely important, as we needed directives from somebody in authority. To be successful, an organisation must have definite aims, and we had to know the task entrusted to our organisation in Poland: was it intelligence, sabotage activities, or an armed rising? And when? We could not answer all these questions ourselves. It was no good to be pushed to extremes by the emotive force of the masses. If let loose, this could prove disastrous.

However, there were many things to be done—such as organising the evacuation of people anxious to reach France, issuing them with identity cards, providing safe shelter, secretly evacuating people from German camps and hospitals in Dabie, the welfare of refugees. . . . A lot of work! We could now answer some of the burning questions

* Later known as General T. Bor Komorowski, Commander of the Underground Forces and Polish C. in C.

which mostly excited the hot-heads. Meanwhile, many self-styled "leaders" and organisers of secret activities established themselves— all individualists, all threatening to do more or less foolish things according to their temperament. We had very similar reports from beyond the San, the Soviet-occupied territories.

I was faced with the necessity of going to Budapest to establish liaison there with Paris. But I decided to go first to Lwow for a few days to find out what the situation was there, and then to cross the Carpathian Mountains with a full report. At the same time, I wanted to find out what had happened to all our families left in Trembowla —including my own. Komorowski agreed to this, and the decision was taken. I went east. That was in the second half of November.

CHAPTER 9

The Demarcation Line

THE EASIEST way to Lwow was *via* Przemysl. Trains ran from Cracow to Przemysl-Zasanie, and no special permits were required. Allegedly, from time to time, the Germans allowed people free passage across the railway bridge on the San, and let a crowd of refugees, mostly Jews, go to the east—to the "paradise". It was necessary to mingle with the crowd in Przemysl and catch another train there to Lwow; such was our information in Cracow, so I chose that way.

I reached Zasanie quite easily. There were huge crowds of Jews waiting at the bridge. The Germans played tricks with them— robbing them of all their gold dollars which they had brought before letting them set foot on the bridge, only to be recalled. Then the Bolsheviks refused them admission. Talks were said to be going on to establish a mixed Control Commission for verifying the refugees.

The idyllic times when it was possible freely to cross the bridge had gone; the demarcation line was closed; to cross it lawfully was impossible: it had to be done secretly. The crowds were as though in a drag-net—they could neither go forwards nor backwards. The Jews would willingly have jumped into the icy water in order to reach the "paradise" on the other side—but the Bolsheviks shot at any desperadoes who did so, and they were swept down with the current.

My enterprising spirit, however, would not let me give up. Some Jews told me that in a village about six miles north of Przemysl a ferry-man would take Jews across the river at night. His name was Fedko; everybody in the village knew him.

I went there and found Fedko, who frankly told me how it worked, as he could see I was one of his own folk.

"I take a full load of Jews in my boat until it almost capsizes. When

77

we have passed the middle of the river, the Jews all shout: 'Long live Stalin!' Bolshevik guards arrive, collect them quickly, and take them away. The Jews are so frightened that they leave half their luggage in my boat, and the other half is taken by the Russian soldiers. That's the procedure—blast them!"

He charged for the crossing twenty zlotys per person. I liked Fedko! He told me there was no other chance of crossing the river, and he even dissuaded me from attempting it. We parted friends.

I returned to Zasanie, rather despondent, hungry and dirty. I went into a pub, which was almost black from steam and dirt. There were crowds at the bar and sitting at tables. Only a kind of broth and plentiful vodka were served. Feeling dispirited, I had a few drinks. There were no Jews there. But there were some petty criminal types— mostly resetters or smugglers, attracted by the frontier and seeking easy prey. I listened to their conversations: all concerned only with prices on this side or the other.

My attention became focused on three typical *batiars*.* They had recently brought some goods from Lwow and were discussing the return journey. I concluded they were the right type for me. I like *batiars*, so I sat down at their table. We had a round of vodka, and then began to talk shop.

It became clear to me that they were penniless, and because of it they had got into trouble the previous evening.

"We went last night to Tarnowce—there's a ford on the San. We persuaded the silly peasant to show it to us for a quid. We didn't pay him, so the scoundrel cheated us! Would you believe it, old man, we went into this bloody icy water and almost got drowned. . . . Blast him!"

They related this adventure with humour; they did not mind it at all. They thought the peasant was quite right: he did not want to appear a fool.

I suggested another expedition to Tarnowce that night, and said I would pay for it.

They immediately agreed.

We started well before dusk—this time about four miles south up the river. We found the same peasant. I gave him on account twenty zlotys and promised to give him another twenty at the ford. He directed us to his brother-in-law, Wasylko, who lived on the other side of the river, where we could wait until the morning and then hire a cart to take us to the railway station in Przemysl. Immediately after

* A *batiar* is a "Cockney" of Lwow.

78

dark we began moving towards the river; at first very quietly along the road, then across country and through osiers; it was drizzling, muddy and cold.

In front of me I heard the guide whisper: "It's a good time for crossing: the soldiers will be sheltering in such weather."

And soon another voice: "Chum, don't bray about 'a good time' —only show us the ford. Look, Joe, what a hero! Blimey! He won't go into the blasted water in this weather!"

It was difficult not to smile at this sample of humour, so typical of Lwow.

As we approached the river we frequently stopped in the dark listening, and became more cautious. At last, through the osiers, we saw the river San. We very carefully crept to the bank; pebbles were under our feet.

"Here is the ford," whispered the guide. "Go in the direction of those willow-trees and then towards that group of tall trees—there is the village where Wasylko lives."

We stooped over the water and, peering against the light, we could observe how the water was rippling, thus tracing the ford.

We discarded our shoes and trousers, as the water in some places would reach our waist.

Suddenly we crouched, as two rifle shots were fired from the opposite bank, and the tracer bullets soared over our heads.

"Don't be silly—they took shelter!" whispered one of the *batiars*.

The guide tried to reassure us: they always used to fire shots into the air just to frighten people; it was a routine patrol. The soldiers were about 300 feet from the ford: they could not see us; we might safely enter the water.

I noticed that my *batiars* had decidedly lost their enthusiasm.

We waited crouching for half an hour; it was silent and calm. I decided to attempt the crossing.

"We'd better not waste time," I suggested; "let's go. One of us must risk first; when we see he's successful the rest of us follow."

The boys agreed with me in principle, but none of them would go first.

"*You* go first, if you're so clever," said one of them to me. This made me angry.

"What do you mean?! I'm the eldest of us, and yet you pups want to hide behind me! Where is your pride? And who gave the forty zlotys—you or I? Forward, one of you, into the water!"

They whispered among themselves, and finally one of them said:

"He's right. He thinks we're afraid. Damn it! I'll go!" And he went, fording like a stork. His features soon became hazy in the dark.

It was completely quiet. He seemed to have reached the other bank safely, so we followed.

A few minutes later we were all on the other side.

I climbed up the steep bank, crouching for a short while. . . . But look! Along the steep edge was a well-trodden footpath, probably used by the patrols. We had better go ahead immediately.

With boots and trousers in my hands, I ran about three hundred yards into the fields, so as to be clear of the footpath as quickly as possible. Although covered in mud, I dressed. The *batiars* linked up with me, and we started to walk in the direction of the group of trees to the village—to Wasylko.

Outside a farmyard we met a boy, who for ten zlotys took us to Wasylko. He did not seem at all surprised at our nocturnal arrival— he probably knew the whole procedure and had often, perhaps, led customers to Wasylko. But disappointment met us: Wasylko refused even to see us! He told the boy to tell us that the Bolsheviks had issued new orders: that they were searching houses at night, and had threatened to arrest anybody who dared to harbour refugees. We must go away immediately: the best thing we could do was to go to the next village, as far away from the river as possible.

We walked on ahead. The rain soaked us, and we were getting tired, but we reached the next village without mishap.

All attempts to get shelter at any of the houses there, however, were in vain. Everywhere we received the same answer: searches and arrests.

At last we came to a decent man, a good Polish patriot. After some hesitation he let us in. Without striking a light, he put up a ladder to the garret and said:

"There is some hay. . . . Lie quietly till the morning; don't make a sound, because if there were a search we should all get into trouble."

We slept there till the morning, our teeth chattering with cold. But we were happy to have a roof over our heads. In the morning we drove in a cart to a spot near to Przemysl, alighting before we reached the town and then walking so as not to be conspicuous. Everything was going smoothly.

What we saw in Przemysl was very different from the German zone we had just left. Here, too, there were crowds of refugees milling about the streets, but these were not Jews trying to reach "paradise": they were Poles trying to escape from it. Exiled from their homes, they had been attracted by Przemysl as a place where one could (at first) legally cross the demarcation line to the West. They now lived, jammed together, with their children and luggage, in unheated schools and other municipal buildings, without food or any hope of crossing the demarcation line.

A number of suspicious-looking touts exploited the refugees by buying for a trifle any valuable goods which they might have—and which they had to sell to keep themselves alive.

The more courageous ones, if they had some money, hired guides and at night attempted an illegal crossing of the San. But the majority were helpless in their misfortune: they were destined to populate the steppes of the Kazak S.S.R.

With difficulty I managed to enter the railway station, and eventually the Lwow train. Finally I reached my destination.

As I left Lwow station I saw a man of outlandish features sitting on a high chair in the ticket-collector's stand, noting each passer-by with a vigilant look. He wore a black leather jacket. I met his eye steadily, then passed him, unmolested, and emerged with the crowd into the street.

CHAPTER 10

Soviet Sector

IT WAS almost incredible how much the character of the town had changed in only six weeks. No longer was it the serene, beautiful, Western town of Lwow. Although outwardly the same—there was hardly any war damage—the whole town was really quite different; it was imbued with the spirit of Communist Asia. Everything I saw aroused my indignation. In streets and on buildings there were huge posters with slogans like "PROLETARIANS OF ALL COUNTRIES, UNITE!" Large drawings of Lenin and Stalin grinned at passers-by; loud-speakers roared music or speeches incessantly. In the Waly Hetman-skie Gardens, next to the monument of King John Sobieski, the invaders had put up a colossal wooden monument covered with concrete—a glorification of the Soviet Union.

In the middle of this dirt and noise, crowds of people walked in the Akademicka Str. (the "promenade" of Lwow Society), but how strange-looking, how different from the genuine townspeople. It was not a mere shifting of people from the busy Mikolasz Passage to the exclusive Akademicka Str.: it was more like a wholesale invasion of complete strangers into the Mariacki Square and its neighbourhood. Different types of "activists", mostly with Oriental features, were in evidence, aping the wear of orthodox Communists but in reality "smart Alecs". They mingled with Soviet soldiers, wandering about and trading at each corner. The Mikolasz Passage looked like a market. There one could buy or sell anything—watches, secondhand suits, underwear, shoes, vodka, and other luxury goods, previously unknown in such quality and quantity to the Soviet people. Soviet officers and soldiers were mostly the buyers; the sellers were re-cruited from casual tradesmen, or came from the gutter. The Soviets bought everything—ladies' underwear, dresses, spoons, forks, torches, etc. Wrist-watches secured the top price, especially if they had black faces and shining hands. The sale of such a watch was not a simple transaction. The potential buyer took a knife from his pocket, with it he opened the cover of the watch, and asked the vendor to show him the jewels. The seller assured him there were at least fifteen (it was the lowest admissible number; the buyer gave himself out as an expert); then both of them very seriously "counted" the jewels, which they could hardly see. In doubtful cases witnesses were called—the seller had his mates, the buyer his Red Army colleagues. A group thus formed examined the watch, each using his knife for opening the cover and listening carefully to the ticking. The final argument to convince the Soviet buyer was an assurance given by the seller that it was a "Cyma" watch. Everybody was then happy, and the transaction was accomplished.

Besides this Eastern Lwow there was another—the old one, carefully concealed, the townspeople trembling and jammed in their flats, where the Bolsheviks, often with their families, intruded as "non-paying guests". It was all done politely, with the landlord's "consent", but it was almost unbearable.

People did not realise how threatening it was: it all appeared rather childish, naïve, and not very dangerous. There was a general opinion that nothing quite so stupid as the Bolsheviks seemed to be could last very long. The *régime* would simply collapse from within. Even the fact that from time to time friends were arrested, to disappear behind the walls of the prison, did not really frighten people. Arrests were being made haphazardly, and were quite understandable in the general confusion. Although there was no news from those who had been arrested, it was said that they were treated not too badly, and that they would soon be released. The authorities must just check up on them; it always takes time. . . .

Everybody was surprised by the amenable attitude of the Bolsheviks. People had expected to see "terrible avengers of the oppressed proletariat": murder and pillage: torturing of the educated classes, or other manifestations of the 1917 Revolution.

Instead, there had been an invasion by naïve Asiatics, whom one could even scold with impunity; at first sight not formidable, but childish, stupid and clumsy. Even the authorities were ridiculous: they introduced an unheard-of confusion in all spheres of life, and nobody could take them seriously. Few people perceived in it the terrible system which slowly, but effectively, was to change our life into a nightmare.

Elections were held to demonstrate the "enthusiastic will" of the inhabitants of the "Western Ukraine" (a name coined by the Soviets for the denomination of occupied Polish territories) to join the Soviet Union. Theoretically, the elections were secret; in fact, they were public. There was only one list of candidates—screened by the N.K.V.D.—for which to vote, so why all this comedy of whitewash? Obviously just another exhibition of childishness, thought the people; anyhow, such elections could not be valid. So they voted, for the sake of peace and in order not to provoke the Soviets unnecessarily; there were so many informers about that people did not know who was reliable and whom to distrust. Besides, Communist militia men called on people who did not vote in the first hours of the morning to urge them to go immediately to the polls. Even people of Ukrainian origin lost their bearings. Khruszczev and Korniejczuk arrived from Kieff, organising big Ukrainian meetings. The incorporation of the "Western Provinces" into the "Motherland" was solemnly celebrated, but it proved to be very different from its face value: only on paper and in many mendacious but loyal addresses, written by the peoples of the "Western Ukraine" to Stalin, the "Father of the Soviet Nations", was there any Ukraine. In *fact*, it was all Russia.

The *"Goniec Polski"* ("Polish Courier"), the only paper in Lwow to be printed in Polish, reported a meeting of Polish professors of the University of King John Casimir in Lwow, who had unanimously agreed to send a telegram of homage to Stalin. The contents of this telegram were nauseating, full of typical Eastern servility and signed by almost all the professors. I met two of them who were friends of mine.

"How could you sign such a disgusting telegram?" I asked them. Both of them answered: "We heard about the meeting, the telegram, and the fact that we had signed it only from the newspaper."

They could not help it: they could not rectify it, as nobody would print a retraction. Anyway, what was the point? Everything appeared so stupid and naïve that the *régime* surely must collapse very soon. . . .

The general opinion could be summarised as follows: "Let us hold out somehow till the spring; the nightmare will be over by then. It cannot possibly last any longer."

There were many Polish soldiers in the town, some who had had the luck to escape from Soviet captivity, others who had come here from the German occupation on their way to Rumania or Hungary. Some of them had already been in Skole or Zaleszczyki—border towns where they had been captured and kept for several days in prison. They had been released and came back here. They would attempt another crossing or would go back to the German side; there was no official organisation to advise them: they only had occasional contacts and help from the railway workers.

There were some Polish wounded soldiers in hospitals, among them General W. Anders, who was treated with special reverence by the Bolsheviks and was looked after by the best Polish surgeons. I wanted to see him and tell him about the situation in the West, but I was warned by his friends not to do so. I heard that, in accordance with his request, he was to be sent to Przemysl on 4th December and handed over to the Germans, so I thought I should be able to see him after my return to the West. I was very pleased with the news, because his personality and name would be invaluable for rallying "enthusiasts" unable to agree with each other.

I met quite a few active people who realised the necessity of establishing an organisation. Of these, Col. Dabrowski was perhaps the most energetic. But everything was in a very rudimentary stage and had quite a different character from that in the German zone.

I concluded I could learn no more in Lwow: I now had a general picture of the situation there and enough insight into its activities, so I decided to return to Cracow.

I sent beforehand for one of my non-commissioned officers from Trembowla, my staff-sergeant, who had gone from Warsaw to the east with a group of lancers. He told me that all of them had happily managed to reach their families in Trembowla, but the families had been thrown out of their flats in the barracks and were all living in the town. The non-commissioned officers and their families were not especially harassed; they managed somehow. But the situation of the officers' wives was much worse. Mrs. Poborowski was in despair about her husband. My wife, threatened with arrest as the wife of the Colonel, had had to escape secretly with our youngest daughter, and they were already in Lwow. When I found her, my wife told me that both non-commissioned officers and railway workers had been extremely helpful in helping her to escape.

I told the staff-sergeant about the fate of the people in German camps, and I committed the officers' wives to the non-commissioned officers' care, as they had no other protection.

"You must help each other, as members of one family, and firmly believe that a change will come . . ." I said to him.

After consultation with my wife, I decided to go to Jazlowiec to see my two elder daughters, caught by the war in the convent school,

85

under the protection of the Sisters of the Immaculate Conception. I wished to find out on the spot if they were threatened by any danger, and whether I ought, perhaps, to take them away to their mother.

I went by train, *via* Stanislawow, and reached Buczacz quite easily. The train ran into the station before dawn, which pleased me as I was able immediately to hire a cab to Jazlowiec (about twelve miles away). I had no desire to rove about Buczacz in the daytime because it was there, not so long ago, on the 15th August—the Soldiers' Feast—that I had delivered an inspiring speech from the balcony of the Town Hall to the local population; I therefore preferred to disappear immediately, unnoticed.

In Jazlowiec, this old grey bastion of chivalrous virtues, my arrival caused tremendous joy. All rules regarding enclosure were suspended. I was immediately surrounded by the nuns, and had to tell them all the news—all about Warsaw, the war, public opinion, the Regiment, and, above all, the rôle that Sundays had played in our history.

I was amazed by their serenity of mind, their strong faith that things would turn out well, and their anxiety about the future of Poland. They did not seem to care at all about themselves. They laughed when telling me about Bolshevik inspections, about the threats to close their convent, and how the population of Jazlowiec and the neighbouring villages—of every religious denomination—had stood up in their defence against the new authorities. I trusted the nuns, and therefore decided to leave my children with them.

After dusk, Sister Lauretta (the same who had demanded "loud bangs") took me to the side gate of the convent, by which I left unnoticed. All four of us walked along the long corridors, my two little ones hanging on to me. Suddenly Sister Lauretta leaned towards me and dropped her voice.

"Sir, I must tell you something—I must ask you something; but it is a terrible secret: the children should not hear it."

At last, I thought, we shall talk in a matter-of-fact way. Probably the nuns have some concealed doubts about the future of the convent and of themselves: this careless serenity was just a mask adopted by these poor trapped women.

She dragged me to an empty cell and whispered: "Is it true that Rydz Smigly and Beck have betrayed Poland—that we are surrounded on all sides by traitors? Is it possible?"

"Haven't you anything else to ask me?"

"Oh, no!" and her eyes, blue as the scapular on her gown, looked straight at me. "That's the only important question."

When I had reassured her, she became quite gay, as if a load had dropped from her heart.

Strange, indeed, was this convent on the Tartarian track!

A few weeks later the Soviet occupation force carried out its threat to seize the convent—the nuns and their charges being forced to disperse, with the Russians giving chase. Sister Lauretta was one of those deported to the U.S.S.R., where she was to spend two years in a labour-camp, before, amazingly, re-entering my story. My daughters (one of whom I would never see again) did, however, at the closure of the convent, manage to reach Lwow, joining their mother and younger sister there. But it was six long years before I knew what had happened to them.

And now, back to that night in the late autumn of 1939.

It was still night when I reached the railway-station in Buczacz and mingled with the crowd waiting for the train to Stanislawow. I was lucky, for nobody noticed me: I should be able to leave Buczacz in peace. . . .

Just before the train was due to leave, I was accosted by a police-man in a leather jacket: "Citizen, how much did you pay the cab-driver for your trip to Jazlowiec?"

I had an unpleasant feeling. "Thirty zlotys," I said, which was the sum I had actually paid.

I heard no more about it; the train steamed into the station and I took a seat. Apparently I had not slipped away unnoticed, as I had supposed! Perhaps the truthful answer saved me—I do not know; anyhow, I was glad when the train started.

I was back in Lwow. I needed information about the route to Cracow. I was not going alone, for I had promised to take Lieut. Lewek Sapieha's wife with me: because of her name the N.K.V.D. were after her. She had had to escape from the Sapieha estate to Lwow, where she had remained in hiding. Now she wanted to go under the German occupation to help her husband, who was in a German prisoner-of-war camp, to get his release from there. When in Blonie I had said goodbye to Lewek, promising to find out all about his wife; now I was glad to have found her and glad that she could come with me.

But it was not so easy to escape from Lwow. The situation had become worse, new restrictions having been imposed a few days earlier.

Special passes were now required to book tickets to stations near the demarcation line, such as Przemysl, Rawa Ruska, or Sambor. Without such passes no tickets could be bought, and the passes were issued only by the Headquarters of the "National Guard". I went there, but naturally I was refused a pass. They asked me so many questions regarding my application that I wondered they did not arrest me there and then. Obviously I had to look for some other way of travelling.

Finally I found it. In the café "Sztuka" in the Legionow Str., was a man who, for thirty zlotys, was taking letters for delivery to Cracow. I thought that he must go himself, so there must be a way through. Perhaps I could join him. . . .

I made my offer; he accepted. We agreed that I should pay for the two of us: four hundred zlotys. The day of departure was fixed for Friday—in two days' time. I asked him which way we should go; he did not want to commit himself, so he gave me merely the general direction of Wlodzimierz Wolynski. On the Thursday—the day before our departure—I again went to "Sztuka", but there I had a very unpleasant surprise. The boy in the cloakroom informed me that my would-be guide had changed his mind and had already left. I was therefore stranded. At least he had not taken any money from me in advance, but that did not alter the situation.

What could I do? I had to get myself out of this predicament. I remembered his mentioning Wlodzimierz Wolynski; that was a hint, at least. I decided to go there, and later we should see . . . perhaps Our Lord would help us. The worst thing would be simply to wait about, inactive, as the situation got blacker every day: it was better to do something, even stupidly, than to do nothing. This is an old military maxim.

My escapade looked like a dangerous improvisation. I explained the risk involved to my companion: perhaps she would like to stay behind? But no. We had no help, so must chance it.

It might be very risky, even fatal—was she afraid? No, she was not afraid, and "Since Lewek asked you to do it and Our Lord has sent you, it will be all right and we shall get through."

There was nothing further to say. All that remained was for us to do as planned.

Saturday afternoon we went to the station. I was distressed because I could not do anything useful for my family and must leave them in suspense, without proper protection; I was only grateful to my wife that she fully understood I was on duty.

The railway station was overcrowded; nobody could tell us the train for Wlodzimierz Wolynski and when it would leave.

At last, on Sunday, we found the right train, which left in the afternoon. We sat in the third class, among a mixture of types such as I had seen in Przemysl and in Lwow in the Legionow Str. and the Mikolasz Passage.

So long as the train remained at the platform it was difficult to guess *why* they were all travelling; but after we had passed a few stations everything became clear. Most of them talked only about the possibility of crossing the German demarcation line, while the "professionals" were interested in prices here and there. There were no secrets for them: they had the most up-to-date information and they knew by which channels the illegal traffic went across the "frontier".

"Wlodzimierz Wolynski?" I risked the question.

"That's ancient history—a mouse couldn't slip through there—reinforcements of frontier guards have gone there; the prisons are overflowing with 'customers'."

"So? Which way?"

"Go *via* Kowel to Bialystok; from there to Zareby Koscielne; and at night you cross to Malkinia; that's the best spot now."

We rid ourselves of all the doubts assailing us. Once again we were convinced that in the times in which we were living any decision was better than none. Once we had decided to take the first step, the next one would follow automatically. I thought of the helpless crowds in the repatriation offices of the Headquarters of the "National Guard" in Lwow, seeking legal permits, and having no guts for this first step—which was so simple. You took a seat in a train, not knowing where to, but determined to go; once the wheels began to roll underneath, you knew everything.

After two days of travelling we came to Bialystok, and with some difficulty we secured seats on the train to Zareby Koscielne.

In the carriage, the old story repeated itself: new passengers, new information.

"Don't be silly! don't go to Zareby. After arrival there the train is immediately surrounded by Bolsheviks, and passengers go straight to prison. You must have a special permit to stay within twenty miles of the frontier. Alight in Czyzew—that's the last station before the frontier zone."

We did not ask any more for information, it would come without asking. We were on the right path.

Indeed, almost all the passengers alighted in Czyzew. A row of peasant carts stood in front of the station, their drivers quarrelling among themselves—almost wresting passengers from each other's carts. Everyone offered his price: the destination was known—nobody asked.

From this time on, we were treated like luggage, passing from hand to hand; only we had to pay all the time—more and more.

First we came to a certain village and had to wait there till dusk. Then we drove in another cart to another village, close to the frontier. Then we had to pay again and walk across country for half a mile; and finally:

Finally we were told: "Walk towards that grove—it is on the German side."

Then the cry: *"Halt! wer da?"* ("Halt! who is there?") and a beam from a torch shone in our eyes. *"Sind keine Juden unter euch?"* ("No Jews among you?")

"No, only Poles."

The guards checked up with the torch again. *"Geht nur weiter geradeaus, dort könnt ihr übernachten, aber morgen müsst ihr euch melden in der Orts-Kommendantur—verstanden?"* ("Go right ahead. You can stay for the night, but tomorrow morning you have to report to the local Commandant. Understand?")

Simply an empty formula. Obviously I would not dream of reporting "tomorrow". We waited in some house till the morning, and then went straight to the railway-station in Malkinia.

At 11 a.m. we were in Warsaw. Sophie Sapieha was overjoyed; I, too.

It was the 4th December.

CHAPTER 11

German "Fist Rule" and Polish Resistance

I FOUND big changes in Warsaw; they kept me busy for a few days. I was almost terrified by what I saw.

The Germans had tightened up. Mass arrests and shooting without trial became common. The Sejm (Parliament) Park in the Wiejska Str. became the centre for daily tortures. Witkowski took me to a house in the neighbourhood, and I watched these scenes from the roof. He wanted to film it and send it to France.

From the time that authority had been taken over from the Army by the Gestapo, terror reigned in the town. There was no fuel at all, and food was very scarce.

Houses were requisitioned in blocks; furniture was confiscated, and the inhabitants expelled.

The Poznan Province had been incorporated into the *Reich*, and its population was being chased out to the east in a most inhuman way, so thousands of refugees were now pouring into Warsaw, thus increasing the misery here.

At the same time, the Underground in Warsaw had become more active. But there was less unity in the organisation than in October.

I renewed my old contacts and made new ones.

Witkowski had an organisation of his own, called the "Musketeers". He had broken off all relations with "Michael"—I think it was a mutual decision—and was now devoting his energies mainly to the Intelligence Service. He had many agents working in all parts of the country, and even in Germany, but he received instructions from nowhere, did not recognise anybody, and wanted to co-operate directly with Paris—at least until he could receive definite orders.

"Gryf" was mainly organising the Kielce area, in groups of five.

91

He was collecting arms and "would not dream of co-operating with 'Michael'. . . ." This "Gryf" was a young Cavalry captain: I did not ask his real name.

"Brochwicz" did the same in the Lublin area. I saw one of his men, Col. Milkowski. Col. Tatar and Major Grocholski were there, too; they would not acknowledge anybody's authority until they had received orders from Paris.

Wlodarkiewicz assembled Warsaw's youth, mainly University students and young officers. He was an intellectual; his group was largely devoted to political discussions on "matters of principle".

Witkowski was definitely the most enterprising of them all. I thought the daring of his initiative, the wide scope of the intelligence service he had organised, and the contacts he had established, made him almost a danger. He was very ingenious: he had many hiding-places, secret flats, cellars with secret entrances, traps and photo-electric cells, etc. In his activity one could perceive the motivating principle, "Art for Art's sake". He was in his element.

All these men maintained that General Tokarzewski was an impostor: that his statements that he had been entrusted with the command of the Underground activities in Poland by General Sikorski with full authority were not true. Behind him was concealed the "Sanacja" (members of the pre-war Governmental Party), which had demonstrated their incapacity in September. There was no question of becoming subordinate to his orders.

It would have been simple to have secured an explanation directly from Tokarzewski, had I been able to establish contact with him. But I could not.

Tokarzewski apparently evaded all contacts with the outside world. In the meantime he did not intend to establish his universal leadership. Perhaps he was afraid of falling into a trap through contact with "hotheads", and he was probably working on a long-term policy.

Under these circumstances, I saw no other solution than to take them all under our leadership. I told them about our central organisation in Cracow and about Komorowski, and asked them to agree to our leadership—at least until such time as I could show them orders received from Paris which would finally settle all the outstanding problems. They willingly agreed, because everyone of them understood the necessity for a united leadership. I gave them precise instructions concerning their activities, delimiting their powers and their respective areas. Witkowski took over, with his "Musketeers", the Intelligence Service. I solemnly promised them I would produce authentic orders issued by General Sikorski, if necessary going myself to Budapest to collect them.

Thus matters were settled and I was free to go to Cracow.

In the meantime, Mary came to Warsaw. She had come straight from Cracow, from Komorowski. Everything was all right there, but they still had no contact with Budapest, and that was the main reason for her arrival here. She was, as usual, wonderful. She tracked down a man called "Richard", who was supposed to be the representative of General Sikorski in Warsaw.

I straightway went to see him. He lived in Marszalkowska Str., under the assumed name of "Kalinowski". I was introduced to him: we did not waste our time on precautions.

He was a political colleague of General Sikorski, with whom he was in contact. He could not give me any information as to the immediate questions which interested me most—namely, who and on what authority could co-ordinate Underground activities? But he did give me some news from France and a general appreciation of the situation. It was obvious that we had to be prepared for a long struggle—one, or even two years; we could not expect any early change in the situation. That was very important news for me.

The same evening I left, with Mary, by train for Cracow. At Warsaw railway station we witnessed a scene which shook us to the core. Some German soldiers on leave, or just travelling, were walking among the crowds, and, from time to time, picking out some Poles to slap their faces. They were not even enraged: they did it quite casually. Was it for provocation or just for sport? It was the *Faustrecht* (fist rule), which would ultimately be their ruin: such soldiers cannot win a war. But how long should we have to put up with it?

I reported to Komorowski all that I had seen in the east and in Warsaw. We decided there was no choice: I must myself go to Hungary to stop, once for all, the menace of unco-ordinated efforts. I began preparations for my journey.

In the meantime, however, another solution presented itself. Mary discovered a reliable and trustworthy man who volunteered to take a report to Budapest and bring back an answer. This was Lieut. Wlodzimierz Ledochowski. We all knew him well and were sure he would never deceive us. As a reward he asked us to promise that if he had a lucky return we would help him get to France to join the Army!

I undertook to write a comprehensive report for General Sikorski. This covered a few pages, written in pencil on very thin paper, as that would be easier to hide; in case he needed to destroy it, Ledochowski

93

had to learn it by heart. Komorowski and I went through it several times, anxious that everything important had been included. In addition to an appreciation of the general situation, we outlined the behaviour of both occupying Powers.

In our view, the Germans appeared to be the more dangerous of the two. They seemed to be aiming at the physical extermination of the Poles. They killed people without trial—not by way of reprisal but simply to exterminate the population, or at least to reduce it to the number of slave-workers required. All University professors had been arrested; high and grammar schools had been closed. But these were only details of the general plan for extermination. The complete political incorporation of the Poznan Province and of Silesia into the *Reich*, and the published reduction of the boundaries of the "General Government" pointed to the object of establishing a *fait accompli* which could never be altered.

In this situation we thought it imperative that the West should act immediately.

In our opinion, the Soviets were less dangerous. They were stupid, and had no culture; but they were not exterminating people indiscriminately. They merely introduced an unheard-of confusion, causing many difficulties and much misery, and it would be possible to eradicate them later, somehow. Their slogans were based on lies, but their lies were so primitive and obvious that there was no danger of the population's believing them. After their return to the East, no trace would be left of their stay.*

Our report described the Resistance movement and the ideological currents flowing through the population. We drew attention to the fact that everybody was awaiting some definite ruling on the questions: Who was to be entrusted by the Government in Paris and the C.-in-C. to form an organisation? What were its regulations to be? And what its aims? We stressed the fact that universal understanding and harmony would depend on the person of the C.-in-C. of the Underground Forces, and that General Tokarzewski was completely unacceptable to the population, especially to the National Democrats. People lacking judgement—understandable under prevailing circumstances—blamed the Governmental Party and the officers who were in Pilsudski's Legion, and adhered to that Party, for the country's defeat.

* How we erred in this appreciation of the Soviets! What we saw superficially misled us: then we did not sense the system so deeply concealed behind apparent chaos. Maybe our incomplete pre-war information about what had happened beyond the Zbrucz (border river) was partially responsible for it.

In this situation we suggested the name of General W. Anders as C.-in-C. of the Underground, as he would be willingly accepted by all groups, of varying opinion. We said that General Anders had been supposed to be handed over on 4th December to the Germans, but as he was dangerously wounded, he would probably be left for a while in one of the hospitals in Poland. We undertook to get him out of the hospital and keep him in safety.

I signed the report with my full name and rank—this was necessary for the first contact; and I mentioned that I signed it also on behalf of two other Colonels (Komorowski and Godlewski), whose names were known to the courier and would be revealed by him.

Ledochowski went to Hungary across the Carpathian Mountains in the middle of December. We then had to wait for his return. Meanwhile, acceleration of the awakened Underground activities absorbed us completely.

Events decided our next move. Mr. Surzycki, head of the National Democrats in Cracow, approached us and asked to take over the command of the armed forces organised by the National Democratic Party. Col. Epler, who up to then had been in command, had to flee immediately, as the Gestapo were on his heels and he was threatened with annihilation.

Komorowski and I decided to avail ourselves of this opportunity, as a step towards the consolidation of our efforts, and thus help to stop the quarrelling among rival Underground groups.

During a conference with Mr. Surzycki, in the presence of a delegate of his Party from Warsaw, Komorowski and I refused to tie up our activities with one Party only, as we were a national military organisation standing above party politics.

Mr. Surzycki agreed with our proposal, and declared that the armed forces of the National Democratic Party would willingly join such a military organisation. Komorowski assumed the command, and I became his second-in-command and Chief of Staff.

In this way we gave up, of our own free will, our hope of joining "real armed forces in France", and we resolved to remain in Poland, prepared to work with all our strength.

We began by looking for safe quarters for our H.Q. and also a few hiding places.

In a huge and always very busy building—No. 5 Zyblikiewicza Str.—we discovered the office of one of the university professors, forgotten by the Germans. Mrs. Zapolska, his secretary, swore allegiance to our cause and enrolled, with all the staff, under our orders.

There were several typewriters and duplicators, a photographic dark-room, and a big library which would serve us as a hiding place for suspicious materials and notes. We appointed a lieutenant from a Horse Artillery Battery to work with Mrs. Zapolska as our A.D.C.

It was the ideal place for our H.Q. There we could, without fear, interview clients and hold conferences. People paid no attention to the numerous visitors, as everybody in the building was accustomed to them, and Mrs. Zapolska still had her own university clients who came to see her as if nothing had changed in the place. It would be difficult for anyone coming in to realise that alongside the normal activities, of a winding-up character, there were other secret activities taking place there.

I myself changed my lodgings from Pieracki Str. to Siemiradzki Str., where I took a modest room on the ground floor. It was well placed, being opposite the Gestapo Headquarters and thus well protected. I thought this the best way to lull the German defensive Intelligence into security.

Unemployed people were liable to arrest during spasmodic "round-ups". I therefore got a job, through Mr. Surzycki, in Mr. Sikora's firm in the Szczepanski Square.

Komorowski remained in Pieracki Str., but he moved to the flat of Mrs. Jaworska, the widow of the well-known university professor.

Mary's flat remained the meeting place for our secret conferences.

Our sphere of activities steadily increased; new districts joined our organisation; we had new military and political contacts. Soon our roots were firmly planted in the mountain districts—Zakopane and Bukowina, Tarnow, Rzeszow, Jaroslaw, etc.

As we spread, we frequently met the organisation of "Michael", called S.Z.P.—*Sluzba Zwyciestwa Polski* (Polish Victory Corps)— which gradually grew stronger. We realised that people did not under-stand political nuances or diplomatic distinctions which are so im-portant among leaders. It was enough for most of them that some-body was issuing orders on behalf of the Polish Government, and it did not matter to them whether this order came from "Michael" or from us: very often they did not know the difference.

In several instances it happened that the same group was under the common leadership of both organisations, and each kept records of them in their own Order of Battle. This did not disturb us: on the contrary, we were pleased—it might lead to future unification. But our political friends did not like it: they insisted on a monopoly. Co-ordination also became a tactical necessity.

We therefore decided to seek out the head of "Michael's" organisation in Cracow.

I was soon on the right track, and arranged a meeting with the Chief of Staff of the Cracow District Command of Tokarzewski's organisation. I was glad to recognise in him my friend, Major Janek Cichocki, who had now assumed the name of Kabat.

We had no secrets from each other, no political reservations: we knew each other well, and each appreciated the other's sincere and soldierly aims.

Soon, other meetings followed between Komorowski and Col. Filipowicz, who was in command of the Cracow District on behalf of "Michael's" organisation. Komorowski and Filipowicz, both Cavalry Brigade Commanders during the September Campaign, were also only soldiers.

We agreed among ourselves to prepare for unification, and, pending definite orders to them arriving from Warsaw and to us from Paris, we agreed to co-ordinate our activities.

We managed, in this way, to tidy up our sector—if not completely, at any rate satisfactorily.

CHAPTER 12

A Parcel of Money

LACK of money was our worst worry. The needs of the organisation increased steadily. Up to now we had managed to cover expenses out of our own pocket; but this source was exhausted, and it became obvious that considerable sums would be required; without it a lasting organisation was impossible. Our needs were augmented by the necessity for finding grants for the evacuation of people from camps, for hiding them, sending them abroad, arranging routes, etc.

Witkowski from Warsaw and "Gryf" from Kielce asked for more money. An authority without money was no authority at all: people expected it; without funds the work became a serious embarrassment.

This problem was solved through mere chance.

One day, Mary, on her usual rounds in Cracow, came across Sister Dzieduszycka, a nun in the Convent of the Sisters of Charity, who had come into possession of 500,000 zlotys, received from a Mrs. Wiktor, who was the owner of an estate on a hillside near Baligrod. After many enquiries, Mary established that, a few days earlier, a stranger, running through a village near Baligrod, had thrown a parcel over the fence of a farmyard, shouting to the woman standing at the house door: "Take it to the priest in Baligrod!"

This stranger, closely pursued by German and Ukrainian guards, had been caught and shot outside the village. The parcel, however, remained undetected.

The farm woman, obeying the man's instructions, took the parcel to the priest, without even looking inside it. The priest opened the parcel, and to his alarm found that it contained a huge quantity of 500-zloty bank-notes—an amount such as he had never seen before in his life. He guessed that it was public money which the unfortunate courier had brought for the Underground movement from Hungary, and he was puzzled as to what he should do about it. Finally, he asked the lady of the estate, she being Mrs. Wiktor, if he could consult her.

They met and counted the money—a million zlotys. After lengthy deliberation, Mrs. Wiktor took half the money, which was as much as she could manage to hide, sewing them into her skirt, and brought 100,000 zlotys to Cracow. The rest she left with the priest.

So far, so good. But Mrs. Wiktor's difficulties were only just beginning. Where should she go? Whom could she take into her confidence?

She eventually decided that the best thing to do was to take the money to Cardinal Sapieha, so she went to Wawel Castle. But there she was disappointed: the Prince Cardinal threw her out with her money; he was probably afraid of trouble—and rightly, too, for he could hardly be drawn into such an unholy affair.

In despair, poor Mrs. Wiktor went straight from the Archbishop's Palace to share her problem with her cousin, the nun. This was just the right place to contact Mary, with her infallible flair.

That day we took possession of the 500,000 zlotys, and told Mrs. Wiktor we would send a courier for the remainder. So as to have a completely clear conscience in using this money, we agreed with Komorowski to seek authority for doing so. Therefore I went to Warsaw to see "Richard"; we thought that, as Sikorski's confidant, he would be the most appropriate person to consult. With me I took about 15,000 zlotys, some to be given to Witkowski and some to others, in case "Richard's" decision was favourable.

It was no pleasure travelling by train to Warsaw. It was cold—36° (Fahrenheit) below freezing point. The train was overcrowded and unheated, and it dragged along for almost forty-eight hours. People carried vodka, petroleum, and other valuable goods, the commodities of the black market.

I quickly settled my business with "Richard". He agreed to our proposal, authorising us to dispose of the acquired capital for the needs of our organisation.

He also asked me to take about 200,000 zlotys in the 500-zloty bank-notes back to Cracow, as it was now extremely difficult to exchange them for smaller notes in Warsaw; and I was to hand these over to Mr. Tempka, with whom we were in contact. I recognised the necessity of this. The General Government had issued an order cancelling all 500-zloty bank-notes in a few days' time. There were long queues at all banks, and there were no other possibilities of exchanging the money. In Cracow it was still possible to do so; we had exchanged some of our money there already. I therefore took the notes back, although it was very risky, as I might have been involved in a round-up or a search.

I availed myself of the opportunity of visiting Prince Janusz Radziwill, who, thanks to Goering's personal intervention, had recently returned to Warsaw after a prolonged stay in a Moscow prison.

The Germans were looking for somebody who would agree to collaborate with them as the representative of the Polish nation. They wanted to create a kind of pro-German government in Poland. If they could set up, in opposition to the Free Polish Government in Paris, some kind of government in Poland, this would be a big political success for them and might influence public opinion in the country.

So far, all attempts to induce Ronikier, Studnicki and others were in vain; now rumours had spread that a similar proposition would be made to Prince Radziwill. I wanted to inform him about the actual situation of the Underground organisation, and let him know our unfavourable attitude towards a compromise with the Germans.

The meeting, arranged by George Czetwertynski, took place in one of the houses in Dabrowski Square.

On hearing my account and my opinion, Prince Radziwill assured me that no definite proposal had yet been made to him by the Germans: he had only been asked, by Goering himself, what his attitude was. Were definite proposals put forward to him, he would certainly reject them.

We then started to talk about Russia. The Prince told me about his sojourn in the Lubianka prison in Moscow and about his talk with Beria, just before he was released and sent back to the German occupation zone.

Beria had said that the order established after the armed conflict with Poland could not be looked upon as a permanent arrangement; many changes must come. He knew well that the Poles would never submit to the established new order, but would, by underground activities or other means, oppose the *régime* on both sides and aim at recovering their independence. The whole heroic history of Poland indicated it. Beria knew the influence that Prince Radziwill could exercise on the Poles, so he asked him to persuade his compatriots, in organising underground resistance, to leave out that part of the country occupied by Soviet troops. Resistance would only provoke reprisals—understandable in this war atmosphere—and would lead

100

to no good purpose. Unnecessary bloodshed and the creation of an abyss between the Soviet peoples and the Poles had to be prevented. After the war the two nations could work out a peaceful settlement to all outstanding questions.

Prince Radziwill then gave me a survey of Russia. In his opinion, the Soviet Union represented a terrific Power, not sufficiently realised by us and others. Her weakness shown during the war with Finland, and the bad showing of the occupying forces in Poland, which was incomprehensible to people in the West, were only window-dressing. Russia was far more powerful and menacing than she seemed. This was a fact which we must take into full consideration, whatever might happen in the future.

This opinion came as a complete surprise to me. I told the Prince that I had just returned from the Russian occupation zone, where I had had a good look at the new authorities, their behaviour and their army. I drew his attention to the fact that he had seen Russia only from the Moscow prison, apart from any literature that was given to him and a talk with a dignitary on the highest level: he hardly had enough perspective, I said, for an unbiased observation, and, in my considered opinion, his judgement was wrong. But he would not give way; he stood firmly on his opinion. So I promised to include his views in our next report to General Sikorski, without any deviation, and I then took leave of him, deeply moved by all he had said.

I went to Zbawiciela Square with "Richard's" 200,000 zlotys, and asked Theresa Lubienska to sew them under the lining of my coat: I would be leaving that night.

I also met there my cousin, Mrs. Clementine Mankowski, with her three-year-old son. She had come from Winogora, near Poznan, having been recently dislodged by the Germans. Her husband, who had been wounded during the September Campaign, was in a Poznan prison.

She told me her story.

In the beginning they had had no cause to grumble. The German army had behaved well; a divisional headquarters, billeted in the Castle in Winogora, had saved the inhabitants and the furniture from pillage. The General and the officers had been very helpful, and had even managed to get her wounded husband out of hospital and brought home.

After some time, however, they secretly warned her that the Gestapo was taking over from the military authorities, that the divisional H.Q. was leaving, and that she must now expect the worst.

101

They advised her to pack her most valuable things into boxes, which they undertook to take to Radom, where they were going, and where they would hand them back to her. She agreed. Two officers—a major from the General Staff, von Hoepfner, and Capt. von Nikisch-Rozeneck—were now looking after these belongings, which would probably be the only things she could save.

Then the Gestapo came.

Everything happened as the officers had foretold. The Gestapo arrived. Her husband was arrested, and, after several days, she was entrained with several thousand of the inhabitants of the Poznan province, in cattle-trucks, and then detrained near Warsaw—as she stood, without any luggage.

From Warsaw she had sent a message to Radom, giving her address in Zbawiciela Square, and was now expecting a visit from the two officers who were looking after her boxes.

We were listening to this interesting story while having our tea in the dining-room. In the next room, Witkowski and Plater were producing faked identity cards and stamps. Suddenly the doorbell rang.

The door was opened, as usual, by Theresa Lubienska: probably, we thought, the expected German visitors had arrived. But no—it was the Italian Chargé d'Affaires, an old acquaintance. He was acting as deputy for the absent Ambassador, and, from time to time, he visited Theresa secretly. He was on our side with all his heart, and usually came to collect news which he then passed on to Rome. He was especially interested in any German atrocities, and was pleased to have some photographs, provided by Witkowski, illustrating their barbaric exploits.

We chatted for a while, then the bell rang again.

Before opening the door, Theresa warned the diplomat that this time it was probably the German officers: he certainly must not meet them. Since he could not leave, he was pushed into a small room, next door to Witkowski.

Major von Hoepfner and Capt. von Nikisch-Rozeneck then walked in. I was introduced to them as a refugee from the Bolshevik occupation zone. They were full of sympathy for "Frau Gräfin" (the Countess) and our "poor country". They had brought the boxes, and were very pleased that they had been able to be helpful and save, even if only a little, something from those barbarians, the Gestapo. They did not agree with what was happening at all. Rozeneck actually called Hitler *ein Teufel* (a devil)! I was unable to make up my mind whether it was a sincere attitude or simply a pose.

During our talk, they mentioned something to which I listened with great interest and attention. Complimenting the Poles and the Polish Army for their stand in September, they said that a detachment of Polish cavalry remained in the Swietokrzyskie Mountains, under the command of a major with a big red beard who sometimes came to Kielce or Radom, probably supposing he was unknown there. Their General had not yet ordered the annihilation of this adventurer and his detachment, because he admired the man and his stubbornness.

"*Ist das nicht romantisch, Frau Gräfin, nicht wahr?*" ("Isn't it romantic, Countess?")

I knew this red-bearded cavalry officer very well: it was Major Henryk Dobrzanski, now using the name of "Hubala". We had already despatched orders to him, through "Gryf", ordering him to disband his detachment: it might be romantic what he was doing, but it was foolhardy and pointless. Now we must open his eyes to the danger to which he exposed not only himself but also his men and the people who supported him. I remembered Henryk well: we had served together for years, in the 2nd Chevaux Légers. And I was afraid it would be difficult to persuade him. Though brave, he was very stubborn, and hated to be "bossed".

The Germans were given tea, and we chatted freely. The little boy, Andrew, became so cheeky that he sat on Hoepfner's knee, and the officer then put his own cap on the boy's head. The child's mother then said: "Andrew, will you please sing for him '*Jeszcze Polska nie zginela*'"? (The Polish National Anthem).

We burst into loud laughter, and the Germans were puzzled. It was an unforgettable situation! There was the little boy, sitting on the German's knee, and wearing the cap with the swastika, while singing our National Anthem in his childish voice. At the same table, I was sitting—a representative of the Resistance; and in the next two rooms, faked stamps and documents were being fabricated in one, and a representative of one of the Axis Powers and an Envoy of H.M. King Victor Emanuel II was hiding in the other!

CHAPTER 13

The Network

DURING my return journey to Cracow I had one rather narrow escape.

This time I travelled by express train, for which I had a faked permit. It was impossible to book a ticket without special permission: express trains were *"nur für Deutsche"* (only for Germans), and only in exceptional cases was a small quantity of permits for them issued to Poles by an office in Chalubinski Str., in the building of the former Ministry of Communications. The journey itself was not at all risky; indeed, safer and more comfortable than by ordinary trains.

What I did not know was that that very day the frontier of the *Reich* had been extended up to Czestochowa, and that our train would, on a short sector near Poreba, cross "German" territory, entailing a check of documents and luggage.

When we alighted, therefore, from the train in Poreba and had individually to pass through the control-post, I thought my end had come—even without my incriminating 200,000 zlotys. In front of me a few persons had already been selected for a personal search.

Something, however, distracted the Germans' attention from me: perhaps it was my free and merry conversation in German with a pretty girl, whom I had met by chance travelling on the same train; or perhaps it was something else. Anyway, they only said *"Passiert"* ("Passed"), and the danger was over.

I was glad to find Ledochowski back in Cracow. He had been kept in a Hungarian prison until our Legation secured his release. Then, by good luck he had returned—but very lean and exhausted, having had a most strenuous return journey ski-ing across the mountains.

He had done everything extremely well. Our report was sent by a courier from Budapest to Paris, whence we received detailed instruc-

tions; also, typed on micro-film, an appeal issued by our Government.
At last we had all the instructions we had desired!

With regard to the problem of organisation, the most interesting development was that our exiled Government had created in Poland a secret organisation called "Z.W.Z."—*Zwiazek Walki Zbrojnej* (Union of Armed Resistance), and General K. Sosnkowski had been appointed C.-in-C. of the Underground Forces, stationed for the time being abroad. The country had been divided into areas and districts, similar to the pre-war administration. The C.O. the Warsaw District had to regulate co-ordination of all Districts, and had the right to issue orders. He was, in fact, the C.O. in Poland.

The instructions said we were to base our organisation on the existing one of General Tokarzewski and his Staff in Warsaw. All armed organisations existing in the country were to recognise this authority.

We were also informed that General Tokarzewski had been appointed C.O. the Lwow District, and had to leave Warsaw immediately to take over his new job; and his Chief of Staff, Col. S. Rowecki, had been appointed C.O. Warsaw District, thus becoming C.O. in Poland.

A statute setting up the Z.W.Z., the text of the oath, and other details, were attached to these instructions.

Receiving these orders in the middle of January, 1940, we were greatly relieved. Quite clearly they restored order to the existing confusion, and co-ordinated the efforts of individuals or groups. They certainly came at the right time.

We had to carry out these orders and overcome both the opposition of the undisciplined and the doubts of the Party men. Therefore we immediately contacted Filipowicz and Kabat, and told them to unite both of the organisations in the Cracow District into one body. Komorowski dealt with this; while I, having received from Kabat the necessary passwords to reach Rowecki, went to Warsaw. We wished to hand over to Rowecki all our units outside Cracow which were still under our leadership—"the Musketeers", "Gryf", "Brochwicz" and Wlodarkiewicz.

After my arrival in Warsaw I became acquainted with the organisation of the security of the S.Z.P. staff. And I was amazed how well it was done. They had a better scheme there than we had in Cracow.

Our colleagues in Warsaw were clearly fitted for Underground activities. For one thing, they had gained experience in World War I, when they had worked in the P.O.W.—*Polska Organizacja Wojskowa*

(Polish Military Organisation): a Polish Underground organisation sponsored by Pilsudski's legion in Austria, Germany and Russia in the years 1914–18. Also, the frightful state of terror that now reigned in Warsaw—incomparably worse than the situation in Cracow, the seat of Frank, the "General Governor"—compelled them to use greater secrecy. We were all deeply depressed by the barbaric murderous shooting of over a hundred men in the suburb of Wawer. I took back with me a list of the names of the victims, which I had received from Witkowski, to send to Paris.

Shootings, as a means of underlining the supposed collective responsibility of the population for even accidental reactions, were daily features in Warsaw. In such circumstances, the S.Z.P. staff had to apply most scrupulous security measures.

The procedure to see Rowecki was as follows.

I first went, armed with the password for January—"*Klemens-Kalina*" (I will personally explain)—to Dr. Pazyra in the Ossolineum in Foksal Str. He told me to go to the beauty parlour of Mrs. Jarnuszewska in Wspolna Str. There I had to give the password again, and was told by Mrs. Jarnuszewska to visit her parlour the next day at an agreed hour to collect the cosmetics which I had to order. Meanwhile they were checking up on me—whether I was being shadowed or whether I was a foreign agent.

The next day, during my visit to the parlour, I was told that everything was all right, and that a despatch-girl would bring word to my lodgings in Zbawiciela Square as to when and where the meeting would take place. A few days later I was given the address of a flat in Marszalkowska Str. and told the way to get there and the exact hour of meeting.

I found the flat without any difficulty, and there I met, not Rowecki, but a man unknown to me who was expecting me and who introduced himself as "Sanojca". It was his duty to find out why I had come, what my business was, and finally to verify my identity.

I was somewhat annoyed, as I was by now anxious to see Rowecki, whom I had known quite well before the war. I felt I had had enough of these formalities: it seemed easier to cross the Carpathians than to pierce the security cordon of Rowecki's staff! But it could not be helped: I had to return to Zbawiciela Square, and again await a messenger with new instructions.

The next day, before noon, a despatch-girl brought me the message that at 3.15 p.m. sharp I was to be outside No. 111, Marszalkowska Str., where I would see Sanojca. I was to take no notice of him, but was simply to follow him, and he would lead me to the right place.

Everything happened as stated, and at last I was able to shake hands with Rowecki, who had grown a moustache since our last meeting. He looked well and cheerful, and he apologised for the lengthy formalities, but explained that caution was essential.

We began to talk business.

He told me that he also had received orders, identical to ours, from Paris, and he was now busy carrying them out. S.Z.P. had ceased to exist; or, rather, it had been transformed into the new Z.W.Z., a strictly military organisation. Tokarzewski, though grieved to relinquish his post, was loyal to the orders received and was going to Lwow, although he well knew that his situation there would be very dangerous, as he was so well known in Lwow. He rejected the advice of his friends to disobey the order and remain in Warsaw. He had always been both courageous and loyal.

I told Rowecki of our views, and the report we had sent to Paris on this subject. He agreed with us. Although he highly appreciated his Chief, he thought that Tokarzewski's departure would definitely help to unify our efforts, and would also help win over the National Democrats to co-operate with the rest of us. He thought our scheme regarding General W. Anders was excellent in theory, but quite unrealistic. The General had certainly been in Przemysl, but had later been arrested by the Bolsheviks, and now there was not the least trace of him; most certainly he was not on *our* side of the demarcation line. The news of his arrest had been brought by an eye-witness, Col. Bokszczanin, who had been lucky enough to escape from the same transport and to reach Warsaw.

Henceforth Rowecki would be mainly concerned with the consolidation of the Underground organisation of the whole country. Undoubtedly he would encounter special obstacles in territories incorporated into the *Reich*, and also with the amalgamation into the Z.W.Z. of the forces organised so far by the National Democratic Party, though he took into account the help available from Komorowski, who was highly esteemed in National Democratic circles. He foresaw, however, that once the unification of both organisations in Cracow had been completed, Komorowski would be transferred to Warsaw. He told me that his final decision would be communicated to us by his personal envoys, whom we could soon expect in Cracow.

We then discussed how he could take under his command "the Musketeers", "Gryf", "Brochwicz" and Wlodarkiewicz.

He was apprehensive of "the Musketeers" because of their lack of caution and their "too exuberant" (as he called it) activity. It would be better just to keep a watch on this organisation, limiting the co-operation to loose contacts: "the Musketeers" were not well disciplined, and it would be better that they continue on their own. Rowecki agreed to take over the other three organisations, and we decided that I had best inform them about the orders received from Paris and tell them how to join the new federation, Z.W.Z.

I told him of my experiences, impressions from my excursion to the Bolshevik occupation zone, and all about my talk with Prince Radziwill. Then we parted.

I went back to meet my people around Cracow.

I had no trouble with "the Musketeers". Witkowski preferred to be left alone and not to be kept in check. He promised, merely, to report all that he undertook.

Both "Gryf" and "Brochwicz" (led by Milkowski) loyally accepted the new authority. But Wlodarkiewicz refused. He questioned whether the instructions were authentic, and outlined his own big political plans—declaring that the country herself had to decide its fate, that Sikorski could not issue orders, etc. Telling him that he was a wrecker, I broke off all relations with him.

I paid a visit to Mr. A. Debski, told him about the orders received from Paris, and asked him to lend countenance to them in the terrain. And then, at the end of January, I returned to Cracow.

The co-operation with Filipowicz and Kabat worked extremely well. The route for the evacuation to Hungary was still improving and was used by people going to France. We issued them with identity cards and passes, and gave them the addresses of guides in Rymanow, Krynica or Sanok, according to which route was at the time the most advantageous; it varied quite a lot.

We had no luck with the remaining 500,000 zlotys in Baligrod. Our despatch-girl found that the priest had already given the money to "a young and very good-looking lady"—he showed her the receipt she had given him. Komorowski and I both guessed who this lady must have been; but unfortunately we had no proof. Our Intelligence Service was told to watch her; we warned all our organisations; and we seriously considered whether she should not be liquidated.* So far as we could ascertain, the money never reached any Polish organisation.

---

* She was later sentenced to death by our Underground court martial, and the sentence was carried out.

I went to Chrobrze to the Wielopolskis, to discuss the latest news and events with Godlewski, who still lived there, and to establish contacts with Hubala-Dobrzanski. Still more disquieting news came about his wanton activities in the Swietokrzyskie Mountains. Having heard the opinions of Hoepfner and Rozeneck, we thought them foolhardy in the extreme.

I met Hubala half-way to Pinczow. He definitely declined to be interfered with. He refused to doff his uniform, or leave his horses, or go underground. He had not signed a peace treaty with the Germans, he said, so he was determined to fight on.

It was a stubbornness full of romanticism: the romanticism of a rogue and a desperado. We could not help it: we had to relinquish him, together with his adjutant Tereska, to their own fate. I felt very sorry for him. I returned to Cracow, having failed in this mission.

In the meantime the question of Mr. W. Witos* became the most prominent. He was confined by the Germans in the Rzeszow prison. We had to get him out of there and manage his escape from the country. As we were in close contact with a delegate of the Polish Peasant Party, the whole scheme was worked out in detail. The chances of success were quite good, but everything broke down because of Witos himself: he absolutely refused to escape from prison and from the country. Probably he had good personal reasons for coming to this decision; nevertheless we, and also our friend from the Peasant Party, were disappointed: his escape would have been such a splendid achievement.

Early in February we were informed by Kabat that, according to promise, the two delegates from Rowecki had arrived for an interview with us.

We met in Zyblikiewicza Str., under the protection of our Intelligence Service. The delegates were Col. Albrecht and Mr. Sanojca, whom I had recently met in Warsaw.

Albrecht communicated to us Rowecki's final decision: Komorowski was to go to Warsaw and become the second-in-command of the C.O. of Z.W.Z. I was offered the appointment as Chief-of-Staff, and second-in-command to General Tokarzewski, in Lwow. They asked me if I would agree. "Of course," I said; "I never was against Tokarzewski as Tokarzewski: I only expressed the opinion that his name was unacceptable for our terrain, but it is excellent in Lwow. Besides, I have strong ties with Lwow, so I will gladly go."

---

* W. Witos was the chairman of the Polish Peasant Party and former prime minister of Poland during the Polish-Russian War, 1920–21.

Thus our role in Cracow had come to an end. Komorowski and I decided to leave immediately—he to go to Warsaw, for good; I to accompany him there to meet Tokarzewski and arrange the details for our crossing of the demarcation line.

This time the formalities were brief. The day after my arrival in Warsaw I went, in the early morning, to Filtrowa Str., not far from Narutowicz Square. On the left side there was a short street, and a house where I was to meet Tokarzewski.

It was a little warmer: a fresh, deep snow had fallen during the night, covering the pavements with a thick layer. It was a long walk, for the tramcars were still not running in Filtrowa, and I had to wade, ankle-deep, in the white downy snow, passing a long row of gutted houses.

The walk gave me time to think and I enjoyed it. . . .

How strangely Fate disposes of one! Can it be mere chance? I did not want to stay in our occupied country—I wanted to go to France, to the Army, to the field. But events had inexorably enmeshed me, and now I had no choice.

One chapter was now closing behind me; a new one opened before me; and I was wading in deep snow, into that new chapter. . . . I was pleased that it was to be in my own Lwow, at least.

I arrived at the *rendezvous*. Tokarzewski was already there, and I reported to him, with Army formality.

"I am not a general—I am a psychiatrist now. So you don't need to report. Sit down, please."

I sat down. He walked about the room and explained to me the principles, political and social, on which he intended to base his work in Lwow: regarding not only the organisation, but the whole creed of a man.

"As we have to work together, we must agree. Are you willing to come with me?" he asked.

"Do you know about my report to Sikorski concerning you, and do you know that I was really opposed to your being here?" I enquired.

"Yes, I know. I understand that, and I don't blame you."

"In that event, then, I will go—for two reasons: first, to convince you that I was not opposed to you personally; and secondly, I come from the Lwow area and Lwow is my town."

We then shook hands cordially, and discussed details.

We agreed that I should leave for Lwow at the end of February and there lay the foundations for his work. He would follow me about ten days later. I was to read the latest reports received from Lwow, from Trzaska and Niewiarowski. These reports were in the H.Q. I was to draw some dollars for the preliminary expenses of the organisation and would receive an authorisation in writing. "Bronka", the chief of the liaison department, could give me information as to where it was easiest to cross the demarcation line: I could then avail myself of the best route.

We then arranged when and where to find each other on his arrival, and I said goodbye to the General:

"*Au revoir*—in our dear Lwow."

The following day I had a short talk with Rowecki. He gave me a common greyish handkerchief. On it were typed a few words in one corner:

"Bearer arrives with full authority by C.O. Obey him."

This was signed in his own handwriting—"Grabina". The grey typewriting was almost indiscernible from the grey colour of the handkerchief and looked like a dirty spot. One had to examine it carefully to discover the inscription. Trzaska and Niewiarowski knew the signature well: it should not arouse any doubts; they were both active in Lwow. I also received a sheet of clean paper, with a little mark to indicate which was the right and which the wrong side. A more detailed instruction was written on it in invisible ink. It could only be deciphered after being developed: I was told how to do that.

Before we parted, Rowecki gave me advice on a ticklish problem regarding the General. He was, according to Rowecki, not cautious enough, and was inclined personally to contact too many people; he trusted them too much. Rowecki asked me to extend strong protection around the General and to organise our activities in such a way that he would be almost cut off from personal contacts: only the most reliable people should be allowed to meet him. He felt compelled to tell me this, though it might savour of criticism.

We wished each other good luck, and I went to see "Bronka".

She was really charming—a grey-haired lady with a young face and deep, intelligent eyes; full of calm, tact and enthusiasm. With her I left my private address in Lwow where couriers could always find me—or, at least, find my whereabouts. They only had to ask at 3 Pulawski Str., on the ground floor, opposite the entrance door, for Mr. Lisowski from Strzalki; that was enough.

She gave me 120 dollars in bank notes, and suggested the use of the route via Lancut; I was also told the necessary password for giving

111

orders to her men. I took them, in case I should need them, although I wanted to use my own men.

I said goodbye to "Bronka".*

I was back again in Cracow. It was the latter half of February.

The final preparations for my journey were almost completed. First of all, I changed my identity card. I kept my assumed name, Joseph Ruminski, but changed the date of my birth to 1893—it was better to appear older—and changed the place of my birth. Apparently I had been born in Dunajow, near Przemyslany. I preferred to be regarded in Lwow as belonging to the "Western Ukraine" rather than as a refugee.

Then I exchanged some dollars for gold coins. One of our men took them, and also my boots, home; when he brought the boots back, four 10-dollar coins were hidden in one heel and three in the other. I took the remaining banknotes so mysteriously packed by Mrs. Komorowski and Mary.

Kabat gave me a companion, a young girl from the organisation; she was to accompany and assist me.

We were careful not to disclose where I was going. The news that I was bound for Lwow might spread and reach the town before me and cause a lot of trouble.

On the 21st February, late at night, I left by train; and the next morning, in Jaroslaw, I found my man. It was Capt. Rutkowski, who was supposed to have organised the crossing for the following night.

Everything went according to plan. The guide in Munina was booked: Rutkowski delegated Sergeant Wozniakowski to go with me. He had just returned, a few days ago, from Lwow, and knew the situation there. I preferred him to my girl companion, who was visibly terrified, although she tried to put a good face on the bad business. I gave her a definite order to return by the next train to Cracow. I was sorry for her: I did not know what would happen to us, and she was so young.

In the evening Rutkowski issued us with one white bed-sheet each —these would be useful as camouflage in the snow. We went by sledge to Munina. I had no luggage, simply a small bundle in my hand containing one change of underwear and a pair of shoes; I wore the ones containing the gold coins!

About 1 a.m. we walked towards the San. We aimed at catching

* Later she became Senior Commandant Bronka Karas, and was killed in a tragic accident, in 1948, in India.

112

the train on the Bolshevik side, leaving Surochow at 6 a.m. for Lwow.

The snow was thick. Sometimes we sank knee-deep. Finally, unchallenged, we reached the osiers on the San. The river was covered with ice; the opposite bank was deserted; at a distance we could see the trees in Surochow. It was really but one bound!

Slowly we descended down to the river and then ran quickly on the ice, across the river. Covered with our sheets, we sat down below the scarp and carefully inspected the field facing us.

We could see the road about fifty feet in front of us, and at its side a stout and lonely willow-tree with branches jutting out like a broom. We were just about to move when Wozniakowski pulled me by the sleeve down to earth.

"Look at that willow-tree, the straight branch on the right of the trunk—it is moving!"

The moon was very bright. I peered carefully. . . . He was right: it was a long Russian bayonet! A soldier was standing behind the willow-tree, and this was what made the trunk appear so stout. We could now see his elbows and the flaps of his greatcoat. We were confident he had not seen us—the bed of the river was so low: perhaps he had been looking in a different direction.

We whispered. . . . It was impossible to cross here—neither right nor left was there any cover. Only about five hundred yards below, however, there were some bushes. We decided to return to the other side. In one bound we reached the opposite bank, and hid in the osiers. The guide was still waiting there.

A short consultation followed. It was too late to try again tonight; we must postpone the crossing to another night, when perhaps it would be darker: now it was too bright, a full moon. We had had some good luck, anyhow.

In the morning, to Rutkowski's amazement, we were back in Jaroslaw.

On the Saturday, it was thawing and cloudy; again we went on sledges to Munina. This time we decided to aim at the left of the fatal willow-tree, where we had spotted the bushes. It was a longer way, and the snow was very deep, but it was safer.

As we were passing the last houses in Jaroslaw I saw, on our left, a big tailless retriever running next to our sledges. Then I heard a sharp shout: "Come back!" as if somebody wished to recall the dog. It was a horrible cry: it pierced me through and through, and its sinister sound remained within my ears. I looked back, but there was no sign of the dog, nor of a man. I had a creepy feeling.

113

"Wozniakowski, did you see a dog?"

"No."

"Did you hear someone shouting, 'Come back!'?"

"No; there was nobody at all!"

It must have been an hallucination—my nerves! And even if it were something other than nerves, I had to put it out of my mind, this "Come back!": there was no "back" now—we must go forward!

We reached the osiers on the river bank without difficulty; this time the willow-tree was far to our right. In front of us, on the other bank, were bushes. It was quite calm. After our last experience, we searched every detail this time, with eyes like gimlets.

After some time we spotted them: two soldiers patrolling along the river. They stopped from time to time, and then walked on again—towards the willow-tree. A patrol or a relief?

The guide whispered: "That's all right. After they've passed, go; no others will come."

We did as he said. Once we had lost the soldiers from sight, we ran across the river, and then walked as quickly as possible through the deep snow into the fields. We had succeeded! The snow drifts, however, made walking very difficult, and we were sweating freely. So we lay down on the snow for a short rest; we had time enough to catch the train.

I do not know how long we lay there—perhaps fifteen or twenty minutes. Then, suddenly, there was a shot and a bullet hit the snow near me. I cautiously lifted my head and saw two soldiers following our footprints, about thirty yards away: one, on his knee, was aiming his rifle at us; the second, with rifle under his arm, was walking slowly towards us.

It had just happened: the tailless dog. . . .

The soldiers came nearer, pointed their bayonets in our backs, and we heard, for the first time: "Forward! Don't talk."

They drove us towards the road. It was the end! That was on Sunday, the 25th February, 1940.

CHAPTER 14

Imprisonment

WE MARCHED quickly along the road, followed by the soldiers.

My mind was working hard to find some means of escape. . . . Should we, perhaps, rush upon the Red soldiers? I believe the same thought struck Wozniakowski, for he gave me an enquiring look. I grimaced—no! It would be murder—which, even if successful, would hamper our work in Lwow. Far better to avoid this and seek other, less drastic, measures.

I slid my hand carefully into my pocket and extracted the incriminating handkerchief and the sheet of paper with the invisible writing. Slowly and cautiously I dropped them in the snow and trod upon them. I was lucky! A good start!

After an hour's walk we came to Wysock, where was the guardroom for this sector. We were searched, and everything was taken away—our identity cards, wallets, personal belongings, etc. The searchers wrote out depositions describing the circumstances in which we were caught; I was chiefly alarmed by the inclusion of a statement that we had, while crossing, both carried white sheets and a torch.

"You have a torch, you bastard! So you are a spy!"

For several hours we were detained in Wysock; then we were marched about ten miles to Stubno, escorted by mounted Cossacks. Without any further search, we were shut up in the cellar of a stone house: it looked to me like a mansion house or a school. The cellar was probably a vegetable store. It had a small barred window, and the ceiling was so low that we could not stand upright.

There were also several other men and women there, who had similarly been caught "on the frontier". More people were brought

115

in during the next five days, and the cellar became crowded. During this time, each of us only once received a slice of bread. Shouting and knocking at the door did not help.

"You're not entitled to food," we were told.

It was dreadfully cold, too—about 30° F. below freezing-point.

At last, on the fifth day, we were called, one by one, into the office for interrogation. Perhaps we were to be freed? . . . A ray of hope dawned. "It happens sometimes," maintained Rena, a fat young Jewess who had been smuggling gum-elastics, for dentists, across the demarcation line. It was not her first attempt: she had had previous experience.

The examination was brief. "Who are you? Why did you cross the frontier? What task did the Gestapo give you?" and so on.

On the table I saw my first deposition and all my belongings that had been taken during the search—except for my identity card and my wallet containing my money. I wondered whether they had been stolen, or simply reserved for a more detailed examination.

The examining officer looked quite good-natured; he was calm and did not raise his voice. I instinctively felt that if asked he might liberate me. He looked at my belongings and waited as if expecting me to ask him; but I was not yet inclined, in my own country, to bow the knee to an Eastern intruder.

When dismissed, however, I did manage to ask: "What will happen to me?"

"Nothing: don't worry—you'll be free in a few days."

This answer reassured me; but to establish complete confidence I repeated the question to the soldier escorting me. His answer was the very opposite.

"Have you heard about the Volga-Don Canal?" he asked. "You'll be sent there to dig. There you'll work for two years. If you're still alive then, your wife will join you and you'll settle down and live there. If you perish, a band will play at your funeral."

My God! What an outlook! My flesh began to creep.

One of the representatives of the Soviet Union was obviously jeering at me; but which one? I hoped it was the second.

That evening we were all herded into a lorry and driven straight to Przemysl. To Przemysl Gaol. The gates of the prison opened wide for us. A search followed. We heard the rattle of keys. We were marched along the prison corridors; cells were unlocked, and we newcomers were pushed in.

Finally, together with Wozniakowski, I was thrust into Cell No. 30.

We could not discern anything at first in the dim light, but there was the noise of many voices. We were only semi-conscious, owing to the frost, starvation, and dirt of the last few days.

Slowly we thawed out and could take stock of our surroundings. The cell was a large one. Perched high up on the wall was a small window, minus its glass; there were no beds or other furniture; the walls were dirty and peeling, and the floor muddy and littered with waste scraps. The smell of unwashed human bodies, cigarette smoke, and general dampness, thickened the air and nearly suffocated us.

The cell was so crowded that one could hardly move, and it would be impossible to lie down at night: probably a transit cell, we thought —surely it would be impossible to survive in it for more than a few hours.

A man with a greying beard and wearing a fur coat came up to me and said:

"My name is Szajna: I was a clerk in Katowice. Have you a cigarette on you?" While his eyes entreated, he only whispered, looking furtively round him.

"I have a few." I got them out of my pocket. "But, tell me, please, how long are we going to be kept here? How long have *you* been here?"

"Six weeks."

"What! In this cell?"

He did not reply; instead he was watching my hand, like a beaten dog or a servile, broken and beseeching slave. Then once more he whispered: "*Please* give me a cigarette."

After several puffs he became more normal. He stuck to me— perhaps expecting another one. Presently, in a whisper, he began to describe the life of the cell.

"It's terrible," he said. "I have never known anything so dreadful in my life. I have never before been in prison. I'm afraid they'll kill me."

"Who are *they*? The N.K.V.D.?"

"No; Spatylak, Pawlowski and Malczyk—their gang." He turned his eyes towards a group of men sitting under the window at the far end of the cell.

For some time I could not understand what he meant. He talked of intrigues in the cell life; described feuds and fights, thefts and bad behaviour . . . all of which grew, as he dwelt on them, to be important events, overshadowing everything else. He did not ask for news from the free world: he seemed to have forgotten there was a normal life;

117

he was caught and soaked in this existence behind the bars. A clerk, he could not get accustomed to it. He was broken, and withered like a plant belonging to a different climate.

I met other inmates. Some were young students—easy to recognise at first sight—who had been going to France to join the Army; others were soldiers, still in their uniforms, returning after the September Campaign to their homes in the east. There were Jews, noisy and aggressive, threatening to settle accounts with imaginary "anti-Semitism"; there were the "*intelligentsia*", both of Szajna's type and of the really educated and cultured classes. But clearly the representatives of the criminal world had the whip hand over all the others. They knew everything, and were on their own. They were experienced in the life and rules of prisons, and were accustomed to force their determined will upon any inexperienced inmates. Obviously, Spatylak was senior in the cell, the uncrowned ruler.

We constantly witnessed conflicts, and the application of rule by the fist.

Middle-class people could not understand that their previous social standing meant nothing in prison. They were pushed down to the depths, beaten with fists, kicked, and maltreated mentally, with biting contempt and mockery.

It was soon evident that Spatylak's rule, though ruthless, had some sense, and was even just according to a special strange moral code. In view of all the beastliness and cowardice, only terror of Spatylak could keep people in check.

The conditions under which we lived, especially the lack of food, brought forth the vilest instincts.

Although in the Przemysl prison there were several thousand prisoners above its normal capacity, there were only thirty iron dishes, of various sizes. Together with the food-containers they were taken round the corridors of the prison, and food was distributed to single cells at different times of the day or night.

We were fed thus once in twenty-four hours.

The sound of the approaching food-containers and the rattle of iron mugs drove the starved people mad. They rushed to the door like beasts, so as to be first in the queue. Before the food had come they were already fighting. Use was made of fists, and the most whining brutes were thrust to the end of the queue. Spatylak's gang, of course, always remained in front. When the door was opened *they* fed first, sipping the soup out of the mugs—there were no spoons. This they did slowly, almost contemptuously, acting according to their law—*viz*: that one should never show any weakness or any sign of hunger—though the covetous, envious looks of the other inmates almost penetrated even their thick hides. Only later did the gang deign to pass on the mugs to others. But the scrounging ones, the weak ones, only received them at the end; sometimes even not at all.

If Spatylak shouted to the guard, "All fed!" the door was immediately shut; any unfed man who might try to reach the door was struck on the face and insulted in a most abusive way.

One could not deny the educative value of the principles instilled by this system: Spatylak could not bear people who were without character—they were beneath his dignity, and weakness was inconsistent with the traditions of the "knights of the criminal world".

In addition to these means of educating people, Spatylak also punished weaklings, as he called them, by stealing their special possessions, typical of the bourgeoisie; as, for instance, watches: but he never harmed people who in his opinion did not violate the moral code of prison life. Only people not up to the standard of the "sublime profession of a prisoner" were the victims of his gang.

Booty thus accumulated was let down on a cord to the street, to be received by the gang's mistresses and by members of "the trade" —who, by the same method, supplied their "heroes" with vodka, bacon and tobacco. This practice was performed with extreme skill: the men knew exactly how to evade the watchful eyes of the guards and of the Soviet soldiers. In their slang, it was called "sending a horse for grub".

I never had any conflict with Spatylak's gang: I even became on good terms with them—from the day I became a "partner" to a theft organised by them in the cell.

Until the opportunity occurred to send a "horse", they had to keep the stolen goods in some hiding-place that would be difficult to discover if there was a search, and was safe from informers and sneaks. They dare not keep it on themselves. By mere chance I discovered such a hiding-place, in the pipe of the stove! According to normal principles of honesty I ought to have given the thieves up and insisted that the stolen goods be returned to their rightful owners, but I did not do so: my subconscious sympathies were with Spatylak and his system of discriminating between various characters. In spite of everything, I preferred strong men to weak, so I pretended not to have seen the loot.

When the stolen goods were lowered later and the "grub" had

119

arrived in exchange, Pawlowski gave me five cigarettes and a piece of bacon, saying "That's from Spatylak." It was my "share" in the venture: it was not a reward, it was due to me. Then I realised that I had become an accomplice. Having adhered to the prison code of morality not to betray my comrades, I had now become one of them, was drawn closer to them, understood them, and perhaps even liked them.

We often discussed the social problems of good and evil, of crime and punishment, of law and social order. During one of these discussions I asked an old prison lag, who had already spent eleven years in many prisons for various thefts: "Mr. Malczyk, tell me: do you think that police, attorneys, and Courts should exist in the world?"

"Yes, of course."

"Do you think that attorneys and judges are honest people?"

"Of course they are honest—unless they have insufficient experience, then one can cheat them during cross-examination."

"And what about you professional thieves—are you honest people?"

"Yes, of course!"

His explanation was not quite clear to me, so he had to explain further.

In his opinion, it was honest to practise one's profession conscientiously, justly and manfully, no matter what profession it was. It was not evil to steal from a weakling or a fool, because he was there for that purpose: he had plenty of everything; but it was evil to betray one's colleague, to allot him a fraudulent share, or not to help him in time of need, and so on. A judge who passed severe, but just, sentences was honest because he did his work conscientiously.

"Mr. Malczyk, have you a son?"

"Yes. He'll be six by now."

"And will you teach him to become a thief?"

"Never! With my leather belt I'd thrash out any ideas like that from his head. I shall send him to school—I myself never went to school."

They were odd people: they had their own morality and their own hierarchy, which they respected. One thief was not necessarily equal to another. At the top of the ladder was a safe-breaker: Spatylak. He was an international specialist, often called to operate in different places, like a specialist surgeon. Next came expert pickpockets, operating in trains: Malczyk was one of those. Then came the

120

ordinary pickpockets, operating in markets and among crowds, and the specialists at cutting open pockets with a razor. Next came those who pilfered from flats and attics. In the lowest category belonged the pilferers of peasants' carts on the roads, and various types of deceivers and impostors.

It was a complete social ladder, well disciplined, with respect for their expert specialists. And any violation of their "constitution" was mercilessly and efficiently punished.

I was interested to know how they reacted to current events—to the Polish question and the enemy invasion. Once I did raise this question. They did not know Poland's history at all. They loved Marshal Pilsudski and admired his strength, looking upon him almost as one of themselves. They had not a notion of what the Fatherland meant, but they were definitely proud of being Poles. The only reason why they molested the middle-class at this time was the fact that they wanted revenge because "those lousy Bolsheviks and Germans had degenerated them". They said: "Look at them! They're no use. They just feed at the trough like cattle. . . . They'd lick the feet of any of those lousy bastards!" They hated the Bolsheviks, and despised them as beneath contempt.

"Stupid mob! Lice!"

The small group of school and university students represented an entirely different outlook. Burning despair was in their eyes: their march to France, their dreams about the Army and fighting—all these had been frustrated. They attempted to adopt a mask of indifference, pretending to have gone astray while returning to their homes.

With staring eyes they watched the behaviour of Spatylak's gang; they grouped together, whispering and protecting each other; in the evening, like Scouts, together they prepared their lair.

I wanted to be friendly, but they were distrustful. I was unable to reveal my identity, though I sensed they made romantic escape plans in order to uphold their morale.

The weakest among them was Szczepaniak. He was afflicted with deep melancholia. He stopped eating, and also stopped killing lice, which plagued us in vast hordes. Eventually he became insensible, broken by despair.

It was with pity I watched how the other students tried to save him, sometimes by encouragement, at other times by coarse mockery; then by a friendly nudge; in it all one could discern genuine goodwill and the true care of friends. Also, they were probably afraid that Szczepaniak, if completely unhinged, would give way to pressure

121

during interrogation and betray them all. They were marvellous youths: the brothers Henry and Sigismund Januszkiewicz, two other brothers, named Hykiel, and Bukowinski (who all became officers later, and fought on the Western front), Kowalski, little more than a child, and many others.

The senior amongst them was Henry; he was married and had a daughter, Alusia, a year old. He often spoke of her and in his knapsack he carried a doll which he kept as his most precious treasure for the little girl. Later on, when we became friends, he told me that this was an excuse, in case of arrest, to make them believe he was on his way home; but really he was on his way from home to France.

"But you see, Mr. Ruminski," he said to me, "I am not lying: I made a vow to bring the doll back to Alusia."*

Sigismund often "pulled his leg", maintaining that the doll was a replica of Alusia: "I think it was for that reason you took it with you."

Mr. Felix Tarnowski looked after this group like a father. He was a short, delicate old man, but extremely intelligent and cultured. While in prison he grew a grey beard. The students all stuck to him. He told them about the marvels of the world which he had seen in his journeys, about the Italian Renaissance, music, about spiritual values and famous men. They seemed to drink comfort from his lips, which helped them to avoid the ruin and the degradation to bestiality which surrounded us all.

Tarnowski had been caught going to the West, in the opposite direction to the students from Lwow, where he had left his wife and two sons. He had tried to avoid arrest as a "bourgeois" and "bloodsucker of the working class"; his wife had made him go.†

There were various other groups and individuals, every one of whom differed from the other. Time was too short to discern them all well, for we were hardly ten days and nights all together. Probably many people concealed themselves behind assumed identities like myself: nobody must guess that I was a member of the Underground, entrusted with a responsible job: that I was interested in Poland's destiny and in her fight for freedom. I had to be very careful not to betray myself by a gesture or by involuntary reaction during a heated discussion. To everyone I had to appear to be just an uneducated little shop assistant from Lankosz Bros. in Cracow, on my way to

---

* He never brought the doll back; he was killed in Italy in 1944 in the battle by the Metauro river.
† He died in a Russian prison from exhaustion.

Lwow, there to find my wife and my three children who had been lost during the September storm.

This was the story I was composing in precise detail in preparation for my approaching interrogation.

I regretted that I could not become more friendly with Tarnowski and his boys: instead, I had to remain apart, rather drawing if anything nearer to Spatylak's gang.

And so day after day passed, and we still lived in the same noise and dirt, plagued by lice, and starving. We had not been interrogated, and were uncertain about our future. Perhaps we should be freed in a few days? . . .

CHAPTER 15

"Parasites!"

AFTER a fortnight there were new developments.

There was a sudden search of the cell: somebody had given information to the authorities. It was incredible, indeed, but in the corner where Spatylak's gang nested they found a hole in the wall, almost bored through. Spatylak had been preparing for an escape.

I could not understand how he had managed to pierce the thick prison wall without any of us noticing it—without any visible sign of rubble or bricks. It seemed unbelievable that he could have done it in the midst of so many people. I could not help admiring his skill. But somebody had spotted it—probably one of the "weaklings"; the scoundrel must have "grassed" out of vengeance.

A terrific uproar followed. The cell was instantly cleared. We were hurled into the corridor, ordered to undress, and thoroughly searched. Then it was that we lost the remainder of our belongings. They even took Henry's doll.

Divided into small groups, we were thrust into other already overcrowded cells.

I found myself in a small cell, completely without windows—a dark room where it was always night. I do not know with whom I was kept there, or for how long. I think for several days; perhaps a week, or even more.

We could barely see the features of our neighbours; though we could feel them with our elbows. The cell was terribly crowded, with only enough room to sit doubled up.

Once a day the door was opened and a mug of soup and a slice of bread issued to each of us.

Amazingly, the prisoners did not rush for the food; on the contrary, an instinct, such as watered animals have during a drought,

124

seemed to impose general good manners. Everyone waited patiently until his neighbour had received the mug and eaten his food undisturbed. Maybe people who have reached the lowest depths of distress do behave in this way.

There was one among them who was not merely calm, but seemed to be really happy. He sat alone, always singing or humming to himself; here he was out of place, irritating. He was a tall, good-looking, fair-haired man about forty; people said he was a sailor. For a long time I watched this enigma; at last I could resist my curiosity no longer.

"Please tell me, why are you so happy?"

He looked at me for some time as if not understanding my question; then, as if suddenly coming to earth, he finally said:

"Why should I not be happy, when I managed without an engineer! I did it myself."

"What did you do yourself?" I asked him, ill at ease.

"The water-pipes."

"Which water-pipes?"

"In the house I am building now." And he gave me a detailed account of his "activities".

He had decided on building a house, himself, without any outside assistance. It was time to get married. He even foresaw in the new house a nursery for children. He had begun to build this house directly he had been shut up in this damned prison! At first he had had difficulties in drawing the plan, but he overcame them. He approached an architect, an old acquaintance of his, to revise this plan. It was a success—the architect was enthusiastic about it.

"It was terribly difficult to find him at this time during the war; the silly man had changed his lodgings—I had to search half the town before I could discover him. Then I had trouble about bricks: I had to economise. I wrote letters to several brick-kilns asking for tenders; only one of them failed to reply. I had to buy bricks at the lowest price. Finally I got enough of good quality, and cheap—they had a beautiful ringing tone. But you'd never believe how difficult the carting was!'

And so he went on for hours, describing in detail his troubles and joys: but he always managed to succeed in the end. After he had built the roof and begun to decorate the interior, he realised that he had completely forgotten to insert the water-pipes in the walls. For two days this problem tormented him. What was he to do now? Should he pull down the house?

He was just going to ask a builder for advice when he himself solved the difficulty. That was the reason for his contentment.

I realised that he was building the house in his imagination, but it was real to him: he actually experienced it. For a long time, however, I did not understand him.

"Is he insane?" I wondered.

Probably he guessed my doubts, for he said seriously:

"Look here, I won't let those bastards keep me shut up. I am not really here—I am free, as before; only my body is imprisoned. You do the same—*please*; that's my advice; otherwise you'll go mad. I know it, believe me. I have been shut in many places during my life —when I was fourteen I went to sea."

He relapsed into silence, and again happiness and joy beamed from his eyes.

The lesson sank deep into my heart: to avoid insanity the spirit must remain free; if it has an indomitable conscious will no power can destroy it.

Soon there were signs that something was about to happen. For two days no food-containers had been circulating along the corridors: we had neither soup nor bread—only one pail of drinking water was brought and put in the middle of our cell: another bucket stood in a corner for sanitary purposes. The first was rapidly emptied; the second overflowed and its contents spilled over. Knocking at the door brought no help, for nobody paid any attention.

We realised that this procedure applied to the whole of the prison, not only to our cell, because the noise of knocking at doors reached us from all sides. Something was evidently happening: perhaps we were about to recover our liberty? . . .

Indeed, on the evening of the second day we were withdrawn from the cell to the corridor by the magic words "Come on!" and were immediately herded into another, larger, cell, which seemed to us unusually well lit; because of this brilliance our eyes, unaccustomed to light, pricked us painfully.

There were already about two hundred prisoners there. At regular intervals the door opened and newcomers were pushed in. The austerity we had previously experienced now seemed to us the acme of comfort. Our actual situation became tragic; our veins pulsated; we sweated; our mouths, wide open, were nervously gasping for air; the atmosphere was becoming foetid; people gradually fell down, suffocated; and several men of short stature, unable to raise their heads above the level of others, fainted. It seemed as though the intention was to suffocate us.

In reply to our wild shoutings and knockings at the door, a senior officer—probably from the N.K.V.D. Corps—appeared.

"Air! We are choked!" came shouts from the cell.

He very kindly agreed to leave the door open to air the cell. He then announced that it had been decided to free us, but we must understand it could not be done in Przemysl, a border town already overcrowded. Tomorrow we would be entrained for Lwow, where we would recover our liberty and everyone could please himself.

"There are plenty of jobs—you'll be able to work," he said; "only don't make such a noise."

"Then give us some food!" somebody shouted from the cell. "For two days we haven't eaten anything!"

"You're not entitled to any—you're no longer on the prison strength. But your food ration has been issued for the journey; besides, we must follow the rule of 'No work, no food.' You must learn to change your outlook."

People reacted to this by making a terrific noise, and the Russian then slammed the door. We heard him bark:

"What a scandal! What uncultured people! Parasites!"

We left the prison before it was dusk, marching in a column six deep to the railway station, watched on each side by a dense escort of Soviet soldiers and dogs, bayonets pointed towards us. Whenever we halted we were ordered to sit down, which we did, often in mud, so that our guards could overlook us.

At last we were entrained in cattle trucks—seventy men to a truck. We were then issued with a piece of sausage and a slice of bread each; and soon the long train steamed towards Lwow.

It was Palm Sunday, 1940.

As we might have foreseen, the promised freedom was only the usual deceitful lie. On its way to the east the train passed Lwow without stopping.

When passing through Podzamcze Station in Lwow, I managed to throw through the window a little ball, made of bread, in which I had stuck a piece of paper with a request to any person who picked it up kindly to deliver it immediately to Mrs. Ela Wolf, 23 Gornoslaska Str.—the address for contacts I had received in Warsaw from "Bronka". In faint pencil I scribbled on this paper: "R—— whom you expected, has been arrested and taken East."

It was brief, but comprehensive. (Years later I learnt that this note reached its destination; the people in Lwow were marvellous.)

I was very despondent. All that I had wished to avoid when escaping from the German prisoner-of-war camp had happened: I would be isolated from active life for a long time, with little hope of return—if one believed the story of the Volga-Don Canal.

I was particularly distressed at losing the job of organising the Resistance in Lwow; the thought kept tormenting me, how would they do without me? I suffered the humiliation of having been captured like a child, and, though somewhat comforted by the thought that General Tokarzewski would be lucky enough to cross the demarcation line, I was gnawed by jealousy of him and by despair.

The train rattled over the rails. . . . We passed Zloczow. Somebody attempted an escape through the loosened boards in the floor of the truck. We heard shots; we did not know if they caught or killed him. The train went on. Then we passed Podwoloczyska, the last Polish station on the true frontier, not the one delimited by Ribbentrop and Molotov. We travelled over the Soviet Ukraine, further to the East. There were great drifts of snow, and the frost became more biting, although it was already March.

The atmosphere in the truck was getting tense. Actually, we were divided into two bitterly opposed parties. On one side of the truck were Jews only—noisy, insolent, and posing as Communists; on the other side were all the Poles, Ukrainians, and one Czech, entangled by mere chance with our crowd.

In the middle of the truck sat the solitary Max, a genuine German Communist, who had escaped from a Nazi concentration camp to join his own comrades, the Soviet Communists, and thus recover liberty. Now he had a taste of Soviet freedom! He did not speak a word of either Polish or Russian, and was completely bewildered by what he saw. He told us of the dreadful conditions in German camps, where, as a Communist, he had spent three years. He had managed to escape after killing the guard and had put on a soldier's uniform, joined an army transport going East, and was lucky enough to have come to Poland. He hoped immediately to be set free when able to talk to some of the Bolsheviks. Up to that time nobody had examined him and he was looked upon as a spy. In my opinion his statements were quite true, but I doubted if he would ever recover his freedom.

Both sides of the truck hated each other!

It was not racial hatred: it was rather the enmity of two opposed political parties, although nobody expressed any political views. The Jews visibly followed the Communist line and called the soldier who brought the pail with water *"Tovariszcz"* ("Comrade"), and not, as the rest of us did, "lousy bastard".

People fought for water. Once a day it was brought in a pail, which circulated from mouth to mouth; no mugs were given, and there was insufficient water for seventy people, so during the ensuing struggle the water was generally spilt. The Soviet soldiers laughed, but would not attempt to bring another pailful.

Finally, agreement was reached that the watering should start from the Christian and Jewish sides alternately. This arrangement, however, was not very helpful, because the side which had the water first deliberately drank at least three-quarters of the pail, thus leaving the opposite side as little as possible. New tussles and shoutings resulted.

Max could not understand this lack of comradeship among people under duress: he thought they must have had an extremely good time when free, and that must be the reason for their anti-social behaviour; but that would pass, and they would all recover their balance, as he knew from his own experience, having been through such things before. He was intelligent and very amicable.

Days and nights passed. The train was still travelling. We endeavoured to remember the dates, and discovered it was Passion Week. Henry and Sigismund Januszkiewicz decided to fast on Good Friday—*i.e.*, not to eat their piece of sausage, which, to our amazement, we received daily with a slice of bread. I admired them very much for this.

One day we passed Zmerynka, noticing that we left the railway line to Odessa on our right: so we were speeding towards Dniepropietrovsk—or perhaps towards the Don—or directly to the Volga-Don Canal. . . .

No! It was on Easter Sunday (*again* a Sunday!) that we were detrained in Dniepropietrovsk, loaded on to lorries, and driven to the building of the N.K.V.D. prison, which was surrounded by high walls, with turrets for the guards.

And again, as in Przemysl, the big iron gate of the prison was standing wide open, afterwards to be slammed tight.

CHAPTER 16

Learning about Stalinism

AFTER our arrival in Dnieproprietrovsk I began preparing for my impending interrogation, having heard much about the methods of the N.K.V.D.

I had trouble in not knowing the necessary preliminaries. I did not know Russia, and I could not guess what the Soviet aims were with regard to those tens—or perhaps even hundreds—of thousands of arrested Poles. I realised quite well that there were only a few, like myself, who were "guilty"; the majority consisted of harmless people captured by mere chance. There must be *some* purpose behind their detention and all the trouble entailed in bringing them there. If only I could divine what that purpose was, I could more easily adopt the proper mode of behaviour. I must, however, decide on some kind of tactics; if they were the right ones for the prevailing conditions, I might be able to lose myself in the mass of people and to swim with the tide. I told myself they could not possibly shoot all of us—we were far too many. So one only had to adopt a suitable attitude. But what?

I absolutely rejected the idea of showing my hand: if I did, our organisation and our Underground activities would be compromised, and the Soviets would hunt for Tokarzewski, and others. It was not feasible.

I had to invent an innocent story; but I did not have the necessary ingredients. I did not know whether my identity card and my wallet were in their hands—I had not seen them during my interrogation. If they did not possess them, it would be better to state another place of birth, not this damned Dunajow shown on my identity card with the faked signature of the issuing clerk, which could easily be verified, for Dunajow was under their authority. But if the identity card happened to be in their hands, then a changed statement would lead to suspicion and I should be trapped. It was not improbable that one of our companions knew me and might unconsciously betray me.

Various schemes flashed through my mind. The thought that I had to lie and cheat during interrogation was unsavoury and haunted me all the time. A lie would always be a lie, even if directed to the N.K.V.D. I was never a follower of the theory that the end justifies the means: to me cheating is dishonourable. However, I could discover no other way: this was the consequence of becoming a conspirator.

It took two days to disperse the whole transport throughout the cells of the new prison, preceded by a new and thorough search. We were stripped naked, and they even searched one's mouth, anus and armpits. The skilful hands of the guards felt every seam in our clothes and underwear, looking for any items prohibited in cells, such as penknives, needles, pencils, pens, paper, notebooks, etc. It appeared that prisoners were not allowed to possess laces to their boots, or belts and braces for their trousers, or any metal buttons. All these were taken away and thrown on a pile. If boots appeared to them suspicious—this especially applied to ski-ing boots—they were cut through and heels and soles torn off in search of hiding places. After this operation we presented a droll appearance, holding up our falling trousers!

Luckily, my boots containing the gold coins were untouched. There was a long discussion between the searchers, though, about my devotional medal; at length they decided to ask me about it.

"What's *that*?"

"God's image."

"Well, you won't need it now—there is no God *here*." And my little medal was thrown on the pile with the rest of the things.

They could not remove more things from me, as I had very few left. But my glasses, bought in Cracow as a disguise, were left to me, as I was said to be "entitled" to those.

Then one had a Turkish bath, went through the business of killing the lice, and had all the hair on one's whole body pulled out by a very old and blunt hair-cutter. After this operation, we were considered ready to be transferred to the "corps"—the name given to sections of the prison, which contained over 30,000 prisoners.

Days, weeks, and months of confinement followed, interspersed every ten days by a bath and search, and at irregular times by summonses to interrogation. Spring turned into summer; then came autumn and a long winter; then spring again; and another summer.

During this time I changed cells and met new people, good and bad, wise and stupid. Steadily the body withdrew from the spirit, withering away from starvation and misery. But the mind found a new liberty and independence of material needs, sometimes travelling far ahead, transgressing the usual limits, visualising strange things unattainable before. Some incident or tragedy in prison life might violently press the spirit down, but it soon recovered its wings, usually at night, to soar into unlimited free regions again.

As time passed, people changed: differences became smoothed out; there were no more divisions into Jews and non-Jews, criminals and non-criminals; there only remained human beings, some of them strong, others weak; but all unfortunate, and all converted to the idea of brotherhood. Even the unavoidable quarrels lost importance; only sometimes, when news about the storm raging in the outside world managed by a miracle to pierce the thick walls of the prison, were old memories stirred, and the sorrow of being incarcerated heavily oppressed our hearts and kindled latent hopes.

At first I was shut in Cell No. 23. Moshe Moyseyovitch (son of Moshe) Nizgorodskij, a Russian Jew about fifty years old, was the senior of this cell. He had been a book-keeper in some Soviet corporation, and now he was kept in prison, still under interrogation, for "carelessness", because he had committed some error in the accounts. Originally he had been accused of the far greater crime of "sabotage", but he vowed that he had managed to convince the examining magistrate that it was not "sabotage", simply carelessness. We asked him what kind of a sentence he expected.

"A small one—I don't think more than three years."

A nice prospect! He called it "a small one"—three years in prison! Just for making an error in book-keeping.

It appeared that we were complete ignoramuses from the capitalist world, who could not, and would not, appreciate the achievements of the Revolution. Moshe Moyseyovitch immediately started to enlighten us on this subject.

He stayed in our cell for about three months. During this time he explained to us, for several hours daily, the principles of Leninism and Stalinism, often quoting Marx and Engels. He talked of the life of the Soviet people, their happiness, and the freedom every citizen enjoyed. His speeches were intelligent and beautifully phrased. He always had a ready answer or explanation to questions; with the patience and indulgence of an experienced teacher, he treated us as

132

unlettered children.

One thing struck us, however: he never would listen to any accounts of conditions of life prevailing in our country. When some of our crowd, exasperated by his boasting, wanted to tell *our* story, he immediately interrupted him, saying:

"Comrade, stop it! Now you live here; you must change your outlook. Your previous life will never return."

We were told by him that before the days of Marx and Engels the world had been ignorant, reactionary, and lacking in culture; the people were cruelly exploited by the aristocracy, and imperialistic wars raged. Only Lenin and Stalin had succeeded in liberating a part of the world and introducing real happiness. Obviously, this was not perfect yet, because we were still living in a period of Socialism, which is only the first step to complete Communism—which, when universal, will bring paradise on earth.

He expounded such marvellous visions to us that once one of our simpletons, fascinated by them, asked: "How many years will it take to achieve?"

Such a question was probably not foreseen in the training of a "pro-agit" (Communist agitator) which was probably the education Moshe had received.

"It will come when it will," he replied. And added: "When Stalin orders it."

Then he enthused again on the happy life of a Soviet citizen. Everybody works, he said; there is no unemployment; and wages are high. You can work in any district you like; and if you dislike it, you can always go to another district and settle down there: everyone has complete freedom. Should a man prefer a warm climate, he can settle down in Tashkent; and in summer he can go to Leningrad or the Baikal Lake. Everywhere are identical houses for the workers; also cinemas, theatres, welfare organisations and assistance bodies. If a man gets married, his wife also works: the State looks after the children, so there is no need to bother about them. If a child is gifted, it will be sent to a university to become an engineer or a doctor. If bored with his wife, a man can get a divorce by paying a fee of five roubles, and he is then able to marry another girl. The second or third divorce would be more expensive, but one could always save enough money for this purpose. To sum up—a paradise on earth!

At first our Polish people in the cell were interested in this information: it might, perhaps, be true, they whispered among themselves. Later on, always hearing the same perfect story repeated, they became bored: there was not even one black spot in this picture. They were annoyed, also, because they could never provoke one work of appreciation from Moshe Moyseyovitch for *our* institutions and *our* way of life.

One day we discussed international politics, and Moshe Moyseyovitch said that "Poland was a prostitute" and that Germany was not waging an "imperialistic war" and must therefore defend herself against British and French aggression. That was enough for our boys! The next time he left the cell, summoned to an interrogation, they searched his knapsack, and abstracted his stock of tobacco and bacon. On his return he made a fuss and threatened to inform the guards.

One of the *batiars*, Jozko Denczykowski, told him: "If you're a Communist, apply Communist principles. You, chum, had better shut up now. Surely you have never been in Lwow!"

Soon after that, Moshe was transferred to a different cell, and another Russian, Nikitenko,* became our senior.

Nikitenko came originally from the Dnieper area, where he had worked in a *Konzawod* (a stud farm) as a stud-groom. He himself did not know why he had been arrested and was kept under interrogation: perhaps somebody had simply denounced him—or perhaps he did not want to tell us the truth.

So long as Moyseyovitch was also in the cell, Nikitenko helped him to indoctrinate us, but after the former's removal, he ceased expatiating about Russia and often asked us to describe *our* way of life. He listened to it as to a fairy tale, murmuring "That's life. . . . A good life. . . . Here it is impossible. . . ."

He had obviously been afraid to describe his true feelings about life in Soviet Russia, but after we had become friendly he began to whisper, to those of us whom he trusted, the dreadful truth: there was no liberty in Russia—only misery and starvation. "Try to change your job, and you go straight to prison. . . ." The N.K.V.D. ruled by terror and through informers. About 25 million people were kept in the *Lagiery* (labour-camps), in inhuman conditions. Anyone who went there would never see the world again. Sentences of three years' imprisonment were simply child's play; usually one was sentenced to anything from five to 15 years—for *nothing*. It paid the Soviet to send people to remote labour-camps, such as Kolyma, to work in the gold-mines, or to cut timber in the Polar Circle. Yet he took comfort from this state of affairs. Once he said: "What's the

* This was a pseudonym: it is dangerous to quote the correct name of anyone still in the Soviet Union because he might get charged.

difference between life at liberty and in a labour-camp? Everywhere it is slavery and misery."

One day Nikitenko told us that Moyseyovitch had in fact been specially selected as a "teacher" for our cell: that he had been paid ten roubles from the prison authorities for this assignment, and had also been promised a lenient sentence if successful at proselytising his cell-mates.

There was one thing, however, on which everyone agreed: the conditions of life in Dniepropietrovsk were very much better than those we had suffered in Przemysl, though still far from ideal.

Between 4 and 6 o'clock each morning, the cell door opened and the overseer shouted: "*Podyom!*" ("*Reveillé!*")—it was getting-up time. The duty prisoners took the *parasha* (the slip-pail) and we were all marched, two by two, to the latrine.

This was always liberally strewn with calcium chlorine, which stung our eyes and choked us. There were some fifteen holes in the latrine, and these were quickly occupied by the first comers, while the rest queued up behind them, the guards incessantly urging: "Come on, now! Empty your bowels quicker!"

We then went to the water-taps to wash our faces and hands before returning to the cell.

About 8 a.m. came the *balanda*—the food-container and a box of bread. Everyone got a ladleful of soup and 1 lb. 4 oz. of bread.

About 9 a.m. the "parade" took place. The "Head of the Corps" and the duty guard from the corridor entered the cell. We stood in a row, the senior reported, and they took a roll-call. Nearly every day the "Head" made some mistake.

This ritual was followed by a fifteen-minute walk round the prison yard. We were forbidden to talk during this exercise, and our hands had to be kept behind our backs. Nevertheless, it was a pleasure to breathe the fresh air.

At about 2 p.m. we again received some soup, with two spoonsful of groats. Late at night we received "tea"—hot water coloured with some herbs.

The food there was much better and more plentiful than in Przemysl; although still very hungry, we could live on the rations: we even had our happy moments. Sometimes, after the round of all the cells, there might be a little food left in the *balanda*, and then the door was opened again and we received a second helping. But this did not happen by chance. It was expensive, for we had to bribe the guards in the corridors. They accepted anything—shirts, pants, socks, or handkerchiefs; one after the other we pulled off what we could spare, to pay for privileges.

Life in our cell was endurable. We even had beds—though, of course, only one to every three men—and the inmates, too, were pleasant. They included Tarnowski and the two brothers Januszkiewicz. Also Mr. Askenazy, a Polish Jew and a lawyer from Lwow, a highly cultured and educated man who was most popular. His stories were charming, sensible and good-hearted—real food for our minds, that helped keep up our morale.

Life in our cell was very different from that in Cell No. 24, next-door, from which we constantly heard shoutings and the noise of scuffles; it was said to be the worst cell in the prison.

Then something new happened. Mr. Wolf, a young man from Katowice, who had an engineering degree, was summoned for interrogation.

"Come out—and leave your luggage!" This meant he would return after interrogation.

We awaited his return with anxiety, for then we would hear about the methods of interrogation and what charges were made against him; perhaps he might even give us some hints which would enable us to adopt suitable tactics.

He returned in the morning, visibly exhausted in some distress. Had they beaten him? He would not say. But he did say that he had been accused of espionage on behalf of the Nazis, of counter-revolutionary activities, and illegal crossing of the "frontier"—in short, criminal charges. He also said that he had had to make depositions, giving precise details of his life and career and those of all his family, from birth till date of arrest. Here were some hints for us, anyway.

The next night, two others were summoned: Wilford, a fifteen-year-old boy from Przemysl, and Jozko Denczykowski, the *batiar* from Lwow. Both were charged with the same crimes as Wolf, but Jozko was additionally charged with smuggling. He did not mind this in the least: he was in excellent spirits and accurately described his experiences.

"Chum, we cooed like two pigeons! When he started shouting at me, I calmly said: 'You bugger, be quiet: you don't know to whom you are speaking. People like you I saw outside the Zolkiew toll-gate.* By now I know your Constitution by heart.' So he cooled

* A toll-gate in Lwow in olden times; now the name is used contemptuously to describe Cockney people.

down immediately, asked me to sit down, and offered me a cigarette."

Then Jozko had asked him what kind of sentence he would get for all his "crimes". Would he be shot?

But it appeared that capital punishment had been abolished in the Soviet Union; also there were no prisons, only labour-camps. "We are a progressive country," the examining Commissar had told him.

"What, in your opinion, is the heaviest sentence?" Jozko had asked.

"Expulsion from the Soviet Union."

"So I immediately said: 'Pass this sentence on me and—goodbye.' The Commissar laughed, and we parted amiably: '*Do svidanya*' ('*Au revoir*')."

Jozko was splendid: always full of humour and willing to resist. Most of us ate our bread immediately after its issue, but he always had at least one slice in stock: there were even days when he ate none.

"Jozko, aren't you hungry?"

"Sure I'm hungry; but they mustn't think I'm after their bread," he used to answer.

One afternoon, during early May, some of us were called from the cell with our luggage, which meant for good. What happened to the others I do not know. But I was thrown into Cell No. 24.

My flesh felt numb: nothing could be worse than being locked up with these semi-beasts.

I stood quietly in the doorway with my beggarly sack in my hand, and was received with spiteful looks from the residents. From that moment I realised that they saw me as an object of hatred—an educated man.

Nobody approached or spoke to me; I heard only growling.

For a while I stood there calmly and looked for the senior of the cell. I had little doubt but that it was the ruffian sitting alone on the bed near the window: the senior always had a bed to himself and nobody else had the right to sit on it.

I said to him: "Senior, please tell me, where is my place?"

"Next the *parasha*."

This—the worst insult one could be given in prison—was received with coarse laughter. Only people whom one wanted to humiliate, outcasts of the cell—educated people, were pushed next to the sanitary pail where men relieved themselves, and where the floor was always wet and smelly.

I could react to it by fighting, which was what they probably expected, or I could show my superiority to such an insult by showing

137

complete indifference. I remembered the sailor, and chose the second alternative.

For two nights I lay next the bucket, and people using it trod on me.

I observed the cell from my corner.

They were poor people; not bad, but completely lost: not professional criminals—just simple, uneducated people. Their instinct for property caused incessant conflicts in the cell, where there was insufficient elbow-room and no leadership. With nobody to lead them, they nagged at each other like beasts, needing an educated man to guide them, just as, when free men, they had formerly been led. But none of them realised this.

One day, from my corner near the *parasha*, I began talking to them, telling them about things not concerning our daily life—about the simple, beautiful, things in the world.

At first they listened half-heartedly, distrustful of me. Then they seemed to long for it, as though through my discourse they were escaping to freedom and to the outside world.

What did I talk to them about?

I spoke of the secrets of Nature—about the moon, the earth, the planets; about Pasteur's discoveries; about bacteria; about people and the human race. Then I told them stories from novels, and together we dwelt on the experiences of heroes. I always included in my stories problems regarding the human soul, optimism, and faith in the other, better world. Out of these simple talks, hope was born —just what they had most missed.

Very soon I left my corner: they gave me the best place in the cell, near the window. I never had to queue up again for soup or bread— they always brought everything to me—and they would not allow me to perform the daily duties, nor in the morning carry the *parasha*; they even washed my mug. I had only to talk and talk.

All the quarrels and disputes ceased; friendship and harmony reigned in the cell. I found that every human being, even the most ignorant, has decent instincts hidden somewhere: one has only to discover its chords and learn how to play on them.

CHAPTER 17

Interrogation

IN THE latter part of May 1940 I was summoned for the first time for interrogation.

It was at night. I was led out of the cell to the prison yard and pushed into the *vorona* ("the crow"—*i.e.* the Black Maria), the interrogation taking place in town in the N.K.V.D. building.

To a novice, the *vorona* was terrifying. It was divided into compact narrow cages, looking like erect coffins. The lid opened like a door; when one entered it, the door was slammed. It was completely dark. One could only stand there and feel around one, with one's limbs the boards and the lack of space, as in a coffin.

A terrible feeling overcame me; I thought I should go mad. I wanted to shout—I wanted to try to escape. But for what? I shut my eyes and tried not to touch the walls, and I said my prayers. The terror passed, and I became calm again.

When, later, for the second time I was driven in the *vorona*, I had no unpleasant feelings at all; I had become accustomed to it.

The interrogation was not frightening. The examining Commissar was young and unintelligent, and looked like a clerk. He took twelve pages to write my deposition. He was good-natured, and put down everything I told him, seeing that I gave as many fictitious details as possible—not only regarding my profession, but even the names and addresses of various relatives (uncles, aunts, etc.). What could they possibly need those for? To me it seemed a sheer waste of time and paper. But I soon realised that there was reason in it—a devil's reason to catch out anyone in contradictions. Should I make an error in stating the name or address of an aunt, this would be a reason for declaring my deposition void and proof that I was guilty, a criminal and a liar.

139

I had composed a precise story of my life, based on the experiences of other inmates' interrogations. I said I came from a proletarian family, had spent my youth in misery, and had struggled with difficulty through life until given the job of a shop assistant in the textile firm of Lankosz Bros. in Cracow. I originally came from the Western Ukraine, I said. I even mentioned Dunajow, of which I claimed to have a tragic recollection—a white house next to the railway station, where, as a child, I had lived with my mother (then a widow) and with a wicked aunt.

Before the war in 1939, when political relations with Germany became tense, I sent my wife and three children (all the names and ages were eagerly inscribed in the deposition!) to some relatives in the East; I myself stayed behind to work. When, after the cessation of hostilities, they did not return, I went in search of them to Lwow. My intention was to cross the demarcation line lawfully; as this was impossible, I then decided to cross secretly—and it was for this reason that I had been kept in prison, while my wife and children were probably living with strangers, in misery!

"We shall find them. We have long arms. Tell us where they are now?"

"That's the trouble: I do not know where they stayed. If you want to help me to find them, I think you could check up with my aunt, Miss Irene Mrozowicka in Lwow, 47 Zyblikiewicza Str., or with my cousin, Mr. Valerian Krzeczunowicz, also in Lwow, 7 Dabrowski Str., or in the white house near the railway station in Dunajow, if my aunt Rosciszewska is still there and alive."

The examining Commissar said: "We'll check up on it carefully."

This was in line with my intentions: I was counting on it as the whole principle for my defence. To make the story still more probable I was compelled to disclose some true facts which, at a given time, might lead to a break of information.

My aunt Mrozowicka died in December, 1939, when I was in Lwow. I saw V. Krzeczunowicz, with his whole family, in Cracow. All the Soviets could find out was that he had really lived previously at 7 Dabrowski Str. I never had an aunt in Dunajow, but for obvious reasons I had to mention this damned place in some way: I thought that some white house probably could be found there not far from the railway station, and this would corroborate my deposition.

"Well, that's fine! But why did you have a torch and a white sheet? You must be a spy! Tell me, what task had the Gestapo given you?"

That was a graver question to answer; thanks to this torch I had been accused of espionage on behalf of the Germans.

Then I was accused of smuggling.

"During the search, they found on you two spare shirts and one spare pair of shoes: evidently you are a smuggler."

The Commissar persisted in this opinion. But at last I managed to persuade him that every cultured man when travelling took with him a change of underwear: he agreed to this very doubtfully. At that time I did not know that the average Soviet citizen possessed only one shirt. Finally this particular charge was dropped.

As a consequence I was accused of unlawful crossing of the "frontier" (Para. 80 of the Soviet Penal Code) and of espionage (Para. 13). The interrogation concluded with the following statement.

"We have finished. Sign here. We shall check up on all you have said. If you have lied you'll live, but you'll never see a fucking cunt again."

I returned to my cell.

Again days passed by, interrupted only by parades, walks, checks, searches, and baths. No news from the outside world penetrated the prison walls, until one day someone returned from interrogation with a scrap of newspaper, found in the waiting-room of the N.K.V.D. The Germans, it said, had attacked France. The war on the Western Front had flared up!

This news kindled my hopes like a spark; perhaps now something really would happen. My inactivity had become almost unbearable.

But then a very old prisoner, who helped the guards in issuing food and thus had some contact through the kitchens with the outside world, brought us Job's news that "the Germans had taken Verdun". To those of us who remembered the previous World War, Verdun meant everything. Verdun was taken; France had collapsed; the Germans were victorious, and, with them, the Soviet Union; there would be no changes—we would all perish in the prison.

Thus the inmates of our cell interpreted this news, and we abandoned hope completely.

One day in July, 1940, the "Head of the Corps" entered our cell carrying a pen, an inkstand, and a piece of wallpaper, previously used for recording the roll-call of our cell.

"Who can write?"

I presented myself.

"Make an alphabetical list of everyone in this cell. Put down the

Christian name, the patronymic,* the family name, and year of birth, and state under which paragraphs of the Soviet Penal Code the prisoner is charged."

He seemed doubtful as to whether I really could write, so he ordered me to put down my own name at the top of the list, in his presence. Thus the "alphabetical" list was headed by the letter "R"!

In the afternoon we discovered the purpose of this list. All of us were ordered to leave the cell with our luggage, the names being called out in the order of the list made by me. The first ten of us—including myself—were thrust into Cell No. 51, called the "Death Cell": not because we had been sentenced to death, but simply because there was no room in the other cells, the prison being so terribly overcrowded. The others were pushed into various other cells.

My new abode was very small and dark; and it was so hot that many of the inmates already there were completely naked.

As an experienced prisoner, I graciously put my sack in a corner and looked around me. I spotted Szajna, my old acquaintance from Przemysl. Now he looked bolder; he had probably become accustomed to prison life.

My attention focused on a naked, middle-aged man with a greyish beard, who was walking up and down the cell. By Jove! Was it a vision or reality? He looked to me like General Tokarzewski!

I could not believe my eyes. Tokarzewski should be working quietly in Lwow; I must be mistaken!

When, however, I saw his eyes—the same pale-blue eyes—I no longer doubted. It was certainly he, only thinner, now, and his skin was grey, like the soil.

I asked Szajna, in a casual way: "Who is that man—the elderly one?"

"It's Mirowy, a doctor from Warsaw—a very decent man."

Later on, I approached him and introduced myself.

"My name is Mirowy," he said, and cordially shook my hand, looking me straight in the eyes; but I knew he had recognised me, from the way he had shaken hands.

Thus both the chiefs of the Underground Organisation against the Soviet Occupation in Lwow met again, but this time in a Soviet prison.

It was only during our walk that I managed secretly to exchange a few words with him. He too had been caught while crossing the de-

* Derived from the Christian name of the father.

142

marcation line, ten days later than I. He believed the Soviets had not recognised him, for he had already been interrogated several times. He had maintained he was a psychiatrist from Warsaw. During one interrogation, they had asked him if he had ever met General Tokarzewski in Warsaw, or had he, perhaps, been his patient?

He was a little excited, but in good form.

For three months we were thrown together in various cells before we were finally separated.

During this time, we met a real surgeon, Dr. Zajaczkowski, the head surgeon of the hospital in Radziwillow. He was a splendid man, with a magnificent character, and he became one of our closest friends. We told him in confidence who we really were, and for our benefit he organised medical lectures. These, he pretended, were for all the inmates in our cell, but really they were for Tokarzewski, in order to give him as many practical medical hints as possible, so that he could maintain his assertion that he was a psychiatrist—and in case he was ordered to practise in some labour-camp!

One day in October, Tokarzewski was taken away from our cell with his luggage. He signalled to us with his fingers from the prison-yard that he had been sentenced to eight years' detention in a labour-camp. He then went away, and only his memory remained.

More and more people were sentenced and taken away, getting terms of from 5–8 years; apparently those were "normal". But the prison got no emptier, as there was a steady influx of newcomers—Poles arrested in streets or in their homes, and Bessarabians from the "liberated" Bessarabia. The latter behaved in prison like wild people.

These newcomers brought news from the outside world, but only sad news: France had collapsed; Norway and Denmark were occupied by the Germans; terror and misery reigned in our country.

One day I came across an old friend, an officer in the 9th Lancers, Professor Z. Stahl; but we only managed to exchange a few words and then were separated again.

I stuck to Dr. Zajaczkowski for a long time. His company was really very enjoyable; and I admired his strength of mind, his culture, and the way he kept up the old standards.

We had at that time a new and fascinating hobby—the study of English. In our cell was a professional teacher of English and Hebrew, Mr. Pozner, a Palestinian Jew. For two months, several hours a day, we learned new words and repeated our lessons. We had to learn everything by heart, as paper and pencils were prohibited in prison.

We had no particular object in doing this—but Zajaczkowski declared that it would help to keep up our morale: men must always have an aim for which to strive; without any aim, they must go mad. Our desire to learn English acted as a vaccine. We studied fervently. Zajaczkowski spent, also, long hours in prayer: he did not mind people watching him. My admiration for him was steadily increased.

After Pozner's departure we spoke fluent English—but it was a peculiar sort of English. I doubt very much whether an Englishman would have understood us. Even without Pozner we went on improving our knowledge of this language, so that, undisturbed, we could discuss secret topics. But its resemblance to English was fading away.

The winter of 1940-1 was very frosty, and it was bitterly cold in our cell. Zajaczkowski had left us; I had no more old friends there: they had all been sentenced and sent away. But I was still detained.

Several times I had been interrogated, always in the same way. The examiner wrote new depositions on twelve pages; I always repeated the same details of my life, which by now I knew by heart, like prayers. All the dates and the names of my aunts and uncles agreed with the previous depositions. I decided that they had now dropped the charge of espionage and that only the illegal crossing of the "frontier" remained.

One day two Commissars examined me. They had checked up in Lwow in Zyblikiewicza Str. and in Dabrowski Str. all right—but they told me there was no white house next to the railway station in Dunajow. Then one of them threatened to hit my face with his fist, and shouted: "You liar! Tell me the truth at once! What task was entrusted to you by the Germans?" Later he said: "Have you heard of Amundsen? Have you seen a polar bear? If you don't tell the truth you will perish there."

At this I showed indignation, in the same way as Jozko Denczykowski had done before me.

"I am in a tragic situation. I have lost my relatives and my family, and you play with me like this! Is this according to your Constitution?"

Immediately they simmered down.

"Don't get angry. Your case is closed. Your files will be sent to Moscow for final decision. In the meantime, you must await sentence."

And I was returned to the cell.

The cold in the cell became biting, but outside it was worse: there was a snowstorm. All the glass in our windows was broken, and the wind had blown down two boards from the shutters. The snow drifted in, but nobody complained: through the aperture we could see the free world, which was always a pleasure.

As frequently happens, some of God's creatures, though free, were even worse off than we were. Through the aperture in the shutters, the sparrows learned to enter our cell, sitting frozen on the cornice of the window, their feathers stiff, their heads hidden in their shoulders. There they gradually thawed out a little—for it was not quite so cold inside. They had no fear of us.

Everyone liked them. Each morning the prisoner on duty swept the snow from the cornice and gave them breadcrumbs. We all gave some willingly, looking upon the sparrows with tenderness: they were guests arriving from the outside world, they were harbingers of freedom.

They soon became very cheeky. And they advertised our abode, so that their numbers soon increased and there was not enough food for them all; therefore they began to squeak and fight on the window-sill.

One sparrow we were especially fond of. He was so eager and energetic, and he was tailless: probably someone had pulled out his feathers. We decided to name him—we must call him something; but what? Different suggestions were offered, but as there was no unanimity we decided to name him by way of a competition.

One of us sat in the middle of the cell and everyone approached him and whispered his suggestion. Having listened to all of us, he began to repeat loudly the proposed names, and we had to decide the issue by public vote.

What odd names were suggested!—Spring, Dear One, Darling, Freedom (of course), and many others. When the chairman announced the name of *"Nyechvatayet"*, ("Short of it"), this met with general applause. People howled with joy, and he was unanimously called *Nyechvatayet*.

The Soviet Union was short of a sparrow's tail, just as we heard so many mornings that they were short of bread or soup in the *balanda:* *"Nyechvatayet"* ("We're short of it").

In this wretched country, something was *always* in short supply. *"Nyechvatayet"* was a word in frequent use in Soviet Russia. It signified both a justification and a reassurance. One should not get upset, just because there did not happen to be sufficient!

To us, *"Nyechvatayet"* symbolised the Soviet Union.

145

CHAPTER 18

Dreams and Prophecies

THE LONG winter dragged on. Although the cell was overcrowded, I became more and more solitary: I did not want anything or anybody; I preferred being alone.

For a long time I had dreams or visions which I could not explain. Sometimes it was difficult to discern which was dream and which vision. My subconsciousness was extremely sensitive: I do not know whether this was due to my ascetic diet or to the illness which gnawed at me (for I suffered from catarrh of the intestines). I ate hardly anything, and yet I was not hungry.

Obviously I was undergoing some transformation, and although my body was weaker, my mind was alert as never before. . . . I became almost clairvoyant. I knew beforehand when I would be called for interrogation, even before I heard the "Come out to the corridor!"; I divined what I should be questioned about; and I visualised the face of the new examining Commissar.

I also visualised the file of my case—which had been sent to Lwow, then to Moscow—returning: I almost divined the decision.

Then I had some strange dreams. At first I did not pay any attention to them; they were nothing but dreams, or delirium. But I began to recognise in them allegories which puzzled me and demanded an explanation. In normal life one would not pay much attention to dreams, but in our situation—when the mind freed itself from the fetters of its bodily cover and roamed round the world—such symptoms gained importance. In time, this second life of mine became the more significant one, the more real one.

One day in April I saw smashed lorries, and soldiers with Polish badges on their collars, killed on a railway track. Then I noticed a colossal naked figure with a cock's head, lying on the ground, still alive, with the smile of an idiot. The Germans trod on it. When, later, we received the news of France's collapse, I thought this was the explanation of my dream.

Then I visualised, quite distinctly, a Holy Alliance signed between Poland and Great Britain—I thought it holy because the covenant was written in golden letters. Looking over their shoulders, I watched the delegates of the President of the Polish Republic sign the document. I could see their faces quite clearly. But I could not understand what this dream meant.

Once I visualised Polish soldiers in a strange landscape that I had never seen before; they were surrounded by people wearing Eastern dresses and colourful Tibetan hats. I saw stooks in the fields, but not of corn; they looked more like rows of cotton. To my surprise, I was second-in-command to General Tokarzewski. I was alone there with these soldiers, and we had just received a huge supply of big wooden boxes, which contained cigarettes; I distinctly saw, in golden letters, the English inscription "SMOKING". And again, I wondered what it could mean.

I had many such dreams or delirious visions. Two soldiers with rifles and long bayonets stood at the cell door, but they looked like children's wooden toys. Suddenly they both fell to the ground and the cell was swarming with new soldiers in strange uniforms—not Polish, German, or Russian ones, but more like Rumanian or Italian. They apparently came to liberate us, but were not our friends. I was aware, the whole time, that it was happening only in my mind but I felt it must have some meaning.

At that time we had in our cell a Viennese lawyer of Jewish origin, called Heller. He was a little crazy, but certainly intelligent. He considered himself an expert interpreter of dreams; and, as so many of us had dreams, they queued up to him every morning as to a doctor. He charged fees for his explanations—a fee of one slice of bread or a spoonful of groats. He took this new job very seriously, and consulted with his clients as carefully as he had done when a lawyer. I believe he required this incentive to fill his life—compensation in some measure for his lost career, for which he still longed. As he spoke only German, I used to act as his interpreter.

The procedure was as follows.

From early morning till about twelve noon he interviewed his clients. Having negotiated the fees, he listened to the dreams—as if taking instructions. He never gave more than three or four interviews a day. Then he would lie down on his straw mattress, meditating sometimes for several hours. When he appeared to be ready, his clients approached him, and, through me, he explained to each one of them the meaning of their dream.

He would not take on every case. Frequently he refused to discuss a dream with a client, saying it had no meaning at all—that it was not a prophetic dream, which was the only kind he was interested in.

He was very jealous of the acknowledged pre-eminence of his interpretations, and, as well as scrupulously collecting his fees, he always treated his clients seriously and courteously.

To me, as his assistant, he explained his method.

He stated he used Freud's method, but greatly improved upon by him as he did not completely agree with the original one. Contrary to Freud, who admitted only sexual stimuli, he recognised other kinds, especially in the specific conditions of existence in prison, where the human mind was as in a hot-house.

He distinguished four categories of stimuli influencing the sub-conscious activities of the mind, each category corresponding to a different type of dream.

He called the first "ein Wunschtraum"—i.e. a dream expressing a wish, usually aroused by a vehement desire for something unobtainable at the moment. He thought it a worthless and meaningless dream, except that it enabled him better to diagnose the character of his client.

The second was "ein Angsttraum", aroused by a subconscious fear. For instance, somebody was anxious to catch a certain train: it was very important to him, but he doubted whether he could manage it and he would be terribly frightened and worried. This anxiety might develop into a vivid dream, with different adventures; but again it would be meaningless. He did not bother about such dreams, and would send the client away—unless he was very hungry and wished to earn his fee.

The third kind was called "Kompensierungstraum"—i.e. dream of compensation. The individual in his dream re-lived happenings in his past life which he missed in prison. For instance, he distinguished himself, he got applause, he astonished others, and so on. Probably it would be as an orator or an actor. "You see," Heller maintained, "Nature tries to balance the mentality of such a man, even sub-consciously. Without such dreams he would go mad."

I found that Heller's interpretations could be dangerous. Once, when I told him about one of my dreams, belonging to this third category, he took me aside and said I had definitely assumed a faked identity: "You are not a shop assistant: you are an officer." But I

148

must not be worried about his discovery, he said, because it was a professional secret and, as a lawyer, he could never betray his client.

His primary interest was in the fourth category of dream—"*Wahrsagungstraum*" (the prophetic dream). He declared that human subconsciousness, having reached a suitable degree of maturity, could completely free itself from the body and receive impulses from a different world.

Contemporary events could thus be perceived, like radio broadcasts—for instance, my dream about the signing of the Polish-British Agreement. But sometimes future events could likewise be perceived, though it was usually very difficult to explain them. Those events, originating from another world, were not expressed by customary ideas. To understand them it was necessary to translate them into our own language. Usually they appeared as queer allegories. It was Heller's speciality to interpret these allegories and transpose the story into everyday terms. He claimed to be a specialist at this. He maintained that, obviously, no rigid scheme could be applied, as any interpretation of a dream had to be adjusted to the intellectual standard of the individual, and therefore he required a long time to find a solution. Besides, it was not easy to distinguish a prophetic dream from the other categories. Various characteristics would point to its being a prophetic dream: he thought that in my case a church, or a part of it, would indicate a prophetic dream.

Then I remembered that when dreaming about the soldiers in a strange country, surrounded by people in Tibetan hats, I had caught a glimpse of a church; so I asked him what this dream signified.

"Surely you will go there," he said; "and the English will send you supplies—you'll see."

What a strange thing! Could I be certain of this? Anyway, I liked to believe it true.

Once, feeling very lonely, I had another vision—when awake, not in my sleep. In a large meadow I saw a distant child. After a while the child came closer, running towards me, and I recognised her as my daughter Christina. She ran at full speed, and the picture was so realistic, retaining all the proportions of perspective as it came right up to my eyes—then it suddenly disappeared.

I asked Heller for an explanation.

"I'm very sorry to tell you that you will never see her again—she'll die.'·*

* Christina was killed in 1944 during the Warsaw Rising, as a soldier of the Polish Home Army.

I was really frightened to ask him for an explanation when later I visualised my eldest daughter, Lena, dying in my arms. I almost sensed the weight of her dead body, which then began to wither away. It dwindled while I tried in vain to keep her there.

"Oh, she will be happy and healthy," Heller declared. "She might die to the world. I think she'll go into a nunnery."*

Again the dilemma: should I believe it or not? Everything was so confused and muddled. It was indeed a bad thing to be imprisoned for so long!

Besides Heller, there was another interpreter of dreams, who also had his own method and his clients. He was less sophisticated, and charged no fees for his interpretations. His name was Reserve-Gunner Burko, a peasant from the Sambor area. His answers came short and pat.

Someone said: "Burko, I dreamed of onions."

He required more details. "Where—on the table or in the garden?"

"On the table."

"Within three days you'll go to a christening."

"Burko, it's impossible! I'm in prison."

But Burko refused to change his opinion. "I can't help that—you'll go to a christening."

Later on we learned that Burko exercised this same business in his home village. For a few pence he had bought *The Egyptian Dream Book*, and he repeated all the answers: he had almost learned them off by heart. It was not his fault that the Dream Book was not adjusted to prison life!

Sometimes he used a different subterfuge, explaining dreams in words which neither he nor others could understand.

---

* In 1947 Lena became a nun in the Franciscan Missionary Order in France.

CHAPTER 19

Existing Realities

CHRISTMAS, 1940, was approaching.

I and Gilowski, an amateur artist from Jaremcze, decided to celebrate Christmas Eve in the customary way and to surprise the Poles by giving each of them a gift. We were only a few Poles, so it was not too difficult.

We found a piece of hard wood, which we cut into small squares with a piece of glass; then we smoothed them by rubbing them against the concrete floor, and cut small medallions out of them with a nail. Gilowski engraved these with a picture of Our Lady of Czestochowa and the inscription:

Christmas Eve, 1940.

These gifts were received with great pleasure, and we consumed our Christmas Eve dinner in an elated atmosphere. We congregated in one corner of the cell and together ate our daily soup and groats and exchanged our Christmas greetings, parting a piece of stale bread in lieu of the customary wafer. As senior in the cell I addressed them all, and afterwards we sang carols.

Members of other religions respected our traditions, sitting quite quietly all this time; later on they joined us in singing carols—Ukrainians, Russians, and even Jews.

Every search of the cell reaped an abundant harvest; but immediately afterwards newly-made utensils reappeared, like mushrooms after rain. I was full of admiration for the human ingenuity displayed.

It was quite easy for "specialists" like Gilowski or Olek Iwanow to make a needle: they drew a nail out of the window frame, or found it during our walk; then they rubbed it skilfully against the concrete floor, bored a hole with glass and the needle was ready made—thin

151

or fat, as one liked it.

Generally speaking, glass was our best tool and could not be replaced by anything else. We used it for shaving: if broken diagonally, it was as sharp as the best razor-blade, and cut hair even without soap.

Bread, carefully kneaded with saliva and coloured with soot, was used for artistic objects such as cigarette-holders or cases, boxes, etc.

It was very easy to make fire without any matches: there were several good ways of doing it. The simplest was to pick out a little cotton-wool from an overcoat or from the padding of a suit, work it into a ball, and then roll it on the floor with a small wooden board. When suddenly rent, it caught fire.

A button threaded with a fibre drawn from a shirt or a blanket and put into a whirling motion would, if touched by a piece of glass or a pebble, immediately spark, and one such spark would set alight a mouldy linen rag.

There were no such secrets the prisoners did not know.

Almost everything we acquired was lost every ten days as a result of the searches, which usually occurred at night. Everyone was pushed into the corridor, stripped and searched. Numbers of trained N.K.V.D. soldiers turned everything in the cell upside down. When we returned it looked as though there had been a fire. The searchers were so cunning that they would even find a needle: they knew so well all the possible hiding places.

However, the prison authorities thoughtfully catered for our spiritual needs. Each month we were supplied with several books in Russian, the old ones being exchanged. But they were all the same.

We received two books on Communist ideology, such as *Principles of Leninism and Stalinism, Aims of the World Revolution,* or *History of the Communist Party*. There was always one anti-religious book, one book describing expeditions, such as *Amundsen's Travels,* and either a volume of poetry or a novel. The books most read were those by Ostrovski, L. Tolstoi, Elya Ehrenburg, and Balzac.

Some of the prisoners read the books; others tore out single pages for use as cigarette-papers in which to wrap their *machorka*—the coarsest kind of tobacco. This often resulted in a few days spent in a dungeon.

From mid-winter there was an innovation. We were told that Stalin took an interest in the prisoners and had ordered an issue of two packets of *machorka* every ten days to any prisoner accustomed to smoke.

The guards checked up in a very simple way on whether the prisoners smoked or not. The "Head of the Corps" entered the cell, wrapped about half a packet of tobacco in papers, licked up the two sides, and gave a lighted cigarette by turns to everybody with the order: "Now smoke."

One had to inhale the smoke several times into the lungs without coughing. Whoever passed this examination received the *machorka*. A smoker who half-choked himself did not receive any: "You lie! you'll get bugger all," was the decision.

This examination, in spite of Stalin's "bounty", resulted in very few packets being distributed.

Quite exceptionally, Olek Iwanow always received not only the *machorka* but also "food for invalids": he saw the doctor and got everything he asked for. He was an interesting youth from Sambor, lean and varicose-veined; he spat blood, but had a voice as loud as a church bell. He shouted and issued orders to the N.K.V.D. soldiers as if he were at home in Sambor. All in the prison knew of him and of his exploits. He had attempted an escape, smashing the *vorona*, and had done everything unruly in prison, without any bad consequences. He was an excellent colleague, and he hated the Bolsheviks, whom he treated with utter contempt.

He used to say, quite gaily: "My God! how long will you let such cattle—such ignoramuses—oppress decent people such as we are?"

Or he would shout at the top of his voice: "Mummy darling!"— he always remembered his mother—"I swear I'll skin and kill them, the bloody bastards, in return for your exile without me and for our defiled country . . .!"

And then, turning to me, he would say: "Daddy, please tell me— do agree with me—we shall beat them, shan't we—those wicked villains, those lousy buggers? . . ."

He delighted in extravagant language.

Siedlecki, a delicate little boy, was another who was always out-spoken. He was often flushed with anger, although full of fun. He was an interesting type: a native of Kujawy. He declared that he was a cook in a country house, and always used to impose upon us in a typical Kujavian way: what had he not seen and where had he not been? He always had to have the last word.

At night he used to steal bread from other inmates, but he escaped being caught at it, as he was so cunning. He never would answer any accusation. He slept next to me, and I knew well that he was stealing.

One day I took him aside and said: "Look here, Siedlecki, you're

153

a decent boy; you should know that it is not fair to take bread from a hungry man. Don't do it again."

But Siedlecki only winked at me.

"Mr. Ruminski, have you ever seen me take bread from one of *ourselves*? I only take it from Russians, Jews or Ukrainians. It is really rather a patriotic deed."

So passed the winter of 1940 and the spring of 1941.

When summer came, they took away Siedlecki, Olek Iwanow, Gilowski, Mr. Kicinski, old Mr. Sokolowski from Volhynia, and many others, but I remained in the cell. What was the reason? Had they forgotten about me?

By this time the majority of the prisoners were Russians—all poor poeple, accused of being late to work. They told me a new law had been issued: being late to work for the first time, or missing a day's work, was punished by three months' detention; when it occurred for a second time, the sentence was raised to three years. This was their crime, and they would have to go to labour-camps. It was quite immaterial to them where: "It doesn't matter where we live."

They did not know anything about the war; they were not interested in it. "What's the difference? You'll perish, anyhow." They hardly looked the happy Soviet citizens described by Moyseyovitch, who "breathed so freely".

One day—I think it was in May, 1941—one of them brought to our cell a scrap of the Russian newspaper *Izvyestya*. Unfortunately, the news section was missing, so we could not discover any actual news. There was only the leader—written, so far as I remember, for the anniversary of the First May, or some military festival.

The article stated that the Soviet Union had always been opposed to imperialistic wars and only recognised war in self-defence. This was just the case of Germany, attacked by Great Britain, the worst Imperialists in the world. The bourgeois and capitalist British Commonwealth, the worst enemy of the proletariat, a country of blood-suckers, would in this war get a well-merited beating at the hands of the German proletariat. The Soviet Union looked at Germany with brotherly sympathy, and on this great festival day they expressed their admiration and sent words of encouragement. . . . And so it went on.

I thought, "Nothing has changed." It was enough that Great Britain was holding out and fighting: that the war was still being carried on.

The tone of this leader did not tally, however, with the incessant questions during interrogation: "What task was entrusted to you by the Gestapo?"—which pointed rather to a rift in the Soviet-German friendship.

CHAPTER 20

In Transit

AT LAST it happened!

In the first days of June, 1941, I was called from the cell with my "luggage". Had the decision arrived . . .?

In the office a senior N.K.V.D. officer read out the sentence to me.

It appeared that the special court in Moscow, according to Para. 80 of the Soviet Penal Code, had sentenced Citizen Joseph Sigismundovitch Ruminski, born in 1893, to five years' deportation, as a free citizen, to Kirov, for unlawfully crossing the frontier.

"Sign it!"

I signed it—greatly surprised that I had received such a lenient sentence. It was unheard of! Only a deportation as a free citizen! Hardly anybody got away with such a sentence! It was exceptional luck, and I did not know what to ascribe it to. Perhaps the sentence had been passed on a Sunday. . . . Or perhaps my left hand, inert from a wound received in 1917, did not encourage them to send me for heavy work to a labour-camp.

But was it really true? In this country I had learned to doubt.

After the sentence had been read to me, they took me to the cellars of the *Witki* department (the transit department) of the prison, where I had to wait for a transport.

There was an incessant mobility here of new people arriving and others being sent away. Days passed. But I was always left behind.

One day we noted a new occurrence: the white electric bulbs had been exchanged for blue ones. Although cut off from the world, we sensed unusual excitement. We asked what had happened.

"Anti-aircraft defence exercises," was the answer; but it did not look like it.

In the corridor we heard the noise of a newly-arrived transport.

Someone opened the cell door and yelled "Give me a fag!"

One of the inmates went to the aperture and said: "I'll give you one, comrade, but please tell me—what is the news from the outside world?"

"War! The Germans have bombarded Kiev."

We all jumped to our feet. At last! It had started! We were mad with joy. It was the second half of June, 1941.

At last came the day of my departure. We were, of course, entrained in the customary way—with the "Sit down!", the dogs, the soldiers on all sides, etc. Mere *numbers* were being transported, not human beings. There was a special carriage for prisoners—with iron bars at the windows and doors. And we were terribly squeezed up. A soldier, with a pistol in his hand, was on guard in the corridor. We were fed on salt herrings and water. From the other passengers, mostly Soviet citizens who had already been sentenced, I heard that we would travel in stages from one transit prison to another, and that the journey would last a very long time. For instance, to Irkuck or to Kolyma might take about a year! To Kirov would not take more than a month.

After travelling several days we were detrained at Charkov. The transit prison there was enormous. Thousands of people passed through it, day and night, crowding its cells, corridors and yards. It looked as if the whole population of Russia was kept in prison: it seemed impossible there were any free people. Experienced prisoners maintained that this same picture could be seen on every route used by prisoners.

They were a mixed bag, of different nationalities—Russians, Kalmuks, Tartars, Turkmen, Tadjiks, Kazaks, coming from both Europe and Asia.

I asked some of them for what crimes they had been sentenced. Actually, nobody exactly knew: they were mostly condemned in their absence, and only knew under which paragraph of the Soviet Penal Code they had been sentenced; one had to memorise it, along with the patronymic, the family name, and year of birth.

Where were they taken to?

Those sentenced for up to three years were going to the nearest labour-camps—Krivoi Rog, Kotlas, or not far behind the Ural Mountains, whither the journey would not last too long. Those condemned to more than three years were sent to distant labour-camps, from which they never expected to return. Even if still alive after having served their sentence, there was no return: the sentence would always be extended by re-examining the case and giving "a second helping", as they called it. But the most difficult thing, as one old hand informed me, was to survive till the end of the sentence—except in the case of a life-sentence, when one would be sure to live to the end.

I stayed for about a week in Charkov, in an over-crowded cell. Prisoners sat doubled up in rows: there was no possibility of stretching out one's legs; it was even impossible to queue for food. To feed, all had to pass their mugs from hand to hand. It often happened that the food was short—"*Nyechvatayet*"—for the last ones. The bread ration was cut down to 14 oz. per day—again "*Nyechvatayet*": we were told that this was our mite towards the communal war effort! We were starved: the groats had come to an end, and the soup was made with stinking fish. After we had been sentenced and were in a transport, we were no longer looked upon as valuable beings. A neighbour of mine in the cell, a Polish high-school teacher from Sanok, became mad; he threw himself upon some other prisoners, with foam trickling from his lips. We handed him over from one to the other until he reached the door, when he was carried away.

Not far from me I spotted Mr. Switalski, formerly a high-ranking Civil Servant. He sat doubled up; he had a wound, or ulcers, on one of his legs. A young Pole took care of him, probably a student or a relation of his.

In one of the corners I noticed an old Cossack captain. He would probably remember the times when the Tsars ruled. He continually sang Cossack songs, interrupting them to shout military commands. He moved his squadrons to right or left, deployed them, charged with them, greeted his men, etc. Like the school-teacher, he, too, had probably had enough.

I was very impressed by an old mine-driller, aged about seventy, from Boryslaw, wearing a long grey beard. He usually stood, half bent, in the third row behind me. He could not sit doubled up as he had a paralysed or sciatic leg, and he suffered terribly. In spite of pain, his face beamed with the spirit of glorious martyrdom; from him we heard only encouragement, full of sweetness and hope: resolution to endure to the end.

"Gentlemen, it's nothing; we'll bear everything. Don't let despair break you. It doesn't matter what they are doing to us, that's a trifle." He, also, in his way, had had enough of it.

After about a week we were again entrained in a Stolypinka carriage. This time almost all were *Urkis*, except for myself and a

Georgian sentenced for political reasons to ten years' detention in labour-camps.

This was the first time that I had met the *Urkis*; until now I had only heard of them.

The *Urkis* are not simply "urchins", as the name suggests; nor are they a nationality or a race: it is the name used for a certain class of people existing only in the U.S.S.R. They are permanent inhabitants of Soviet prisons or labour-camps, having lived in them from their childhood. They are recruited mostly from homeless children left behind after the 1917 Revolution, and at this time again their numbers were being increased by new additions. They would never recover their liberty, as they could not be squeezed into the framework of Soviet society; therefore they had to be isolated from the normal community. One could not even say that they are professional thieves or bandits, in our meaning of the word. No, they are simply savages, who, never having known a life of freedom, have grown up behind iron bars. Labour-camps are the environment they know, and they have their own code of law. They do not steal, they only take away; and if they encounter resistance they simply murder. But they do help each other, like members of a close sect. "One for all, all for one" is their motto. They work only when they like, and they pay no regard to any orders, regulations, or guards.

Prison authorities treat them with an embarrassed indulgence; they do not oppress or destroy them—on the contrary, they protect them. Politically, they are not a dangerous element. Often they prove to be useful by playing the rôle of a jackal in the desert in the labour-camps: of disinfection and sanitation. They kill the weak prisoners, and thus increase the rentability and efficiency of the labour-camps. Moreover, they are innocently joyful and easy-going: a prison, a labour-camp, or a transport, are all home to them; there they feel unfettered. I found them interesting, and I rather sympathised with them.

They looked at me, like children, from my feet up to my head, and enquired into every detail of my clothes. Then one of them said: "Look here, old man, you've got a nice shirt and I've a very bad one; let's swap them." To make his request quite clear he added: "You're old and will soon perish; there is a long life before me, so give it to me."

I was amused, and convinced. I pulled my shirt from off my back and said: "Take it, chum." Afterwards I put on his dirty and ragged one.

They were very pleased with my comrade-like behaviour. To me it was all the same what I had on my back; this was the least important question. I had often in my life had good shirts, probably they never had; let them have some pleasure, too. So I gave the shirt without the slightest regret; they realised this, and we became friends.

It was much worse with the Georgian. He was very attached to his possessions—probably never in his life had he had too many of them. He resisted and refused to exchange, and during the night the *Urkis* beat him terribly, took everything away, and left him naked. The duty guard removed him, bloodstained as he was, but said nothing to the *Urkis*: such was the unwritten rule.

We passed Moscow, and, after a week's travelling, we were detrained at the next transit point, in Gorkij. Again the transit prison, with its searches, baths, and overcrowded cells. A few more days, and we were put in another Stolypinka for the next stage of the journey.

Finally we reached Kirov (formerly called Viatka).

The formalities of receiving the new intake lasted for two days. People were pushed, one after the other, into cells, but I was still detained in the corridor. At last some high-ranking officer came up to me.

"Christian name? . . . Patronymic? . . . Family name? . . . Year of birth? . . . Sentence? . . ."

When I had told him everything, he shouted: "How did you get in? We don't want you here. Come along now!"

At last, a beneficial *Nyechvatayet*—the prison was short of accommodation for me! Perhaps I should be freed!

They led me out of the prison and put me into a hooded lorry, not a *vorona*, and we drove away. I was the only passenger in the lorry, and realised my importance.!

I alighted before a small house with an entrance direct from the street. Normal people walked there. So they did still exist! I was directed into, and shut up in, a small room with beds made of wooden boards, all along the walls. A few persons, men and women, were already sitting there. They informed me I was in the cell of the local police-station. It was not a proper prison, only a place for detention. My hopes were rising. All the people here were detained by the police: they would be freed or put on charge, in which latter case they would be transferred for their further interrogation to the prison which I had just left.

For three days I had to wait for further developments. On the morning of the fourth day I walked, accompanied by a policeman, into the street, and we went to a nearby building of the N.K.V.D. of the district of Kirov.

My situation was improving again. I believed it was a Sunday, but was not quite certain as I had lost count of the days.

For a little while I stood in the waiting-room, then was called into the office and saw the N.K.V.D. Commissar. He looked at my papers, made some notes, then said: "Now, citizen" (this was the first time I was so addressed), "you'll be freed. You're to live and work here in Kirov."

He explained the duties of a Soviet citizen to me, and ordered me to report every ten days to the Police-station. Then he gave me thirty roubles for my urgent needs, and told me to go to the Police-station of the First District, where they would register me and find me a job.

A policeman directed me to the Police-station of the First District, and, at last, I walked along the streets unescorted!

CHAPTER 21

I Become a Soviet Worker

STRANGE are a man's feelings when, after a year and a half of imprisonment, he finds himself alone in the streets of a town, unwatched by agents, scoundrels or dogs—a free man once more.

It is even stranger if one also finds oneself thrust into Soviet conditions, like a sealed parcel dropped from the Western world deep into Soviet Russia.

Walking along the street at noon, in the July heat, with my shabby bag under my arm, I felt very strange indeed.

I was hungry as a beast. Passing a shop, I saw in the window heaps of tasty-looking dark bread and beautiful white Vienna loaves. I had thirty roubles in my pocket, and thought I would walk in and buy a loaf, trusting to have enough money.

When I asked for it, the astonished salesman looked at me and said: "There is no bread." I looked towards the window and suddenly realised the displayed bread was only nicely painted wooden dummies.

I strolled along the streets as though on holiday, until, at one corner, I was arrested by a militiaman, and taken back to the police-station which I had left only that morning! Shortly after, I was released and went along the same road again, but quickly passing all the shops, until I found the Police-station of the First District. After waiting there for about an hour, I was directed to work in the "Kirpicznyj Zawod No. 2" (Brick-Kiln No. 2) in Bolshaya Subotnica. I was told the brick-kiln was about three miles outside the town, and I must cross the bridge on the Viatka.

I walked slowly, and suddenly realised how exhausted and weak I was. I could hardly drag myself along.

The bridge was outside the town; it was quiet and deserted. The

162

river was so beautiful that I could not resist its temptation; I slipped off my rags, put them on the grass, and bathed. At last I could do what I wanted! I revelled in freedom and in the blessed coolness of the water.

Hungry as I was, I wanted to stay there far longer. In prison one misses nature, and for a year and a half I had seen neither trees nor rivers. But the sun was declining to the west and I had been told not to delay as the kiln's office closed down as 6 p.m.

So I walked on, and arrived in time. I was interviewed by the "comrade manager".

"What do you want?"

"I have come to work here."

"From the prison?"

"Yes."

He looked at my long greyish beard and my suspicious-looking figure, and decided sharply: "We don't need men like you. This is heavy work. Go away."

I explained I had been directed by the police, but it did not help.

"To hell with your police! Go away."

I took my sack and walked off. But where to go? It was getting dark. Hunger twisted my intestines so that I could hardly walk. A foreman working in the kiln, named Limonov, had pity on me and took me to his hut where he lived, together with his wife, in a small room. There I slept on the ground until the morning. He could not give me even a slice of bread because he had already eaten all he possessed.

"We are awfully sorry," he apologised. "If we had expected you we would have left something."

I was thankful even for this shelter. But I thought prison was better as far as food was concerned. As a free man one could easily perish.

In the morning Limonov brought me some *kipiatok* (boiled water) and managed to produce a slice of bread. After this meal I again hurried to the Police-station of the First District.

They looked surprised. "What! Here again?"

I explained that the manager would not give me any work.

"Oh, the son of a bitch! Let's talk to him on the telephone."

He rebuked the manager, and demanded: "Employ this man immediately; it is the N.K.V.D's order." Turning to me, he said: "Get back to the kiln."

Again I took up my bag and walked off.

This time the manager was kinder to me; he muttered some inaudible words and gave an order to "register" me—*viz*: to employ me in the kiln. I received a ration-book, which entitled me to buy one kilogramme (2 lbs. 3 oz.) of bread daily, and to have meals in our works' canteen.

I could not get bread at once, as it was only supplied at about 5 p.m.; but I had a lunch consisting of soup and groats, similar to the prison diet—the only difference being that now I had to pay for it! There was nothing else; but I could order a second helping, so I did, paying 2 roubles 40 for it. There are some happy moments in one's life!

I then started work. It was quite a big "mechanised" brick-kiln, consisting of wooden huts where everybody worked. It was called "mechanised" because the clay was carried on a conveyor-belt. There were no other mechanical devices, all the work being done by hand.

About fifty people were employed in the Works' office, which consisted of a planning office, supplies' department, transport department, and accountant's department employing about twenty clerks who had to calculate every worker's pay according to his productiveness, basing it on the established "norms" calculated for every job.

The workers were organised in "brigades" under the leadership of a "brigadier", whose duty it was to find out daily how much of the "norm" the worker made and to send daily reports to the office.

Pay-day was every Saturday—at least, so I was informed.

The Works' fire-brigade formed a quite separate group. Besides performing their duties of fire-watching and fighting they kept a watch on the whole premises and on the behaviour and political orthodoxy of the workers. Really they were a part of the N.K.V.D., and the head of the fire-brigade was the most important person after the manager. He was also responsible for the *Krasnyj Ugolok* at the recreation-hall, where people attended political meetings and listened to agitators, and where there was a box for anonymous letters of denunciation or observation.

All the workers lived the *Obszcze zytie* (communal life). This meant living in leaky wooden huts, divided into big compartments serving as sleeping accommodation for men and separate ones for women. The beds were two-tiered, but there was enough room. Everyone had a straw mattress and a blanket—at least, in theory. Between the compartments stood a big boiler for the *kipiatok*. There was continuous movement and noise in the huts, as the kiln worked twenty-four hours a day. And the huts were infested with bugs, which seemed to be everywhere.

Married couples had their own private "communal life", and were allowed a single room where they could live as they liked.

Everybody fed in the canteen; married couples did not cook. Women worked like men, so they would not have had time for housework; besides, there was no possibility of buying food. There was only one shop in the factory, which sold a ration of bread to registered workers.

In theory—it was stated in the ration-book—everybody was entitled to buy once a year in this shop a pair of shoes (for four roubles) and one pair of combinations; but in practice "*Niechwata-jet*"—none was available, and nobody remembered any such allocation of goods to the shop.

The people varied: old and young, of the various nations and races composing the Soviet Union. They were not bad, but simple and unpretentious; some were wild, but all were very poor and ragged—much the same as those I had seen in prison. Very seldom did they possess more than the clothes they had on. Anyone who possessed a second shirt was looked upon as a rich man. Nobody even dreamt of a lounge suit: where could he go in it?

One worked six days of the week and ten hours daily: the seventh day was free. I was told that the free day varied for different people, but at the present time Sunday was the free day for us.

There was a Works surgery, looked after by a woman "doctor". She was called "Doctor", although she was really only a nurse, her medical training having lasted only three months.

Allegedly there was everything there; but in fact there was nothing except bugs, misery, dirt, and the "norm".

There was also the manager. He lived outside the kiln premises, in a separate house, had a scratched old Ford car, and was supposed to draw three thousand roubles monthly. He looked very similar to the workers, though he was a trifle better dressed, and visited the hairdresser's shop daily. He smelt obnoxiously of a cheap kind of *eau de Cologne*.

I was lucky to be put far away from the Works itself. I think the manager was frightened I might endanger the productivity of the Works, so he gave me the task of a sawyer. The kiln was heated with logs, so men in couples had to saw wood for this purpose, right on the bank of the Viatka, about a mile and a half from the Works. A small wooden hut served for living accommodation.

Logs were floated and tied up at the bank; aided by rollers, we had to pull the logs out of the water. This job was called "fishing out logs from water".

Then the logs had to be put on trestles (which we had to make ourselves) and sawn into yard-long pieces. Stouter logs had to be split; they were put into cords, and daily the "brigadier" checked the length of the cords. Two sawyers worked as a team, together, and the pay was divided equally between the two.

If a log was found that was suitable for timber, it was put aside; this was called "timber classification" and was paid for according to different norms.

Liminov was the Works' foreman; he instructed me as to what to do, and gave me a saw, an axe, an iron bar, and a file for keeping the saw sharp. He took me down the river and appointed a mate to work with me and teach me.

Liminov was born not far from Kirov; he was kind and easy-going and very guarded when talking. Looking at me he could not conceal his curiosity, as he never had an opportunity of meeting people from "the rotten West". He remembered it slightly from the time of the First World War—he had even taken part in the Battle of Gorlice—but it was so long ago, and things had changed so much since. He also looked at me with some respect. "They were educated, those Western people." Eventually he took off his rubber boots (everyone wore rubber boots, there being no leather), unwound the rags in which his feet were wrapped, and showed me the ulcers on them.

"Comrade, perhaps you know what I should do? For more than a year I have had these abscesses, but our doctor doesn't understand them."

I told him to leave off rubber boots, because they kept the feet hot and damp, which caused them to rot.

"You are right; but I haven't any leather ones. And I couldn't walk barefooted."

We arrived at the Viatka's bank. This splendid river flows from the north and her banks are covered with osiers.

Limonov showed me how, without any great effort, two men could pull logs out of the river with the help of a lever; and then he left me with my new mate. I was surprised to find that he was also a Pole, who, like me, had been sentenced to five years' deportation.

He was a few years older than I, and was called Dobrzanski. He could not speak Russian, and he was terrified and helpless as a child, and very low-spirited. He clung to me as his last hope of rescue. Very soon he told me he was a retired Major in the Army Ordnance Corps. In the summer of 1940 he had been arrested in Lwow, and had been terribly beaten during the interrogation. They tried to make him confess, first that he was General Tokarzewski, and later on Colonel Rudnicki, and that he was an organiser in the anti-Soviet Lwow Underground activities. They broke a few of his teeth and ribs. After that they left him in peace—and rightly, too, for he had nothing to do with any organisation. At last they discovered his identity, sentenced him to five years' deportation, and, a few months later, brought him to this place in a very bad state. However, he had recovered a little.

What an amazing encounter! I still had my teeth, and he had lost his because of me. Fate seemed to persecute some; others were luckier and escaped.

I did not immediately tell Dobrzanski my true identity: I thought I had better get to know him first. After all, it might only be an N.K.V.D. trick!

We started working, agreeing to labour only to earn enough to buy our bread and food; nothing more. We would not overstrain our hearts, already much fatigued by starvation and prison life.

We made a budget of our bare necessities:—

Bread	1 rb.
Lunch	2·5 rbs.
Supper	1·5 rbs.
Total	5·0 rbs.

It was necessary to make five yards of our log cord in order to earn five roubles each on which to live.

For the first few days we could not make more than three or four yards: not having enough strength and experience, we simply could not do more. So we cancelled our suppers, and reduced our evening meal to hot water and bread. Later on, we managed to work better, although we were never able to exceed our goal of five yards daily.

But we were blessed by tranquillity, nature, warm weather and the river. We worked in our pants only. The fresh air and July sunshine improved our health, and we became stronger every day.

Our "brigadier" was a young woman, her husband being somewhere at the front. Every evening she came to check up on how many yards of cords we had made that day. She was also keen to talk to anyone from the West, and very often she stayed longer than was necessary. She was an intelligent girl, educated in a Komsomol school (a public school for Communist youth), and listened with pleasure to our discussions and to our teasing—doubtless quite different from those to which she was accustomed. The West was fascinating, on the bank of the Viatka.

I told Dobrzanski to go ahead with the girl. "Our future is in your hands: you haven't a beard, and don't look so old."

He only looked sadly at me. But it often happened that our "brigadier" added a trifle to our yards. "The pencil can do *some* work," she used to say.

At last, on Saturday, we went to the office to collect our pay. There was a long queue outside the cashier's office. We waited patiently for the window to be opened.

At last the cashier's head appeared. "There is no money today— we haven't received it from the *Gosbank* (State Bank)." And the window was closed again.

I thought there was probably not sufficient money sent. The workers, however, started to shout: "It's not true! We want the manager! How shall we buy bread, or pay for our food? What shall we give to our children?!"

Eventually the manager arrived, and after much argument everybody was paid "on account" five to ten roubles of his earnings.

Later I heard that at almost every pay-day such scenes occurred. The workers lived by payments "on account" and the Works always owed them money. It was wrong for anyone to possess too much money: he might think himself free, and stop working, or run away from the Works, which might thus run the risk of being involved in difficulties. And so the money was kept, as in a Savings Bank; and thus the management ran no risk of losing their workers.

Sometimes we had pleasures as well.

One Sunday people were rushing wildly about, crying: "They've brought beer today!" Something unheard of—beer! Everybody took what vessels he had—pans or tins—and went to the store. The draught beer was poured out of the casks into the containers provided. It cost only a few kopeks, and the people carried it away to their huts, everyone enjoying it enormously. Stalin, "the nation's leader and the people's sun", had told them to give it to us.

The same day we had a big Workers' Meeting. The manager was the speaker. He spoke about the heroic efforts of the Red Army, which had fought so successfully against the Fascist-Nazi invaders, and about the necessity for the united efforts of all of us to support the achievements of the Red Army. He therefore begged us to vote for the abolition of our one free day in the week, which would mean working on Sundays, and to give the earnings of this day to a special "fund" for the State.

"Victory will be with us," he concluded. "Now, who is against the motion?"

Nobody opposed it, so the motion was carried.

From this time on, we had no Sundays.

CHAPTER 22

A Decision

I LIVED with Dobrzanski in a river hut, which consisted of three small rooms. Both of us, together with an old man of about seventy, who came from Polesie and was employed in watching the logs on the river, lived in one of these rooms. We made ourselves beds of boards, also a table and some shelves. No straw mattresses were issued— they were not available. Perhaps this was just as well, because they would only have provided an excellent breeding-ground for bugs.

The second room was occupied by a very poor married couple. They owned nothing, not a bed or even a straw palliasse; they just slept beside each other on the bare ground. They had two children— a girl of ten and a boy of eight. Every day they went to the school attached to the Kolchoz, in Sobotnica. The father was still young and had recently returned from a labour-camp, where he had been kept for three years. The mother looked old and worn out.

Like us, they both worked as sawyers, only they tried to work as hard as possible to increase their earnings: they had to feed their children. Sometimes they managed to make twelve or fourteen yards daily if the work was not too difficult.

Their children liked me, and very often we chatted together. They treated me with some condescension, apparently to prove their superior knowledge. In their opinion I was a lost capitalist sheep, desperately needing proper education. They often started discussions with me such as the following.

"Tell us; do you believe in God?"

"Definitely—yes."

"How *can* you believe that?! You are quite educated, so how *can* you believe in such nonsense?"

They would get very excited, and explain to me that thunder and

170

lightning were not signs of God's anger—as I probably believed—but simply discharges of electricity.

Or again: "How, according to your belief, did man come about?"

"He was created by God."

"You went to school, and yet you don't know about evolution! A long time ago Darwin proved that men descended from apes."

There followed a long exposition of the evolution theory, in which they simply repeated the same phrases that I, while in prison, had read in the textbooks of anti-religious propaganda.

The third room was inhabited by another couple. The man came from Siberia. He was quite young, and was the Works' chief electrician. His wife was expecting her second baby, so for the time being she was now working. Their first child, a boy, was not aged two. They seemed a little better off: they had a bed, sheets and pillows, and even a green cover on their table; but actually they were in financial trouble.

As a skilled worker, the husband was earning 220 roubles monthly—supposed to be enough for three of them; but they could not make both ends meet. They had to pay 8 roubles monthly for their room, and food for each person cost at least 5 roubles daily; so there was a gap. To fill it he used to bring only one meal from the canteen: they then diluted it with water and shared it. They were an exemplary, loving couple. They had terrible difficulties with the bringing-up of the boy. He needed milk, but one litre ($1\frac{3}{4}$ pints) cost 12 roubles and could only be bought in the Kolchoz or in the bazaar. To enable her to buy some for the child, the woman cut osiers on the river bank to make baskets, the husband helping her in this work at nights; and they sold the baskets in the bazaar. Without this additional income the child would have died; as it was, he used to cry all the time.

This man was scared of being called up, which would mean disaster for his wife. But one day the militia came and put him on the conscripts' list.

As the war went on and soldiers got killed, more people were called up. It was a tragic prospect, and nobody wanted to join the forces. I could not discern any of the patriotic enthusiasm described in all the newspapers.

I had to report personally every ten days to the police of the First District—so I had a day off, though others did not. I could thus get acquainted with Kirov.

It is a very large, widely spread town, mostly of bungalows; only in the centre of the town are there a few storeyed houses. There are

171

over 700,000 inhabitants, but no tramcars or taxis: everyone has to walk. There are no general stores, as every corporation or institution has its own shop, which can be used only by people working there. But there is one exception—the Univermag Stores, houses in a huge building of several floors, rather like Selfridge's, for instance. There one could buy everything one liked: shoes, clothes, underwear, needles, and thread, with only one restraint—the prices. I studied them well; they were marked on labels: one pair of shoes, 600 roubles; one suit, 2,400 roubles.

I wondered who could afford to buy them, when a qualified electrician was only earning 220 roubles a month. But the shop was filled with people—mostly, though, just passing through, to enjoy the knowledge "that there is plenty of everything in our country. . . ."

However, there were *some* buyers! I could not make out who they were for certain: obviously not workers or clerks, but perhaps artists or high-ranking N.K.V.D. officers.

There were no restaurants or cafés in the town, only two canteens —one for travelling Kolchoz workers, the other for industrial workers. Every citizen could go there, but one had to queue for at least two hours. Once one was in, everything ran smoothly and one could get the same sort of meal as in our canteen and for the same price; they even gave half-an-ounce of bread.

There was a bazaar in the town—a place for the uncontrolled exchange of goods. One had to beware of "speculators" selling other people's property. Special sections were allocated to dealers in old, second-hand clothes, footwear and underwear. There anyone could sell his redundant clothes, asking any price he liked for them. It was a place where people could buy necessities for personal use. For a pair of old shoes, one had to pay about 60 roubles; for a suit, about 200 roubles; and for a shirt 30 or 40 roubles.

The readiest buyers came from the farms. They used to have money, for in another part of the bazaar they sold their own products. Every member of a Kolchoz had the right to sell all he produced himself in his house and garden—*e.g.* cucumbers, tomatoes, hempseeds, eggs, cheese, milk, and sometimes butter. They sold these to buy clothes.

Prices were very high: 3 rbs. for one egg, 1 rb. for four cucumbers, etc. A rapid calculation showed that, working as a sawyer, I was earning daily less than two eggs or half-a-pint of milk.

Only then did I understand what a blessing the system of factory canteens and the enlistment of workers was. Without it, one would
172

have starved and perished in misery in this wealthy land of the Soviet Union; but with such an arrangement one could vegetate tolerably under the protection of the powerful Stalin, "bright sun of the nations".

So that the people should not develop any doubts about Stalin's greatness, one heard almost incessant propaganda issuing from loud-speakers, interspersed with noisy music and proud words of comfort. For instance, we were informed that "men and women workers in the Stalin Metallurgic Works in Svierdlovsk produced 150% above the norm"; and a war *communiqué* stated that "in the central sector of the south-western front the enemy managed to take forty-five villages, but our heroic Red Army, in a counter-attack during the night, routed the enemy, taking 26 guns, 93 machine-guns, and 3,561 rifles. Victory will be ours!"

They were simple, clear and definite statements: everyone could understand them. How encouraging it was to listen to them!

Extracts from *Pravda*, giving the chief news of events in the front line and in the world, were exhibited in the recreation-hall. It was impossible to buy newspapers because of the paper shortage: they were available only for a few people.

In the last days of July my attention focused on news concerning the Czechoslovak-Russian Agreement; it puzzled me very much and I was expecting similar moves towards Poland. The loud-speakers transmitted speeches from the Pan-Slavonic Congress in Moscow. Besides Czechs, Bulgarians, Jugoslavs, and Ukrainians, I also heard Polish speakers—Mrs. Wanda Wasilewski, and, to my amazement, General Januszajtis. I did not like their statements—the style was too Sovietish—but it was a hint that something unusual was happening and that some basic change in policy was being prepared. I went regularly to the recreation-hall with Dobrzanski to keep abreast of developments.

At last, in the first days of August, we found a *communiqué* telling us that General Sikorski and Ambassador Majski had signed the Polish-Russian Agreement* in London: both Governments had joined forces to beat the common enemy. An "amnesty" was pro-claimed for all Poles serving sentences in Russia, and a Polish Army was to be formed in the U.S.S.R.

After all our experiences, we could not believe it. It was too good to be true!

But in the middle of August we were summoned to the N.K.V.D.,

* The Agreement was actually signed on 30th July, 1941.

173

where we were notified of the "amnesty" and told that we were free: that we could choose our domicile, and need no longer report to the police-station.

We chose to remain in Kirov. It was better to stick to our job as sawyers, and await further developments under tolerably fair conditions.

In the last days of August we heard the news that, as a further development of the London Agreement, a Polish-Russian Military Agreement had been signed on August 14th in Moscow. Professor S. Kot became Polish Ambassador there, and General Szyszko-Bohusz the Head of the Polish Military Mission.

The situation became clearer, but we still had serious doubts. We did not trust the wireless and the *communiqués* in the recreation-hall, especially as we were unfamiliar with the names of Prof. Kot and General Szyszko-Bohusz, and we awaited further evidence before believing the news.

At last it was announced that General Anders had been appointed Commanding Officer of Polish Units in the U.S.S.R.; he was free in Moscow, and had begun to form the Polish Army there.

I said to Dobrzanski, with whom I had become very friendly: "Look, I believe it now, and I'm going to join the Army. It is not a trick of the N.K.V.D.; it is wonderful reality." By this time I had told him who I was.

Dobrzanski still had doubts, and implored me not to be precipitate; but I paid no attention to his warnings; I went straight to the manager.

"Comrade Manager, I want to join the Polish Army. Will you please release me from your factory?"

"You can't leave this place; you're here for life! Now we need workers." And he added: "The Army doesn't need old men."

And that was the end of the interview. Now he needed *me*, the scoundrel! But I would find some way of going.

How to do it, though? I could not escape from the factory—I should be caught immediately, and once I became involved in all the enquiries, checks, examinations and other routine measures in prisons, I might never get out of there. In Russia, the gates of the prisons are wide open for the incomers, but only small fissures are left for the outgoers.

I had no choice but to place my cards on the table—a decision made against Dobrzanski's advice. I went to town and posted two registered letters to Moscow: one to Ambassador Kot and the other to the

174

Head of the Polish Military Mission, General Sryszko-Bohusz. I stated frankly that I was working as a labourer in the brick-kiln in Bolshaia Subotnica, near Kirov, under the assumed name of Joseph Ruminski. Among other things I wrote: "As I have no other possibility of being released from my job, I have decided to tell the N.K.V.D. who I really am, and to demand an immediate transfer to the Polish Army." At the same time I asked them to intervene in my case should my risky decision have bad consequences for me; for there was no joking when the N.K.V.D. dealt with one. I signed the letter with my full name and rank, and kept the postal registration receipts carefully.

I was uncertain whether these letters would reach the addressees: they might be intercepted by the N.K.V.D's censors, and then I might be arrested again, and maybe not a trace of my existence would be left. But without risking something one could achieve nothing, and I wanted to join the Army as soon as possible, no matter what it involved. Having overcome so many difficulties, I had to try to master this last one.

I had some very amusing problems to overcome in the writing and posting of these letters—difficulties which could only occur in the Soviet Union. A stamped envelope for a registered letter can be bought in the post-office; but where to get the paper? There was none in the post-office itself, so I walked round all the shops in the town (of 700,000 inhabitants!), but nowhere could I buy a scrap of paper, a diary, or a copy-book. At last a girl behind the cash-desk in one of the shops took pity on me and tore two pages out of her receipt-book, and I used these for my letters. It is almost unbelievable that there should be such a scarcity of paper in a large town, but it is true.

Three days later, when I might assume that the letters had left Kirov and were on their way to Moscow, I chanced the next step. I wrote a *zajawlenie* (petition) to the Military Attorney of the Kirov District—having got the paper from an accountant in our firm, whom I knew quite well. In this petition I briefly informed the attorney that my depositions during the enquiry, which were the basis of my trial, had been false. I was not Joseph Ruminski, son of Sigismund, a merchant from Cracow, but Klement Rudnicki, a colonel of the Polish General Staff, and a close colleague of General Anders before the war. With regard to this, I asked the Military Attorney, in accordance with the Polish-Russian Agreement, immediately to inform the Polish authorities in Moscow of my whereabouts, and to transfer me without delay to the Polish Army just formed in the U.S.S.R.

175

At the same time I mentioned that, three days ago, I had posted in registered envelopes (I gave the date and the registration numbers) a similar report to Ambassador Kot and to General Szyszko-Bohusz.

I had previously told Dobrzanski of my intentions. He was very much opposed to my plan, but seeing he could not change my mind he said: "If you want to be hanged, do it, but don't get me mixed up in it."

I took my petition and went to hand it in personally. The Military Attorney's office was in one of the N.K.V.D. buildings. The door was open, as everybody could go to see him—to denounce their neighbours! He raised his head from his papers and said: "What do you want?"

"I have come with a petition."

"Give it to me."

He took it and began to read. First he appeared to be indifferent; then he began to clean his eye-glasses and the colour changed in his face. He looked at the petition for a long time, and I could see he was puzzled and uncertain what to do.

At last he arrived at a decision. He got up and shook hands with me. "You were right, sir, to do this. I hope you'll be able to join the Polish Army." He then asked me to sit down.

I felt relieved—this was not too bad. I asked what he thought I should then do.

"Nothing," was the answer. I must return to my job and work as if nothing had happened. I was not to talk about it until I received a reply. "You know, this is a very serious question. I must report to Moscow; we must check up on it. . . ." He looked at the postal registration receipts, wrote down their numbers, and said goodbye to me.

I walked out. I did not like the fact that he had so carefully noted down all the details regarding the receipts, but this could not be helped.

For ten days I cut logs, every day expecting good or bad news—I was almost indifferent which. Dobrzanski expected the worst, but I tried to calm him.

"Don't be afraid; I will get you out of here. You won't be a sawyer all your life," I used to joke, although I did not feel too sure.

CHAPTER 23

"Now We Are Allies . . . "

AT LAST, on the tenth day, a girl messenger called me "to go immediately to see the manager". I went straight away, dirty as I was from work.

In the manager's office I saw a young, attractive lady.

"She has come to see you," said the manager, looking a little puzzled.

The woman asked me sharply why I had stopped reporting to the local police-station.

"Why should I? The amnesty was granted," I replied.

"It doesn't mean anything," she answered, and then said I must go with her to the police-station immediately.

This puzzled me. But suddenly I thought she might be a messenger from the Attorney. So I said: "Citizen, perhaps you have come with regard to the petition ———"

I did not finish the sentence, because she discreetly gave me a warning sign, which I took to mean that this was to be kept secret from the manager.

"Well, I'll come with you," I said. As I followed her, I noticed how scared and puzzled the manager appeared: he probably thought I might denounce him and perhaps he would be put in prison.

As we walked outside the precincts of the Works, a misunderstanding arose between my guide and me. She told me to follow her down a path leading in the opposite direction to the town, into some bushes. I thought she had made a mistake, and pointed the right way out to her.

"No, no, we'll go this way," she said stubbornly.

"But it isn't the right way to town!"

She remained adamant. "It doesn't matter; we'll go this way."

I was now becoming suspicious of her intentions.

I did not want to go with her into the bushes, so I refused to follow her, determined not to be drawn into any ambush.

She took my hand, and almost pulled me after her by force.

"Am I arrested again? Why not be frank? Why all this nonsense?"

"You offend me!" she answered sharply. Then, with a charming look, she added: "If you don't believe me, as N.K.V.D. agent, then believe the *woman*."

I argued no more, but followed her down the path.

After we had walked about half-a-mile, we found a car, hidden in the bushes. She pointed to it, and, to dissipate my remaining doubts, she said: "That's for you, Colonel."

So she really was a messenger from the Attorney! Things did not look so bad. We got in the car, she driving, and I seated next to her. I tried to elicit from her where we were going—obviously not to the police-station: "They do not have such cars," I said jokingly. "Yours is a beautiful one."

She only smiled mysteriously. My brain was busy. I wanted to be prepared for any emergency, so I must try to get some information out of the girl. . . . I therefore started on another tack.

"You know, I was reminded just now—please don't laugh, but our situation reminds me of something I experienced in 1937, in Paris."

"Oh, in Paris! Do tell me, please."

And I told her a story, partly true, partly fictitious: how once, after a night spent in Montmartre—"You know, Citizen . . . Montmartre . . . I passed a beautiful car driven by a lovely lady, very like you. . . ."

"What on earth are you talking about?" she protested. "But what happened then?" She was evidently interested.

"Well, she stopped the car, opened the door, and said to me: 'Since we are both going in the same direction, could I, perhaps, give you a lift?' And suddenly I found myself seated next to the lady, as I am now sitting by you."

"And what happened then?" She was very anxious to hear more. The breath of Paris has its charm, even here.

"We drove along, talking charmingly—as now with you. She asked me to have a drink—obviously *she* was very keen to have one herself. I couldn't refuse—I didn't want to, anyway."

"What next? What happened then?" She was becoming very excited.

"We drove to a suburban restaurant. I ordered champagne. We drank—one bottle; then the second. . . ." I went on, suggestively. "Oh, it was fine! Then it was time to leave, and I called for the bill. The waiter brought a chit for an unheard-of-amount—for six thousand francs! I was fully aware that it should have been for no more than two or three hundred francs; it was sheer robbery. So I refused to pay the bill. A row followed. A policeman was called, and took the side of the waiter. My pretty lady began to cry hysterically that I had brought her to this place by force: that I was a 'sal étranger' (a bloody foreigner), and that I should immediately pay the bill. The policeman threatened me with arrest. I realised then that they were all in conspiracy and that I had become the victim of a band of suburban robbers.

"So you see," I continued jokingly, "that is the story of my journey to an unknown destination with a pretty lady-driver. Since then I have always been very cautious! I am sorry—I don't mean that this story is connected with us—only, you see, it seemed so similar."

"But it's all blather!" She laughed heartily, though still remaining the controlled N.K.V.D. agent on duty. We drove along to an unknown destination.

Finally she stopped her car in front of the main N.K.V.D. building and led me to the head of the N.K.V.D. for the Kirov area—Comrade Gavorik, as he introduced himself to me.

"Pleased to meet you, sir," Gavorik greeted me heartily. "Do sit down, please." Immediately he began to talk "shop". He was pleased to inform me that, according to instructions received from Moscow, he was to send me there immediately. My petition had been granted. The Polish Army was expecting my arrival, and he hoped that I would serve the common Polish-Soviet cause well. He would like to know what my political views were, and whether I really and sincerely desired the full co-operation of both our Governments.

"But definitely yes," I answered. "I am only a soldier, and as my Prime Minister has entered into an Agreement with your Prime Minister, I must approach the matter loyally and do everything to forward the terms of this Agreement."

"That's so," he agreed with me; "but do all Poles think like that? I doubt it."

"I am sure they do."

"I am sorry, but you are wrong," he said. "We know that there are Poles with different views—as, for instance, General Sosnkowski and his group."

179

I was overcome by this news, but I could not possibly enter into a discussion about it. Here, on the banks of the Viatka, I did not know the circumstances under which the Polish-Soviet Agreement had been signed; nor did I know anything about opposing views. Apparently seeing my point, Gavorik ceased questioning me on this subject.

Then he said, almost carelessly, something which affected me directly. He spoke about the Soviet Government's awareness of subversive activities by enemies to our Agreement, and pointed out the necessity of fighting them. He suggested I should sign a statement in which I would undertake to denounce to the N.K.V.D. all persons suspected of activities obnoxious to the Polish or Soviet Governments, or to their common cause. All my reports would remain secret: I could sign them with a pseudonym, upon which we could agree, and send them directly to the N.K.V.D.; my activities would remain secret, but I must give a formal pledge that I would not divulge my undertaking to anybody—not even to my Commanding Officer in the Army, or to my friends and my family.

He spoke easily and freely, as if it were just a matter of mere formality. Although it galled me, I continued to talk imperturbably, hoping to find out a little more.

"Well," I asked him, "why should my reports go directly to the N.K.V.D.? In the Army, General Anders will be my direct Chief; how could I go over his head by sending such reports to you?"

He gave a very naïve explanation: it really did not matter who received the reports, as both Governments would co-operate closely, but General Anders' staff was not yet fully instructed, and it would be difficult for them to deal with such matters. So it would be easier to forward them. . . . Perhaps later there would come a change. . . .

I refused, categorically. He seemed annoyed, and told me that, unfortunately, according to his instructions, he had to insist on this point: that he was sorry, but. . . .

"What, then?" I asked. "Back to prison?"

He made a gesture with his hands. I realised that my situation was getting hopeless. I tried argument. A cold shudder ran down my spine when I thought of a return to prison—especially now, when I was on the threshold of liberty and of an active life. I suggested I might sign a statement that I would send such reports, but only through General Anders—I could not do it otherwise.

He tried to alter my stubborn attitude. Finally he acceded to my request, but decided to send me, under an escort, to Moscow direct, to the *Narkomindiel* (the Foreign Ministry), where they would take the final decision. I signed the required statement, on my terms, and all was friendliness again.

After settling this unpleasant dispute, Gavorik looked at me—my suit in rags from head to foot—evidently disliking my appearance.

"You can't go to Moscow, our metropolis, in such rags. A Colonel on the General Staff! It is quite impossible."

He called a clerk, and ordered him to take me to the Univermag Stores, and there dress me completely.

"You have to buy everything—breeches, tunic, a shirt, greatcoat, forage cap—everything." He gave a definite order.

I was actually driven in a car to the stores, and after an hour I left the shop completely dressed, with even a white handkerchief in my pocket! What an unexpected change, I thought! What would my manager or Dobrzanski say? I wanted to return to them, to tell Dobrzanski what had happened to me—though the adventure was not finished yet and I did not know what the final outcome would be.

After my return to the N.K.V.D., I told Gavorik that before my departure I wished to return to the factory to collect my few belongings.

"What for? You don't need them. You'll get everything in Moscow."

I insisted that I wished nevertheless to visit the factory, and he could not refuse my last argument: that I had to report my departure to the manager, get crossed off the register, and receive 40 rbs., which I had earned by my labour and which were due to me. "You see, I *earned* them."

He agreed to this, but only on condition that I resumed my rags, went in the car to the same bushes as previously, and that I told nobody about what had happened.

We drove back. I walked from the bushes straight to the manager and asked for my release. He flatly refused. "Wait a moment," I thought; "now I will use against you the same weapons you used against me!" And in his presence I lifted the telephone-receiver and got through to Gavorik, whom I asked to talk to the manager.

The manager took the receiver with trembling hands, and I listened while he kept stuttering: "Yes, Comrade. . . . Yes, I understand, sir. . . . Yes, I see. . . ."

In five minutes, all formalities were over. I received my forty roubles and shook hands warmly with the manager, who said: "*Do swidania*" ("Hope to see you again"), and I replied "*Proszczajtie*" ("Goodbye"), adding that I did not expect to see him again.

When I departed he was smiling stupidly, and I was amused to note the contrast between our farewell and my previous welcome. I considered the N.K.V.D. a magic institution!

I then saw Dobrzanski and (Gavorik forgive me!) whispered to him what had happened, and how.

"In a few days you'll either receive a telegram asking you to join the Army, or no news at all. In the latter case, you'll know that I am missing, and in future you'll tell anyone it may concern that you were the last person to see me alive," I said—half-seriously, half-jokingly.

"My goodness! God bless you! It's terrible what may result from this!" And we embraced heartily, as we had become very good friends.

CHAPTER 24

To Moscow!

AT 1 a.m. I left Kirov by train for Moscow, escorted by a civilian with an attaché-case. He carried all the documents, the tickets, and the food for our journey. We travelled on a slow passenger-train, with ordinary passengers. Nobody would think he was escorting me and that I was under guard as we chatted amiably.

Our journey lasted five days and five nights. On the evening of the fifth day we reached Moscow, at the end of September, 1941. From the station we went straight to the Narkomindiel.

My escort was very helpful: he arranged all the formalities by telephone, got all the necessary passes, and handed me over to the local N.K.V.D.; then we parted.

I was taken to an office upstairs. An officer in the N.K.V.D. uniform greeted me in good Polish.

"A hearty welcome! I am Colonel Fediczkin. For many years I was in Warsaw in the Military Attaché's office." This explained his fluent Polish. "General Anders," he went on, "will be very pleased to see you here. We have been looking all over Russia for you! Luckily, you reported your*self*." And he produced one of the letters posted from Kirov, which, he said, General Anders had handed over to him with a request to have me brought there as soon as possible.

I was pleased. My idea of posting these letters had not been a bad one, after all; perhaps I was lucky they were not intercepted before they had reached their destination. Anyhow, it was all over now, and my situation appeared very satisfactory.

"Soon we'll hand you over to the Polish Embassy; only my boss would like to see you first."

We waited for the "boss" until 2 a.m. Finally, Colonel Fediczkin and I were summoned to his office.

The "boss"—a man with Eastern features—was, I discovered later, Beria himself. He was wearing a general's uniform, but was very uncivil.

"You're a dishonest man! You've cheated Soviet authorities and concealed your identity," he sharply reproached me. He maintained that they had many generals and colonels in prisons who had all honestly confessed their identity, and I was the only one who had lied. "For this you should rot in prison. You are not supposed to make fun of the N.K.V.D. or other Soviet authorities."

While he spoke he sat at his desk, hardly deigning to look up at me. What contrasts one finds in this country! I was furious. How dared he moralise to me—he, who had helped keep a million-and-a-half Poles in prison; and who, on the 17th September, 1939, while I was fighting against the Germans near Grehina, had helped to drive a knife in Poland's back by invading our country in collusion with the Germans!

I could not stand this, and burst out: "You can send me back to prison if your only purpose in bringing me here is to insult me! Do you really think I am such a fool? Do you think that I don't know that if I had disclosed my true identity during my interrogation I would be rotting—or would perhaps have perished—in Kolyma or some other place in Siberia, and would never have lived to stand here today in front of you? Do you think I am so naïve? Then we were enemies, and one is allowed to use any ruse to cheat an enemy. As soon as our Governments had signed the Agreement, I, of my own free will, disclosed my true identity. I think that fair play; what more do you want?"

He could see that I was shaking with genuine rage.

"Don't get excited," he said, in a more kindly tone; and he asked me to sit down. Like Gavorik, he asked me about General Sosnkowski and the opposition of some Poles to the Polish-Russian Agreement, although I still could not know anything of the details.

I explained, as before, that I was taking a serious view of the Agreement, and that I was convinced my Prime Minister, General Sikorski, looked upon it similarly. After that we discussed military questions.

Beria asked me about the strategic position of Skala, a town on the river Zbrucz. I was puzzled by this unusual question.

I told him: "To us, in Poland, it has no strategic value at all."

"How is it possible that you—an officer of the General Staff—can tell me this?" He seemed surprised.

"I know Skala," I said, "and it is just a small Jewish town on the
184

way to Kamieniec Podolski: of no importance for military operations whatsoever."

"But if a Staff came to the town, for instance—an Army Headquarters—where would you billet them?"

"Probably in Count Coluchowski's palace, which I know and remember well."

"Could you make a sketch for me, please?"

"No, I couldn't do it now—it would only be inaccurate; but you can make a copy from any map."

I did not know the meaning behind this enquiry. Perhaps he wanted proof of my Intelligence activities by possessing a sketch drawn and signed by myself; or perhaps it was simply an innocuous question. It was difficult to decide which, but in any case I preferred not to comply with his request.

He then brought our talk to an end. He got up, stretched out his hand to me, and begged me to forget all the discomforts I had endured in prison; for his part, he would try to forget the offence I had committed against the Soviet Union in concealing my true identity.

"Now we are allies, we have to unite our forces against our common enemy." And he told Fediczkin to hand me over immediately to the Polish Authorities in Moscow.

He rose to bid me goodbye, and I said: "I don't know if you are aware that your subordinate, Gavorik, the head of the N.K.V.D. in Kirov, extorted from me a revolting statement, which I had to sign in order to get to Moscow. I must say that such behaviour is contrary to the friendly principles which now unite our countries. If you endeavour thus to implement our Agreement, we shan't get very far. I am determined to report this to General Anders directly I see him. If you wish to avoid this, you must detain me here."

He looked at me, then smiled, and, going to his desk, opened a drawer and produced my statement. He handed it over to me, and said: "Were you concerned about it? It's trash—a foolish idea of that idiot Gavorik. I will teach him a lesson."

I tore the statement to pieces in his presence, and walked out.

An hour later I was in the Polish transit centre for Officers in the Stromynko Street in Moscow, and was heartily welcomed by Captain Zunft, who was the Commandant there.

I had now rejoined the Polish Army.

CHAPTER 25

The Embassy

THE FORMATION of the Polish Army in the U.S.S.R. was a bold attempt at international co-operation, but it resulted in failure, in spite of the goodwill of the Poles. We—all of us prisoners or deportees —approached this venture with the greatest faith and energy. We tried to blot out the memory of our dreadful personal, and national, sufferings, and hoped to build a new future based on neighbourly co-operation. We aimed at a sincere and lasting settlement with Soviet Russia according to the Agreement signed by General Sikorski and Ambassador Mayski on 30 July, 1941, and reaffirmed in December that year, during the personal talks in Moscow between General Sikorski and Marshal Stalin.

Unfortunately, the Soviet side approached this partnership in reverse. They wanted to capture us, and once and for all use us as tools to further the realisation of their aims. From the outset, the Soviets schemed in deceit and treachery. They endeavoured to persuade many Poles to become informers for the N.K.V.D., just as Gavorik did with me.

We became convinced that co-operation with the Soviets, on their terms, meant complete surrender by us of our Christian principles and culture, our ancient traditions and our national sovereignty. And we refused to accept this arrangement. This resulted in more suffering for the Poles now in the Soviet Union. Of 1,500,000 people deported into Russia, only 118,000 managed to leave that country again; the rest were left behind, most of them for good, to die of exhaustion and starvation.

At first, however, life in Moscow seemed to me like a fairy-tale. From now onwards, I have my diary to consult, as well as memory. On my first morning, 28th September, I received, from Capt. Cumft,

3,000 roubles, for myself! According to the military agreement, this was the amount due to every officer as compensation for his imprisonment. This large sum, compared with my earnings as a sawyer, seemed fabulous. And the unaccustomed speed with which all the formalities had been settled encouraged further co-operation.

After receiving the money, I went (by the underground-railway) to the Polish Embassy.

The first person I met there was Prince Eustace Sapieha. I thanked him for the "loan" of his suit from his Warsaw flat—of which he, of course, had no knowledge. He, also, had been recently released from prison.

General Szyszko-Bohusz gave me a Polish Army badge—the Polish Eagle—as a symbol of rejoining the Colours.

I was then received by Ambassador S. Kot. I gave him a written and comprehensive report about my activities in conspiracy, and all my experiences in gaol. It included a list of all the Poles I had come across in various prisons: I hoped this might facilitate their release. I also described the way in which declarations were extracted to recruit Polish informers for the N.K.V.D., but I was told that this was already known—almost every released person had met with similar proposals. The Embassy feared that many of those who had signed were now ashamed to admit it, foolishly trusting that the N.K.V.D. would forget about them, whereas now they could easily be blackmailed. The Embassy was debating whether to lodge a protest with the Soviet authorities regarding this matter: it was the first friction in the newly initiated co-operation.

General Szyszko-Bohusz sent a telegram to Kirov, requesting the immediate release of Major Dobrzanski to join the Army.

The Polish Red Cross, which had offices in the Embassy, gave me a letter written to them in 1940 by my wife's parents, asking for help and for news of me. They had been deported to the Kazak Steppes in the spring of 1940, together with their daughter-in-law and her little children, from Lwow, and eventually died there, either in tents or mud huts. They were among the 1,500,000 Poles dragged far into Russia. It was difficult to understand why they were deported: both were aged—my father-in-law being over seventy-five. According to their letter, I assumed that my wife and children had been left in Lwow.

Masses of similar letters were received by the Polish Red Cross. People wrote from different parts of Russia—from the Kazak or Kirgiz steppes, from Siberian hamlets, or from the Far North. They begged for help, for advice, for food and clothes, to stave off death. But what could be done?

General Anders was in Buzuluk on the Volga, in the Chkalov Military District where our Army was being formed: I had to await his return to Moscow, expected in a few days because of the visit of Lord Beaverbrook, then British Minister of Supplies, and of the conferences to be held with him regarding our equipment and supplies. I thus had time and opportunity to observe Moscow.

General Szyszko-Bohusz had invited me to lunch with him at the Metropol Hotel. What a contrast to the canteen in Kirov! The tables were beautifully laid, and there were waiters in tails, carpets, and easy-chairs covered with damask—almost like Western Europe. On the menu were caviar, a most luxurious choice of *hors d'oeuvres*, even hazel-hens, and various sweets and cakes as well as vodka and a selection of wines.

The General told me that there were only three restaurants of this kind in Moscow—the Metropol, the Moskva, and the National. In theory, everyone could enter them, but in reality only members of foreign Legations and high-ranking Soviet dignitaries frequented them because of the astronomical prices, and more especially because they were watched by the N.K.V.D. Ordinary citizens, as in Kirov, fed in canteens.

I received from the General a quick summary of the main events during the one-and-a-half-years' break in my life. I heard about our determined attempts in France to reform our State and Army; about the Poles who had fought there (which perhaps I had visualised in my dream about the railway track); about France's tragedy ("Verdun"); about Narvik; about Great Britain; about the secret background of the Sikorski-Mayski Agreement in London. Everything was new and interesting to me.

He intimated the clauses of the Military Agreement signed in Moscow on 14 August, 1941. We were to form a sovereign Army fighting on the side of the Allied Red Army against the Germans. The Army would be organised according to Polish laws and regulations, but tactically would be subordinate to Soviet commanders. The equipment would be supplied by the U.S.S.R. and by the Polish Government in London from the Lease-Lend Fund.

To begin with, it was agreed that the Polish Army should be 44,000 strong, but with volunteers forthcoming the number could be increased.

The General told me about the difficulties raised by the Polish

Opposition Parties during discussion of the Polish-Soviet Agreement, demanding that General Sikorski obtain a definite and precise statement by the Soviets regarding the inviolability of our Eastern frontiers. The Soviets bluntly refused this, confining themselves only to a vague statement that the Ribbentrop-Molotov Agreement from 1939 was void.

He explained that agreement had only been reached because General Sikorski had carried it through the Polish Cabinet simply by sheer weight of his authority: this had created many opponents. So Gavorik was correct in telling me of the internal tension among our politicians.

Personally, I could agree with the opposition only in the event of there being a possibility of obtaining more favourable terms. Anyhow, it would have purely a nominal, not a real value. I knew that force alone would receive the respect of the Soviets.

The postponement of the Agreement by juggling with formal questions would only delay the release of prisoners and deportees, and I knew from my own experience the value of each day spent in freedom.

I was glad to learn that General Tokarzewski had been traced and had already joined the Army, being put in command of one of our Divisions.

At the beginning of October, 1941, General Anders returned by air from Buzuluk. He still had to use a walking-stick, and was very exhausted, but was in excellent spirits. He expressed pleasure at seeing me, especially as only a small number of officers had yet rejoined the Army—the group from Griazovetz and a few ex-prisoners: altogether only a few hundred. Officers from the reputed prisoner-of-war camps in Starobielsk, Kozielsk and Ostaszkov were still missing. All the soldiers, although exhausted and in rags, were in excellent form and began to work enthusiastically.

General Anders offered me an appointment as deputy to Col. Okulicki, the Chief of Staff, and I was delighted with my new job.

The Soviet authorities had given the General an extremely well-furnished flat in Moscow, with a cook, servants, and a car. There were no difficulties with supplies. If the slightest wish was expressed, the tables would groan under the weight of the choicest dishes, fruit and drinks for himself and his guests. Naturally, the General did not transgress ordinary frugality, but he was amused by this Eastern lavishness. For him, too, it seemed a magic transformation after the misery suffered in prison.

189

He was fully aware that all his servants were simply N.K.V.D. agents, watching and spying on him, but this did not perturb him, as he had nothing to conceal from the N.K.V.D. Our aims were quite sincere and obvious: as soon as possible we desired to create a strong Polish Army to fight side by side with the Soviet Army against the Germans. We made no plans for secret activities: everything was aimed at fulfilling the agreement reached. If they thought it necessary, or were prompted by reasons of expediency, they could spy as much as they liked. With a little goodwill, one could, knowing Russia, even understand this attitude.

From the Soviet authorities themselves the General met only with far-reaching, almost cringing civility. He could always get anything, from a box in a theatre to facilities for releasing from prison soldiers or civilians discovered by chance. It appeared as if the authorities wanted to satisfy his every whim. At that time he could do far more than the Ambassador, over whom he was deliberately given precedence. It was difficult to know whether this was due to his personal value, his knowledge of the language, his sincere attitude, or what. Perhaps there was some concealed purpose in it: they maybe hoped to cajole him. I thought the Embassy seemed somewhat annoyed by these civilities.

It soon became apparent that our trust that the talks between Lord Beaverbrook and the Soviet Government would result in our obtaining equipment was unfounded. Lord Beaverbrook was not prepared to discuss the issue separately with us, and was interested only in Soviet needs: eventually we should share in the global supplies to Russia. Therefore, the issue of equipment to our Army depended on our direct talks with the Soviets. However, since we were to fight together, I considered it logical enough that we shouud have the same equipment as the Soviet Army.

Our Embassy became more and more embarrassed by the masses of letters and telegrams arriving from deported Poles, asking for guidance. They had recovered their freedom in accordance with the "amnesty",* but what next? Being free, they did not want to die in

* The only judicious reason for signing the Polish-Russian Agreement on 30th July 1941 was the urgent necessity of liberating all Polish soldiers and civilians who, contrary to international law, had been deported to Russia and kept there in prisons and labour-camps. The Soviets reluctantly acceded to this request. They obstinately maintained that this "liberation" of Poles should be called "amnesty", as this was the proper legal term used in such cases in Soviet law. To speed up the liberation of the incarcerated Poles, the Polish Government did not dwell on the choice of expression, and agreed to this unfortunate term of "amnesty", quite incorrectly applied in this case.

The deported Poles were guilty of no crime, and were not granted a pardon by their ruling authority, which is essential in an amnesty. They simply were to be the appalling conditions in which they were left: they were frightened of being unable to survive the coming winter without supplies of clothing and food. Frequently they left their quarters—mainly in the North—and caught southbound trains, travelling into the unknown, hoping that there conditions would be better, or at least warmer. They had delusions that the Polish authorities in the U.S.S.R. had foreseen all this and had prepared for their rescue. We were deeply perturbed, wondering whether this unco-ordinated move of the population might not result in more tragedy.

It was extremely difficult in Moscow to know how best to react to this spontaneous activity. It might, perhaps, have been more sensible to have bidden people to stay where they were and await further instructions, but this would have been unrealistic, for the population expected different advice—and they wanted practical assistance. Telegrams were sent by the Embassy recommending calmness, and telling those who had already left their living quarters to go to Samarkand and Tashkent.

In the meantime, the situation in Moscow became more tense. The front was approaching: fighting was going on in its immediate neighbourhood; actually, it was a battle for Moscow.

It was very difficult to form any opinion of the military situation. Food supplies were getting short in the town; nevertheless, order reigned. In spite of the vicinity of the front line, one did not notice any nervousness or increased traffic, which is customary in the vicinity of a front. Moscow was allegedly sealed off by special cordons of constabulary, and rigid discipline was maintained. At night we heard the powerful roar of anti-aircraft artillery repelling German air-raids. Losses sustained by bombardment seemed negligible; anyhow, we saw none.

The Embassies secretly prepared for evacuation, while the Soviet authorities assured them that Moscow would be defended.

General Anders left Moscow for Buzuluk again in his aircraft. I myself left Moscow on the 14th October in a Lasalle car supplied by our Embassy, bound for Buzuluk *via* Kuibyshev.

I already wore uniform, tailored by Soviet military outfitters. General Anders took with him ten similar suits for his staff officers. I had received special passes, identity cards, and vouchers for petrol, issued by the Narkomindiel (Home Office).

released from captivity or detention in which they were wilfully kept by Soviet authorities, who occupied a part of Poland even without declaring war. Thus the "amnesty" granted by Soviet authorities to Poles deported into Russia became a shameless mockery of justice and international honesty.

It was not easy travelling by car. In spite of all we had been assured, there was a good road only as far as Gorkij (about 300 miles from Moscow); from there to Kazan, it could hardly even be called a road. Only with difficulty could the car move over the frozen mud. On the ferry over the Volga in Kazan we were detained, with our car, suspected of espionage. After they had checked up on us the guard apologised and let us proceed. We started on the road to Ulyanovsk, but after driving for about twenty miles we had to return to Kazan as the road was completely impassable. Only by using force, efficiently assisted by the N.K.V.D., did we manage to embark with our car, on the s.s. *Lomonosov*, sailing down the Volga to Kuibyshev.

Some of the travellers were Poles released from the Northern labour-camps. They were clad only in rags, their feet wrapped in clouts, and were starved and suffering from scurvy. They crowded all the landing-stages and climbed on passing boats. The stronger and luckier ones reached the decks, the weaker were left behind. About sixty were embarked on the *Lomonosov*; some of them had been travelling in stages for over a month, coming from the Polar Circle. All of them enquired about our Army and the place where she was being formed, for the Army was their one hope of escape. The Volga was only one small artery of this Polish current flowing from the North to the South. I was told the same thing was happening on the railways.

At last I reached Kuibyshev—more than 800 miles' journey from Moscow. To my amazement, I found all the Embassies there, including the Polish one. They had been evacuated by rail, and had arrived before us. The Government and President Kalinin were also in Kuibyshev; only Stalin, with the highest executives, had stayed behind in Moscow.

I stopped in Kuibyshev for several days, waiting for better weather, in order to be able to drive the remaining 125 miles to Buzuluk. There was a terrific snow-storm, and the roads were unusable. I therefore stayed in the Embassy, where we all had to sleep on the floor.

The Embassy was billeted in a small house in the town, and was continuously besieged by people needing assistance. There was a transit camp organised for them, but everyone liked to visit the Embassy, as the source of all help. But the help we could give was really insignificant, for our means were very limited. Certain people, however, were selected from this needy crowd by Ambassador Kot

General T. Bor-Kumorowski,
Commander of the Polish
Home Army, 1943-5

Polish soldiers discharged from Soviet concentration camps joining
the Polish Army in Russia, 1941-2

With the Russian liaison officers in the Polish Army in Russia, 1942

A detachment of the Polish Army in the Middle East, 1943

for preferential treatment—mostly old, active members of the Polish Peasants' Party and the Polish Socialist Party: among them Ehrlich and Alter.

The heavy snowfall would make the roads impassable for a long time. So I left the car behind in the Embassy and went by rail to Buzuluk, arriving there on the 1st November.

CHAPTER 26

The New Army

THE Polish Army H.Q. in U.S.S.R., as it was officially called, was billeted in two different parts of the town. The Staff was in a one-storeyed spacious building, which stood out prominently from a mass of wooden bungalows, while the Staff Company was billeted, in lieu of barracks, in wooden huts on the outskirts of the town. We called it the Depot. Polish flags flew proudly over both H.Q. and Depot.

Some of our officers lived in the only small hotel in the town; others were billeted in various houses. All the other ranks, orderlies, and the Staff company responsible for the protection of H.Q., were billeted in the Depot. There was also the Town Major's office and the newly-created Company of the Polish Women's Auxiliary Corps.

The Depot also acted as a centre for receiving and sheltering any volunteers arriving from prisons and labour-camps who, in spite of all the Soviet cunning, managed to get through to Buzuluk. They were retained at H.Q. or sent to one of the Divisions.

In the Depot there was perpetual chaos. The wind and the snow blew through the leaky walls; lice, brought by newcomers, jeered at the lice-killing operations carried out alongside the steam baths and the Medical Inspection Room. People slept crowded on benches made of wooden boards, in the same way as they did in prison. But in spite of the appalling conditions of life, and the insufficient food rations, all of us in Buzuluk were in good spirits. Soldiers still wore clouts instead of boots and ragged wind-jackets instead of uniforms; but they had a good military spirit. They were drilled, they attended lectures, and on Sundays they went to Holy Mass, celebrated by Father W. Cienski, our Army Dean.

Father Cienski lived in the barracks, on the communal benches—

to share the life of his flock. He refused to go to more comfortable quarters in the town, to which he was entitled as Chief Chaplain to the Army—he preferred to live and work in the Depot. He was an exceptionally brave and honest man. Formerly parish priest in St. Mary Magdalen's Church in Lwow, he had been arrested by the Bolsheviks for "counter-revolutionary activities" and sentenced to death, but was saved by the "amnesty". He was one of the first to volunteer for the new Army, and thus became Chief Chaplain to our Forces in the U.S.S.R.

From the first I had been very favourably impressed by Colonel Okulicki, whom I had known slightly before the war, and who was our Chief of Staff in Buzuluk. We became close friends.

He was an intelligent, energetic and sensible man, full of youthful energy, verve and initiative, which he had not lost during his ordeal in prison. He had been arrested in Vilna as C.O. of the "Z.W.Z." District. In that capacity he had gained considerable understanding of Soviet aims, having witnessed their realisation in his territory. While in prison he had undertaken a thorough study of Soviet literature, thus making himself acquainted with the main principles of Soviet ideology and methods; and, thanks to this, he always remained doubtful, or at least cautious, despite his enthusiastic good-will.

I noted with surprise that during our most confidential talks he used to tap the metal inkstand with his pencil, as if sending a telegram by Morse. He explained to me that it was an excellent way of jamming any microphones which might have been installed by the Bolsheviks in our offices for intercepting our talks. In any other country in the world, such a statement by the Chief of Staff of an Allied Army would be highly inadmissible; but there it only indicated suspicions which many shared.

But we never voiced these suspicions openly, for we remembered the extorted declarations to co-operate and act as informers for the N.K.V.D. Many of our officers at H.Q. from before the war were unknown to us.

One group of officers from the Griazovetz prisoner-of-war camp had been selected by the Soviet authorities to be billeted in the "Bungalow of Bliss", where they underwent a political training. We heard of the aims and syllabus of this course: they were strictly Communist and had nothing in common with Polish aims. It was there that the Bolsheviks tried to recruit and train Communist agents for Poland and other European countries.

Only the "graduates" in this course were sent as officers to General Anders when he first began to organise the Army. They were almost thrust upon him as his closest colleagues. But the General looked upon them in the same unbiased way as upon all others, without any inhibitions. He himself had been through prison life; he understood human weakness and knew how to forgive it. Even if they had erred, they should not be deprived of an opportunity of atonement and of working for our cause, which, almost miraculously, had brought so many of us back to the Colours.

Disregarding the opinion of their fellow-officers that they were "Reds" and opportunists, he gave them appointments, and collaborated with them in the same way as with the others.

The most Red group was led by Lt.-Col. Z. Berling, thrust upon us as Chief of Staff of the Division, and included Lt.-Col. Bukojemski, Major Rozen-Zawadzki and Lt. Wicherkiewicz.

Another group from the "Bungalow of Bliss", working in Army H.Q., were less active, and it was difficult to be sure whether there were any ties, and if so how deep reaching, attaching them to the N.K.V.D. Col. Gorczynski (Chief of the Engineers) and Lt.-Col. Tyszynski (Chief of the IVth Section), were members of this group.

It took a lot of Okulick's time and effort to prevent other officers in Army H.Q. from showing their hostility towards them. Perhaps their only guilt was that they had been regarded by the N.K.V.D. as worthy of training: we were not at all sure that they had been converted to the Soviet creed like Berling and his group.

Okulicki's caution was therefore prudent. The Army Commander might show generosity, but the Chief of Staff had to keep his eyes open.

A Soviet Military Mission, under Col. Wolkowyski, was attached to our H.Q. Wolkowyski was a Jew, coming from Wolkowysk in Poland. He understood Polish—maybe he could also speak it, though he would never do so. He was very polite, almost submissive, to General Anders—he was probably frightened of him. He pretended to be friendly, was very garrulous, and always tried to introduce unsavoury propaganda in conversation; we were therefore discouraged from closer contact with him. His behaviour was that of a sly fox: sometimes insolent, sometimes servile. He was not on good terms with Okulicki, as the latter had caught him out several times in lies and discreditable dealings.

General Anders had full confidence in Okulicki, and left the organisation of the Staff to him. This had the effect of increasing the authority of the Chief of Staff and resulted in better co-ordination of the work, but it also enlarged the scope of his responsibilities. So he was pleased with my appointment as his deputy.

In addition to the complicated political questions and the military organisation, the problem of the Polish civilians' welfare fell—despite the prevailing tendency in our Embassy to retain it in their own hands—on our shoulders. It necessitated the creation of a special network of Polish liaison officers in the most important centres in nearly every autonomic Soviet Republic. Various and complicated difficulties connected with it occupied much of our time and energy. Thus the Chief of Staff was overburdened and had insufficient time to organise the Staff and the Army for their principal duty—*i.e.*, to fight.

We agreed that I was to take over responsibility for purely military questions, and I became the head of Lt.-Col. Wisniowski's 3rd and Lt.-Col. Gielgud Axentowicz' 2nd Section, and we went ahead rapidly with our work.

Soon we published instructions concerning the training and work of the Field Staffs. We studied the latest war reports and the Soviet methods of work in the Staffs and in the Army, thus preparing for the imminent co-operation in the front line. We also passed over to the Committee responsible for the publication of official documents the various Soviet Army regulations for translation into Polish for the use of our troops.

It was a heavy task that we had, from the very beginning. There were no publications in Polish on these matters, so we had to provide everything ourselves; but, thanks to our strenuous efforts, we were very soon able to publish many valuable instructions.

According to the Military Agreement signed in Moscow, the strength of our Army was limited to 44,000, consisting of two Infantry Divisions, a Regimental Depot and Services, Signals and Engineers.

The 6th Division, under General Tokarzewski, was organised in Totskaya, not far from Buzuluk; and the 5th, under General Boruta Spiechowicz, in Tatishtchev. The Regimental Depot, under Col. Rakowski, was with the 6th Division in Totskaya.

On November 12th I went to Totskaya. Apart from my desire to see General Tokarzewski, whom I had last met when we were both inmates of the Dniepropietrovsk Prison, I wanted to see for myself the conditions in which our soldiers were living, and to discuss with the Divisional H.Q. various questions concerning their training.

197

I found Tokarzewski in good health and temper. He had shaved off the beard that he had worn as a "psychiatrist", and he brought his story up to date since we had parted.

Sentenced to eight years' detention, he had been sent, as a doctor, to one of the labour-camps in the North, not far from Archangel; but before very long they had discovered his identity.

It had been revealed in Moscow that Tokarzewski was in Soviet hands, but under an assumed name, unknown to them. The N.K.V.D. then procured a photograph of him, which was sent to all prisons and labour-camps, and had thus managed to identify him. He was immediately taken to Moscow, and kept in the Lubianka prison until he was freed after the "amnesty".

In Moscow the Soviets had offered to send him back to Warsaw, there to resume command of the Polish Underground Organisation against the Germans—only on condition that he agreed to keep in constant touch with Moscow, which really meant complete subordination to Moscow instead of to our Government in London. He was also required to give full information of Underground work to men thrust upon him in Moscow.

These plans did not materialise, however, because he rejected the Soviet conditions, preferring to remain in prison.

These treacherous Soviet proposals, made almost on the eve of the Sikorski-Mayski Agreement, show clearly how far-reaching were Soviet plans regarding Poland, and how opposed they were to our own aims.

Tokarzewski was right to reject the Soviet offer, although it must have been very tempting, as it would have secured him his freedom and given him a chance to work.

I then visited our soldiers of the 6th Division.

Never did I have such a shock in in my life! Certainly no other army in the world has ever been created in conditions like those of the Polish Army in the U.S.S.R.

There were various types, old and young; but they were all in rags, their feet in clouts; and they were suffering from exhaustion and scurvy—the dreadful disease of the North. They came to the Division from prisons, labour-camps, or hamlets. The women who came with them formed separate units of the Polish Women's Auxiliary Corps.

In spite of the fact that already in November the frost had reached 40° F. below zero (72° below freezing point), the Army was housed and trained only under canvas, in fields and woods.

The food was insufficient, and they were really hungry. Despite these appalling conditions, their morale was excellent. They had faith in the future, and even under these difficult circumstances of life they looked forward to the realisation of their most cherished dreams and of their personal deliverance. They were well disciplined, and tried to salute with their benumbed fingers, as if to prove their will to become soldiers.

The ingenuity of these people was amazing: there were practically no secrets for them. As protection against frost, they covered their tents with snow. They had built, almost without any tools or materials, stoves for heating. Thus life became tolerable, and even allowed for some kind of military training. Obviously, however, this was merely nominal: they could only be drilled; anything else was out of the question. We had no rifles, and no equipment for Signals, Engineers or Artillery.

Most of all, we lacked uniforms, boots and underwear. The men had no coats or blankets. All that the Soviet authorities had supplied was an insufficient number of *fufayki* (a kind of padded wind-jacket).

Soon issues of clothing were expected to be radically increased, thanks to announced supplies from Great Britain. We had already sent a detachment to the port of Archangel, there to meet and receive British transports with equipment for 100,000 soldiers. We anticipated receiving them for our units early in December.

In the meantime there was a struggle going on against debilitation, and against the deadly frost and the lice; briefly, a struggle for life. Only by being victorious in this strife could we think of creating a real Army.

I left the Division full of admiration for its very high morale, but definitely worried, and wondering if, under such conditions of life, we could possibly produce real soldiers fit to fight.

I did not visit the 5th Infantry Division, in Tatishtchev; but I had reason to believe that the situation there was similar to that described above—perhaps even worse, because there the wood was further from the tents than in Totskaya, and therefore they had fewer logs for heating, and must be paralysed by frost. However, there they had received their equipment, and could thus train their soldiers properly. Maybe they owed this advantage to Berling's presence.

CHAPTER 27

Tricked

IN SPITE OF our goodwill, certain facts increased our vigilance. The first was the incident of the hidden microphones. It proved that Okulicki was right to tap the metal inkstand with his pencil while discussing confidential matters.

In several places in our H.Q. our experts found microphones installed for the interception of private talks. For instance, one ingeniously-fitted microphone was found in General Anders' room in the ventilator above his desk. The wires led to a room in the basement which was not occupied by us because, allegedly, the Town's records were kept there as no other place could be found for them.

Instead of records, the telephone exchange had amplifiers for the interception of our talks. We disconnected the microphones, and General Anders hid them in the drawer of his desk. Then he asked Col. Wolkowyski for an interview, in the presence of Okulicki and me.

After we had discussed various questions, the General took the incriminating microphones from his drawer and smilingly handed them over to Wolkowyski. He said, jokingly, that his Staff had found these innocent toys—one even in his own room. He apologised for having taken them down, and wished to return them to their rightful owners. He averred that he was not annoyed: he could well understand the need for caution. But he could assure Wolkowyski that we had nothing to conceal; our approach to the co-operation and organisation of our Army was quite sincere, and Wolkowyski could obtain any information he required by asking us directly without having recourse to any such subterfuges.

Wolkowyski reacted instantly. He said there must be a tragic misunderstanding somewhere, which had nothing to do with him, and our assumption was a direct offence to the Soviet authorities. He thanked us for having discovered the microphones; he would immediately report to Moscow about the incident and ask for an enquiry to be made, to establish how the instruments had found their way into the H.Q. building.

Indeed, the Court of Enquiry came from Moscow three days afterwards. After making a "thorough investigation", they communicated their findings to General Anders.

It was "irrefutably" established that the net of microphones dated from old—probably Revolutionary—times; they had never been used since, and had only through carelessness been left in the building handed over to us. The Court of Enquiry was most apologetic, and assured the General that the culprits would be severely punished.

We had to accept it at its face value because of the annoyance already caused to the Soviet authorities. Thus the incident was closed and normal relations were again established between us and Wolkowyski. Nevertheless, this incident aroused our suspicions, and drew our attention to the cunning Asiatic methods of our Ally.

The second question which worried us was our military establishment.

During the Moscow talks it had been agreed that because of the unification of equipment, etc., our divisions would be organised according to the war establishments of the Soviet divisions.

Having assumed my duties, I went through our establishments and found that they were ludicrous. They were below our standards of 1919–20, and not by any means up to date. The equipment allocated to Signals, for instance, was sufficient to serve only one Battalion in the front line. The same applied to Records and to the Ordnance Corps.

We came to the conclusion that we had been blatantly cheated. It was inconceivable that such could possibly be the establishment for a Soviet Infantry Division in war-time. It must be very different for fighting units.

Having made this discovery, we immediately reported it. We were put off, however, and Wolkowyski maintained stubbornly that our establishment was accurately copied from the actual Soviet one. At the same time we were requested to reach our fighting preparedness as soon as possible!

Thus we could only conclude that the Soviet authorities were against our divisions becoming fighting units; they were probably necessary to them for political or propaganda purposes, but not for military ones. They desired to use us as submissive tools, deprived of our will, solely for the realisation of their aims and completely disregarding our interests.

General Anders, having reached the conclusion that it was possible to increase the numbers of our Army beyond the limit of 44,000, as agreed in Moscow, immediately applied for permission to do so, but was met with a blunt refusal. We had understood that the agreed figure was only a tentative one, because at that time nobody had reliable information about the numbers of available Poles. To us it seemed obvious that once we had more men at our disposal, we could increase our numbers until all potential recruits were absorbed. We aimed at the creation of a Polish-Allied Army at its full capacity, and not at an arbitrary limit.

This refusal put us in a very difficult position. We had already transgressed the ceiling of 44,000, and, meanwhile, new volunteers, for whom we had neither lodgings nor food, were arriving daily.

The Soviet authorities then issued secret instructions to the railway stations on the Buzuluk line that newcomers should bypass our encampments and be directed South. Therefore transports of those poor wretches passed Buzuluk and overflowed the Uzbek, Tadzhik and Turkmen S.S. Republics. There they expected to join our Army; instead, they were distributed by force in *Kolchoz* farms and compelled to work in the vast spaces between the Tibetan border and the Caspian Sea.

Transports of people sent from Farabu along the river Amu Darya to the marshy area of Nukus in the Turkmen S.S. Republic were most affected by this deception: they underwent harrowing experiences when their barges were pulled by tugs for several hundred miles and they were then disembarked in a desert, completely cut off from the world and civilisation.

Every day we received telegrams full of despair from those who looked after the transports—from Farabu, Samarkand, Fergana, and Alma-Ata—most of them phrased in some such terms as:—
"*We have been disembarked and directed to 'Kolchozes' instead of joining the Army. People are dying of starvation. We have no food. Women and children are with us. We refuse to disembark. We beg help.*"

We requested that food should be issued to them; but we also advised them to follow the orders issued by the local authorities. What else could we do? We were helpless, and had to watch our potential soldiers being wasted in this way.

These facts convinced us even more strongly that the Soviet authorities were counteracting our recruitment and the organisation of our Army. Other signs pointed to this, too. We found that the clause about the "amnesty" had in many cases been disregarded. From time to time, officers from various prisons and labour-camps came to Buzuluk with lists of their colleagues whom the Soviet authorities would not release.

First we attributed this to local disorders, especially as immediate personal intervention by General Anders always bore positive results. Later on, we decided that the Soviet tactics were the result of deliberate policy, since they were mostly applied to *young* officers. They aimed at depriving us of the officers so sorely needed!

We were seriously disturbed by the fact that no officer from prisoner-of-war camps in Starobielsk, Kozielsk and Ostaszkow reported to us. General Anders, anxious to find out more about them, instructed Capt. J. Czapski to compile lists of these officers and to examine all who had arrived, or were still arriving, to find out if they had met (in prisons or labour-camps or in transit) any of the officers on these lists. But all our efforts to trace them remained futile.

Our Soviet Liaison officers, headed by Wolkowyski, hinted to us that they were probably kept in camps in the Far North, so we might expect their arrival only late in the spring of the following year, as in winter there was no communication with these areas. Faint hope, therefore, still glimmered that one day we should see them.*

Capt. Czapski conscientiously compiled his lists of the missing officers, and the General requested copies to show personally to Stalin so as to prompt his intervention.

About mid-November, 1941, we were notified that General Sikorski intended to visit Russia, to inspect our Army and to have talks with Stalin. We were greatly pleased with this news: every soldier wanted to see his C.-in-C., whose name had become for the ex-prisoners the symbol of all the ideals for which he had suffered so much. So there was a great deal of exaltation, understandable after the ordeal suffered and the almost miraculous rescue.

With this emotional and joyful approach, we, in H.Q., also linked some practical expectations with Sikorski's visit.

The situation was becoming unbearable; it called for radical

* Later, their bodies were discovered in the Katyn Forest. We can assume that this monstrous murder was prompted by a desire to deprive the future Polish Army of her framework. This possibility had probably been envisaged in 1940 in the far-reaching plans and provisions of the Politbureau.

change, and this we hoped for as a result of the General's arrival in Russia and his personal talks with Stalin.

Tricks like secret microphone fittings could be endured; but the recent new and unexpected request directed by Vyshinski to our Ambassador Kot—that the strength of our forces be forthwith reduced to 30,000—was directly menacing our very existence. Not only had they refused to increase the strength of our Army beyond 44,000—which had, in fact, already happened—but they now insisted on reducing it to 30,000. This demand simply could not be acceded to by us. We had no way of releasing the surplus 14,000, and it was definitely contrary to the London Agreement, which stipulated that we were to use all available human resources for the creation of an army as strong as possible.

By then we had sufficient proof that we could recruit 300,000–400,000 men, and we wanted them all—not just a fraction of them.

We arrived at this figure as follows: We reckoned the number of civilians who had been deported from Poland in 1939–40 to be 1,500,000. To this figure we had to add several hundred thousand prisoners of war and men recruited by the Soviet authorities from Polish territory for the "Stroy-battalions" (Pioneer Corps). Even assuming that a high percentage of these men had died in labour-camps from starvation, the computed figure of 300,000–400,000 men able to join the Army seemed to be completely justified.

Under these circumstances, the request to reduce the strength of our Army and the threat to cut down our food allocation looked like a tragic misunderstanding. It seemed a hopeless *impasse*, from which we could find an outlet only by a vehement shock liable to occur during a personal meeting between Sikorski and Stalin.

It was to our advantage that Sikorski arrived in Moscow not only as Polish Prime Minister and C.-in-C., but also as a representative of our Western Allies.

The following demands were included in the agenda of the Sikorski-Stalin talks in the Kremlin:—

—the immediate release of all Poles still kept in prisons and labour camps;
—the increase of our Army to its full capacity, including the Poles recruited illegally by the Soviets and incorporated into the Soviet "Stroy-battalions";
—the transfer of the Polish Army to the South, giving it better living accommodation and thus ensuring the most rapid

training to a state of military preparedness, which, while living under canvas in a temperature of 75° F. below zero, was quite impossible;
—consent to despatch immediately 15,000–20,000 soldiers from the Polish Army in U.S.S.R. to Great Britain, there to increase our Air Force and Navy.

In the latter part of November, General Anders flew to Teheran, in Iran, there to meet General Sikorski. With him he took a memorandum prepared for the General by our H.Q., outlining all the acts of ill-will displayed by our hosts.

Three unquestionable conclusions were drawn:—

1. That the Soviet Union was unwilling to carry out the Polish-Soviet Military Agreement, or else intended to carry it out in a different way to that previously agreed on and serving its own—to us unknown—aims.

2. That the Polish military authorities were completely cognizant of this situation, and there was no danger that they would be used unwillingly as a tool for an alien policy.

3. That only a decisive move at highest level could safeguard the existence of a strong and sovereign Polish Army in the U.S.S.R.

I thought that the second conclusion, proving our sober and clear-sighted appreciation of the situation, was the most essential, for it meant that one could be sure we would never give way to the impostors or fall into their trap.

The third conclusion was highly tragic. After two and a half months' lasting attempt at co-operation, things had come to the point that the problem of the very existence and sovereignty of the Polish Army depended on a hair's-breadth, and required great effort at the highest level to save it. How fragile, after all, were the principles of our mutual co-operation!

It was agreed that General Sikorski should first go to Kuibyshev to our Embassy, then on to Moscow, and, after his talks with Stalin, should inspect our Army, visiting Buzuluk, Totskaya and Tatishtchev.

Immediately after General Anders' departure for Teheran, Okulicki left for Kuibyshev, so as to be at hand there if additional excuses or explanations were required. I myself was left in Buzuluk, with the task of organising a worthy reception for our honoured guest. I had to prepare a time-table of official meetings and inspections and a plan of festivities in honour of the Prime Minister and C.-in-C.

On the 3rd December, after talks with Stalin in the Kremlin, an agreed statement was issued. General Anders took part in all the talks with General Sikorski in the Kremlin.

Anyone can easily understand our impatience to hear the result of these talks, and Okulicki had to inform me immediately. They were unexpectedly good—almost too good to be true.

Stalin took into consideration all our claims:—

1. He agreed to release from prisons and labour-camps all who were still retained there.
2. He agreed to allow the strength of our Army to be 100,000, increasing accordingly the number of our Divisions.
3. He agreed to transfer our Army to the South to Central Asia to better climatic conditions.
4. He did not oppose the evacuation to Great Britain of reserves for strengthening our Air Force and Navy.

But the enigma as to what had happened to the 14,000 officers previously detained in the P.O.W. camps in Starobielsk, Kozielsk and Ostaszkov had not been solved.

Stalin, when pinned down, suggested the possibility of their escape to Manchukuo, and made a gesture with his hands expressing his bewilderment to explain.

Obviously, after such excellent news, the world seemed to us brighter, and we looked forward enthusiastically to greeting our C.-in-C.

We had arranged a big public meeting in Buzuluk, during which a private soldier was to greet General Sikorski, not only as the Polish Prime Minister, but as the man who had saved him from death and enabled him to continue in the fight for liberty.

We prepared a reception in our H.Q. officers' mess for about 150 guests. Besides officers from our H.Q., we had invited the top-ranking Soviet military and political authorities.

In the Divisions, we laid stress on the parades and the march-past and on personal contact of General Sikorski with the men.

General Sikorski arrived in Buzuluk on 10th December, 1941, accompanied by Vyshinski, then Deputy Foreign Commissar, and by our Ambassador Kot. With them there also came from London General Klimecki (Chief of the General Staff), Lt.-Col. Protasewicz, Dr. J. Rettinger, and Major Cazalet, M.P.

I had seen General Sikorski for the last time several years ago: he now appeared to have matured, to be full of authority and majesty; his eyes, especially, had acquired an unusual expression. He won my liking easily, finding time for a long talk with me, when I had to tell him everything about our Underground activities in Poland, my experiences in prisons, and my opinion about actual events.

He thanked me on behalf of our country for my work till now, and presented me with a gold watch, appropriately engraved. He told me he had already signed my promotion to full Colonel. This proof of memory and thoughtfulness was, of course, most gratifying to me.

The official reception to General Sikorski went off smoothly. There were a few very moving moments, some amusing incidents, and, as usually happens, a few unpleasant ones, too.

The public meeting in Buzuluk was moving, especially when Mrs. Domanska, an actress from the Vilna theatre, a courier in the Underground, a Soviet prisoner, and finally a Polish A.T.S. in the U.S.S.R., recited a poem written for General Sikorski already in a Soviet prison, by another prisoner, who afterwards became a soldier (A.T.S. Biesiadecka). The poem was very expressive—probably because it was composed almost in the other world, by the half-starved inmate of a labour-camp. It expressed all the emotions we had gone through, and showed what General Sikorski's name meant to prisoners and deportees. And it was proof that Polish patriotism was still alive. To listen to this poem at a time when the prophecies contained in it had already come to pass, and in the presence of the person to whom it was addressed, was most moving.

If Sikorski had been annoyed by the political friction after the signing of the Agreement on 30th July, 1941, I think that this moment must have recompensed him. Manifestly deeply moved, he shook hands cordially with the author, Biesiadecka, and the reader, Domanska.

Direct contacts between General Sikorski with the soldiers in Totskaya and Tatishtchev, the parades and march-past of these strange troops, were also very affecting.

Among the strange events at this time I must put General Sikorski's impression of the dinner-party in Buzuluk. General Klimecki told me about it afterwards. He and Sikorski had been rather shocked by the applause with which our officers greeted Vyshinski's speech, which, though ostensibly about Panslavism and its historical value, was really a badly-camouflaged challenge for us to realise Soviet political aims, disregarding Polish interests and traditions. Then Col. Svoboda, the C.O. of the Czech Forces in the U.S.S.R., who servilely supported and enthusiastically developed Vyshinski's ideas, met with similar applause, much to Sikorski's distress.

I reassured Klimecki: our officers on such an occasion would applaud even the Devil! In this country, applause did not mean anything: every speaker was applauded—it was the custom. Any audience in the U.S.S.R. was used to being vulgarly subjected to Soviet propaganda by the speaker, who would obviously be a member of the Communist Party; they also knew well that many N.K.V.D. agents attended the meeting, and that was the chief reason for applause. This behaviour had already got into the blood; people soon learned to cheer without blushing. Our officers were still only half awake, intoxicated by their comparative freedom—no wonder they applauded, even if without conviction.

It was difficult for Klimecki to understand the logic of my explanation, and I was not surprised; I realised how puzzling it must be for a person of Western mentality to comprehend the situation in Russia at all.

General Sikorski spent a few days with the Polish Army in the U.S.S.R., and then he left by air from Tatishtchev for Teheran and London.

We decided that this inspection had had positive results. First of all, a sense of unification in the Polish Army had been given to both officers and men. The soldier who had met his C.-in-C. better understood that his companions in arms were fighting in Tobruk, in ships that flew the Polish flag, or in the air, and that he was a member of the same family, bound together by the same oath of allegiance, aims and duties, although separated by such great distances.

This recollection was timely, because the troops did not always know about the achievements of their colleagues on other fronts; and it was all the more needed when life was supervised by Soviet Russia.

The visit to the Kremlin led us out of the *impasse* reached, and opened up again, as we thought, new possibilities for our already dwindling activities. With reaffirmed faith, we progressed towards the building-up of our Army.

CHAPTER 28

Visitors from the Past

ONE DAY in November, through Wolkowyski we got news from Moscow that in the front line, near Orel or Tula, three suspected individuals, calling themselves Polish Army officers and couriers from the Polish Underground to General Anders, had been seized. The Soviet authorities asked us immediately to send the head of our Intelligence Service to Moscow to identify them, and expressed their willingness to pass them over to us if we could establish, without any doubt, that they were not spies. The circumstances of their capture had aroused suspicions that they were in contact with the German Intelligence Service.

The whole story looked very suspicious.

Major Bakiewicz immediately left by air for Moscow. At the same time we sent a wireless message to London asking if "Grot" (meaning General Rowecki), had despatched any couriers to us.

From London we received a negative answer.

After several days, Bakiewicz returned with the three suspects, and a Soviet request that General Anders would deal with them as he thought fit.

This suggestion, in view of the facts which had prompted it, looked like an attempt to catch us out in a slip!

The story was as follows.

In Moscow, Bakiewicz had, first of all, been shown different objects found on the detained men. He was assured that these objects had not been examined by the N.K.V.D. Bakiewicz considered this most unlikely; nevertheless, he pretended to believe it, and went forward with their examination.

Among other things, they included a piece of shaving-soap, used as a hiding place. When he cautiously cut it in two, he discovered a microfilm which was, to his amazement, already developed. It is against general practice ever to send out secret mail in this way; such a film would be despatched undeveloped, because if captured by unauthorised persons it would automatically be spoiled by exposure to the light. It was obvious, therefore, that the film had been developed by somebody before it had been handed over to Bakiewicz, and only the N.K.V.D. could have done this.

He was greatly alarmed when he read the message on the film and realised that the N.K.V.D. must have read it too. The note was terribly incriminating: it was a letter from Witkowski, the head of the "Musketeers", whom I knew, to General Anders, asking him to attack the rear of the Bolshevik armies when sent to the German front. There was a postscript containing the words *"Greetings for Klimek from Inia"*. Obviously Bakiewicz could not understand this: he had never heard of the "Musketeers": he did not know their rôle in the Polish Underground, nor their relations with the "Z.W.Z."; neither did he know who "Klimek" and "Inia" were.

In spite of the incomprehensible message, all the couriers undoubtedly were Polish officers, who really had come from Warsaw, and they seemed to be brave men, expecting rather to be praised than punished for crossing two front lines. In this confused and bewildering situation, Bakiewicz thought it advisable to transfer further investigations to Buzuluk. The Soviet authorities agreed to this and Bakiewicz returned by air with the three officers and all the material collected from them.

We had no doubt but that the Soviet authorities had agreed to hand them over to us only to ascertain what our reaction would be and thus put us to a severe test. Should we declare that everything was all right, it would mean that we agreed with the message and were in contact with the German Intelligence Service; otherwise, we must shoot the couriers as German spies. The situation was very grave, and investigations were carried out under General Anders' personal supervision.

It soon became apparent that the whole story was unimportant: it was not pro-German espionage; it was simply one of the incalculable and irresponsible ideas of Witkowski and his insane ambitions. I knew Witkowski so well that I could easily understand that the only purpose of this exploit was to appear to be a perfect conspirator, able to send couriers deep into Russia across two front lines. He would not hesitate for his purpose to avail himself of the assistance of the Gestapo. For this reason he adopted the subterfuge of writing his message asking us to join the German side. This was no more than a pretext for reaching the front line near Tula.

The couriers were to explain everything orally to us, their real task being to inform us about the feeling and the situation in Poland. The "postscript" was supposed to be their password. Witkowski knew that I had already joined the Army H.Q. and was confident that I would vouch for his loyalty. "Klimek" was the diminutive of my Christian name and "Inia" was Mrs. Mankowska, from Winogora—but only I knew it. The "postscript" was really a message to me in code, meaning:

Col. Rudnicki, tell General Anders that the couriers are trustworthy. Although they were assisted by the Gestapo, they are not spies; it was only a subterfuge.

This incident might be looked upon as a romantic episode, adding splendour to unusual exploits; but it caused considerable trouble for us in our situation while forming an Army: we needed the full confidence of our hosts, so that any suspicion that we were collaborating with the enemy could not be tolerated.

Witkowski was responsible for this criminal indiscretion, committed because of his insane megalomania or through sheer stupidity. For this purpose he abused the confidence of his couriers—honest and brave men acting on his behalf in perfect faith.

We could not find any other way out of this *impasse* other than declaring that the three officers had apparently collaborated with the Gestapo and must therefore be court-martialled.

During the hearing of the case, in the presence of Soviet observers, two of the officers were acquitted, because they were definitely carrying out their orders blindly without initiative. The third, Capt. Zaremba (a pseudonym), who was in command, was found guilty of collaboration with the enemy and sentenced to twenty-five years' detention. However, he was not handed over to the Soviet authorities for the execution of the sentence, but was retained under our own detention.

This solution was accepted by the N.K.V.D. without further comment, and thus this insignificant but disturbing incident was closed.

Another very worrying incident concerned Prof. Leo Kozlowski, a former Polish Prime Minister.

He had been arrested in the autumn of 1939, immediately after the Bolsheviks had entered Lwow, where he was professor of prehistory in the King John Casimir University. As a personality known in Polish politics from the pre-war Pilsudskist *régime*, Kozlowski had been detailed in the Lubianka prison in Moscow, and had been through a terrifying interrogation. He was accused of being "an enemy of the working class", and threatened with the death sentence. But he had eventually been liberated, not so much by reason of the "amnesty" of 1941, which the Soviet authorities refused to apply in his case, as by the personal intervention of General Anders.

Since Ambassador Kot would not assist a member of the pre-war Governmental Party, whom he personally hated, General Anders, prompted by purely human feelings, incorporated Kozlowski into the Army as a lieutenant (his previous rank) and gave him an appointment in one of the Army H.Q. offices.

Thus Kozlowski came to Buzuluk. He soon caused a compromising incident, which might have had serious repercussions.

One day in mid-November he disappeared from Buzuluk. The Soviet Intelligence Service found out that he had crossed the front line near Tula and given himself up to the Germans. The Soviet report was soon confirmed by a German *communiqué* from Warsaw and Berlin, giving the details of a Press conference with Kozlowski.

This incident caused a great deal of trouble. General Anders and our Army were suspected of disloyalty to the agreed co-operation, involving an act unbecoming to Allied honesty during the war. The very fact that this man had been released from prison, in spite of Soviet misgivings, solely because of General Anders' guaranteeing him, indicated apparently that we were playing a double game. His escape, also, was very puzzling: anyone might think that he had been sent, with our help, as a special courier to Germany. As a consequence, our hosts might get the impression that there was some kind of political co-operation between us and the Germans, especially viewed in conjunction with the incident with Capt. Zaremba and the "Musketeers".

These episodes occurred at the worst possible time for us—just when we were struggling for the very existence of our Army and an increase in its strength, and when sincere relations with the Soviet authorities were so essential. The incidents, in view of the well-known suspiciousness of the Soviets, cast deep suspicion on General Anders' sincere statements about our good faith and soldierly honesty. They definitely harmed us, though they had happened against our will and conviction, for the arrival of the three couriers and the departure of Kozlowski were both examples of individual exploits, completely out of step with our policy.

In order to prove this, Kozlowski was charged, similarly to Zarem-

212

ba, with desertion from the Army and joining the enemy during the war, and was sentenced by court-martial, in his absence, to death. The sentence was passed to our Government in London, with a request for its transmission to our Underground authorities in Poland for execution. I think that this soothed the feelings of the Soviet authorities.

One day in December, news reached Buzuluk which revived in me memories of the Lancers from Malopolska, which had seemed almost obliterated by my recent experiences.

This news came in a letter written by the wives of several officers and N.C.O's in Aya-Guz, near Semipalatinsk, in the Kazak S.S. Republic. They had all been dragged there in the spring of 1940 from Trembowla, when the Bolsheviks began to clear the town from "rotting elements". The letter told of their misery, and expressed tremendous joy that they had discovered me: "Now we know we shall not get lost."

Among them were the wives of Capt. Ksyk with their six-years'-old boy; of Capt. Zahorski with their boy; and of the late Capt. Poborowski with a little daughter. The wife of Capt. A. Bielecki had been with them but had died of starvation, leaving behind two little sons under Our Lord's protection. There was also the wife of my pre-war second-in-command, Lt.-Col. Golaszewski, with their son and her sister; the wife of Capt. A. Rogawski, another old 9th Lancers officer; and many more. And there were the wives of many N.C.O's: Tyblewski, Sobol, Ostafin, Maznas, and many others.

Apparently somewhere in Heaven it was noted in the appropriate files concerned with the welfare of the 9th Lancers that, even if the husbands were imprisoned in German Oflags, their wives must get proper assistance. Needless to say, I sent them help, and told them that we would soon bring them to our camp once we had moved South.

A new breeze from Trembowla, Podolia, had blown in upon me! The Regiment and all the hours of our Warsaw tragedy vividly returned to my mind.

Then, one day I got a letter from Sister Lauretta, the Convent gate-keeper who was so fond of loud bangs, and I almost smelt Jazlowiec, and poignant memories flooded my consciousness.

Also some of my fellow inmates from Soviet prisons came to Buzuluk: the honest Wozniakowski, Kicinski, the brothers Janus-zkiewicz and Hykiel, Bukowinski, Olek Iwanow, and others. One day I spotted Siedlecki, cutting wood in the yard of H.Q. He was terribly emaciated, but talkative and resolute, as usual. I asked him to become my batman; but only on condition that he must promise never again—even for "patriotic reasons"—to steal bread from his neighbours!

"Oh, my God, Mr. Ruminski!" (Siedlecki could not collect his wits when he heard I was not a shop assistant, only a Colonel.) "Is it possible that it's really you! Although I always thought that you weren't who you said you were. Now we never shall part again," he said. And so it was.

He was a decent lad, and had many good qualities; above all, he was an excellent cook and could always provide some eatable food! But in spite of better feeding, he did not recover his health after the appalling conditions of life in labour-camps on the Petsera river; he coughed perpetually, and used to say: "Something is wrong in my inside."

I appointed as my A.D.C. another starveling from a labour-camp, Lt. Casimir Godlewski, a reserve officer from the 8th Lancers. His pre-war weight had been over 18 stone, but by now he could probably have gone through the Biblical eye of a needle, although he was as healthy as an ox and had an appetite like a wolf. He got on very well with Siedlecki.

CHAPTER 29

To Central Asia

IN THE last days of December, 1941, orders came from Moscow regarding our Army's move to the South, in conformity with the agreement reached between Sikorski and Stalin. We were to go to the Central Asiatic military district called "SAWO", whose H.Q. was in Tashkent, the metropolis of the Uzbek S.S.R.

This military district comprised the Uzbek, Tadzhik, Turkmen and Kirgiz S.S.R's, its southern boundaries being the Iranian, Afghan and Indian frontiers, and its eastern boundary the Chinese. Very exotic, indeed!

The disposition of our old and new divisions had to be decided by the C.O. of the SAWO, after the arrival in Tashkent of the advance echelon of our Army H.Q., with a representative endowed with full powers. I had been appointed by General Anders as this representative.

Far-reaching powers were given me, laid down in written documents; also a Staff, consisting of members of all sections, inclusive of the services, and a powerful wireless transmitter for keeping in contact with Buzuluk, about 1,800 miles away from Tashkent. I was to:

—negotiate with SAWO on the disposition of our existing divisions and the ones to be newly formed;
—discuss with SAWO the expansion of our Forces to seven Infantry Divisions, with the necessary Services and Army Units;
—discuss with SAWO and agree upon all other questions which might arise on the spot in connection with the disposition and growth of the Polish Army.

My advance H.Q. Echelon was ordered to leave in the first days of

January, 1942. The transfer of troops had to be carried out during the months of February, March and April, by rail, along the only existing line *via* Aktyubinsk, Aralsk and Dzhambul.

Meanwhile, however, the only indications on the Soviet side of adherence to the new agreement were the issuing of orders regarding our move and the stopping of previously announced reductions in our food rations.

The question of the return of Poles recruited into the "Stroy-battalions" was still only a promise; we were told it would be done later on. All the battalions had to be found and their nominal-rolls checked, as all the men were mixed up. When, by chance, we found one such battalion in the vicinity of our 6th Division in Totskaya and requested their return, giving the names of our men, we met with refusal, and the battalion was transferred to an unknown destination. Only about a dozen soldiers from this battalion managed to desert and find shelter in the ranks of the 6th Division. They did not even disclose their late whereabouts to their commander, who, according to agreements, was bound to return them.

The release from prisons and labour-camps, in conformity with the clauses of the "amnesty", did not improve. We constantly found many detained people, by mere chance. Only by telegrams signed by General Anders, addressed to the district N.K.V.D. authorities, did we manage to secure the release of these poor people; and we were well aware that we only touched about one per cent of these detainees, who were still serving their sentences. And still no officers reported to us from the P.O.W. camps in Starobielsk, Kozielsk and Ostaszkov.

Despite these unfavourable symptoms, our hopes for a better future were high. The agreement to expand our Army, in improved conditions of life, left all other drawbacks in the shade. We still believed that our co-operation might stand a chance of success. Perhaps Stalin now saw the situation more clearly, or had been convinced by Sikorski? Perhaps the still-existing omissions were due to the immense distances hampering everything in this country? Perhaps this also affected the change in the Russian attitude towards us?

We went to Central Asia in good spirits, leaving Buzuluk immediately after the New Year. There was a hard, biting frost—about 72° F. below zero.

Having passed the Aral Sea, the railway-line followed the valley of the Syr Darya. At last the snow disappeared, and then all we could see, as far as the eye could reach, was the vast Kazak Steppe, covered with thistles and dried grass.

Later on, somewhere near the Turkmen S.S.R., we plunged into spring. In wayside stations we were able to buy water melons, a piece of goat's milk cheese, or a cupful of mare's milk, sold by bare-footed and half-naked children. But most of the time we were surrounded by an immense desert plain. Only a keen eye could some-times spot the outlines of low, square, clay boxes, which mingled in with the yellowish-grey landscape—a perfect example of camouflage! Half-naked, dirty, and almost wild figures crept out of these mud huts to the stations, standing about in isolation, or, if they were *Kolchozes* (co-operative farms), in groups. They did not speak Russian: they begged for bread in a strange guttural language—a true picture of Eastern misery.

Several times in these wayside stations our train picked up some of our compatriots, hardly alive and swollen by starvation, who had been left behind by transports going from the northern labour-camps to the south. They had perhaps alighted to buy food and the train had left them behind, or they had had no more strength to continue the journey.

At last, on the tenth day, we reached Tashkent.

I immediately contacted the SAWO and called upon General Lipatov, second-in-command to the District Commander. I asked for billets for our Army H.Q. and for the appointment of officers with whom I could discuss the disposition of the Army and also recruitment.

I was informed that unfortunately SAWO had not received any detailed instructions from Moscow regarding the Polish Army, apart from the intimation that we were arriving. SAWO could not hold any discussions with us before the receipt of appropriate instructions! They were just preparing billets for our Army H.Q., and probably in a few days' time they might be able to give me more information.

I insisted on the right to be consulted about the choice of H.Q., as I knew best what we needed; but I was told the place had already been chosen, but they could not show it to me before the District Commander had approved it; however, I must not get worried about it—it would be done in two or three days. In the meantime, they advised me to remain in the train.

The answer seemed reasonable, especially as SAWO had probably been taken by surprise by the decision to transfer the Polish Army to their district, and had had no time to prepare plans for its disposition.

I took advantage of the enforced delay to establish contact with the Polish Delegate's office in Tashkent, who, on behalf of our

217

Embassy, organised the welfare of Polish civilians. Mr. J. Kwapinski was the Delegate, and Mr. J. Kazmierczak, appointed by our H.Q. in Buzuluk to deal with military questions, was his deputy. They gave me an outline of the situation—which was tragic.

Tens of thousands—or perhaps even more—of Polish deportees and ex-prisoners, with their families, peopled this area. The Delegate had only a vague notion of the numbers, or of where they were kept. In spite of the fact that there was no room for more people, masses were still arriving, camping for weeks in the streets of Tashkent, Samarkand, or Bukhara, until they were sent by Soviet authorities as workers to *Kolchozes* (co-operative farms) or *Sovchozes* (nationalised farms). They lived in appalling conditions of misery, decimated by typhus and other illnesses. The same situation existed in localities to which they were directed, as the whole country was starving.

Formerly, the Central Asiatic area was renowned for its rich agricultural production, especially of rice. Now, according to the requirements of the planned economy, it was forbidden to cultivate crops, as emphasis was laid upon the production of cotton, and corn was imported, theoretically, from other parts of the Soviet Union. However, because of transport difficulties and war requirements for corn, which was directed to other, more important, destinations, the Central Asiatic Republics were almost starved The people primarily affected were the native rural population—*i.e.* the *Kolchoz* workers on cotton farms—as nobody cared for them. And our people were just pushed into these same areas!

Recently, new instructions adapted to war requirements had been issued, ordering the reintroduction of the rotation of rice. This meant that malaria would inevitably spread again, for the irrigated rice fields made excellent breeding-grounds for malarial mosquitoes. Theoretically, improvement could be achieved only after one year. provided that the necessary seeds, implements, fertilisers, etc., were supplied in time.

All this aroused some doubts in me as to whether our optimism, encouraged by the transfer of our Army to the South, was justified. But both Kwapinski and Kazmierczak agreed that the arrival of our Army in this area would be a godsend to the civil Polish population. All those fit to join the Army would find shelter in our ranks, and their families could gather round our garrisons and live under their protection.

After leaving the Polish Delegate's office, I visited the town. It covered a wide area but was rather dreary. Mostly there were low wooden bungalows, with some ordinary town houses. There were only a few shops, all of them typical Soviet-nationalised co-operative ones. Everywhere one could discern misery and destitution.

In one part of the town there were several modern blocks, probably offices, but they did not improve the general view. This part of the town looked as if it had been modernised by force, lacking as it did any of the beauty of Asiatic folklore or architecture, and presenting a colourless suburban appearance.

The Uzbek part of the town had probably once been beautiful, but now it was in ruins. Dilapidated houses, with Eastern arches and canopies, courtyards with mulberry, almond or bread-fruit trees, and half-demolished mosques decorated with a few blue enamelled tiles, bore witness to the old culture.

Many street vendors sold *shashlyk* (mutton cooked on iron grills and dripping with fat), *uruk* (small fruit similar to olives) and *kysh-mysh* (raisins and walnuts). There was Eastern mobility and noise. Little donkeys passed, succumbing under the heavy weight of their freight or their riders; and sometimes a small caravan of camels, attached one to another by strings and heavily loaded with cotton. The streets were narrow—one could hardly move in them; along them were many *cafés* serving green tea or coffee, where one could sit on worn mats.

It was the East, but not the ancient East, where, alongside misery, one could have seen splendour and riches.

During my wanderings in the ancient part of the town, I met an old Uzbek dentist. When he realised that I was a Pole and not Soviet Russian, he invited me to his room and told me about his country and its slavery. He spoke about the last Uzbek rising, in 1924, and about the bloody "pacification" performed by Budionnyj, in which all the old mosques, dating from Tamerlaine's times, and other national monuments were destroyed. In its place, the new Soviet way of life was inculcated, utterly alien to local traditions.

He believed that the Uzbeks would one day recover their freedom, and hoped that this war would bring it about. He was surprised that we Poles were going to help the Bolsheviks to fight against the Germans, instead of the reverse: he ascribed it to our peculiarly different political situation. Surprised that he was so outspoken, I asked whether he was not afraid to talk so freely; but he said he knew to whom he was talking, as he knew Polish history and could trust us. Polish traditions were vivid to him because they were connected with the golden age of Uzbek history under the reign of the Gengis Khan dynasty. He certainly knew far more about Poland than I did about Uzbekistan.

His national pride was enthusiastically expressed, and he fervently believed that soon freedom would come to his country.

This was the first time in the Soviet Union that I had met views expressed in such a way. Perhaps it was due to the fact that for the first time we were outside the national limits of Russia. It was a new and interesting discovery within the "voluntary and spontaneous Union of Republics".

On the third day, Major Kireyev, the Soviet liaison officer, brought me news from SAWO that the District Commander had agreed to the proposed site for our H.Q. in Yanghi Yul, about six miles from Tashkent; but I could not go and see the allocated buildings for a few days yet, because they were now being redecorated and they could not be handed over to us before completion of the work.

"Why not? Why shouldn't I see them now?" I enquired of Kireyev.

"No," he said firmly; "the building is guarded and cannot be shown earlier." Kireyev explained to me: "SAWO prefers that the site should impress you favourably. At present, on account of the mess made by the builders, it would not do so."

My opinion differed: I was sure they were installing a network of microphones for the interception of our talks, and I should therefore be an inopportune witness.

Three days later I was taken to see Yanghi Yul, shown to me by SAWO's chief engineer. They were still working there, but probably the work that had to be done secretly was now finished.

I liked the buildings and the surroundings. It was a two-storeyed agricultural school—a "polytechnic", as my informant explained—situated in the middle of a beautiful orchard on a small river. Not far away was a large bungalow, having about fifteen rooms, provided as quarters for General Anders and the senior Staff officers. One wing of the house was reserved for Wolkowyski, which I did not like. Several sheds in the garden could be used as shelter for our stores and as our car-park.

There was also a second bungalow, where about forty people could be billeted. No lodgings were provided for the remaining Staff officers and the Staff company, but we were promised tents, which would not be too bad in this milder climate.

Generally speaking, I was favourably impressed, and I sent a telegram to General Anders saying so.

Simultaneously, discussions started on the disposition and re-cruitment. Eventually, the following scheme of disposition was agreed upon:—

5th Infantry Division	in Dzhalyal Abad in the Eastern Kirgiz S.S.R., almost on the Chinese border;
6th Infantry Division	in Shachrizyabs, near Samarkand, South Uzbek S.S.R.
7th Infantry Division	in Kermine, Central Uzbek S.S.R.
8th Infantry Division	in Pachta; later on, because of lack of accommodation, transferred to Czok-Pak in the Western Kirgiz S.S.R.
9th Infantry Division	near Ferghana in the Uzbek S.S.R.
10th Infantry Division	in Lugovoye, South Kazak S.S.R.
Artillery centre	in Karasu, Tadzhik S.S.R.
Army Training Centre and Engineers	in Vrevskoye, East Uzbek S.S.R.
Centre of Armoured Forces	in Otar, West Kirgiz S.S.R.
Army Depot	in Guzar, South Uzbek S.S.R., near Bukhara.

I was told that details of this disposition would have to be discussed by billeting officers on the spot, but if they needed outside help they could send reports to me, and I would discuss them with SAWO. This question was thus settled satisfactorily—though, of course, it was in theory only, as we could not check up on what the billeting conditions were, on account of the great distances between the various areas, for only Vrevskoye was near Yanghi Yul.

The 6th Infantry Division was the nearest to us—only about 400 miles away; others were 600 miles away and more. The distance between the 7th Infantry Division in Kermine and the 5th Infantry Division in Dzhalyal Abad was about 1,600 miles! There were no highways at all, and roads were out of use in the spring. There was a railway-line, but it did not run to all the places and only ran an irregular train service.

I visualised the difficulties with which our H.Q. would be confronted, having so great a distance between our units. However, it would have the advantage of providing more favourable conditions for our recruitment, which was most important to us; being scattered over such a wide area, we could that much more easily be reached by the masses of Poles dispersed in this vast Russian Empire, who might reach our Army centres and join the Colours.

The first billeting groups from all our units began to arrive in Yanghi Yul almost immediately after the disposition had been agreed upon. The still largely non-existent 7th, 8th, 9th and 10th Divisions arrived as small nuclei with their commanding officers: the 7th under General Szyszko Bohusz, the 8th under General Rakowski, the 9th under Col. Boleslawicz, and the 10th under Col. Schmid. Soon afterwards, the nuclei of different Army centres arrived, together with that of the Armoured Forces.

Only then did the deficiencies become apparent. With the exception of Shachrizyabs and Dzhalyal Abad, there was nothing prepared at all—no quarters, no tents, no food, nor the necessary tools which were indispensable for carrying out the most primitive works.

In Yanghi Yul we began to receive indents from different units, reaching us only after much delay because of the bad communications. Finally, when we approached SAWO, it transpired that they had nothing to give us. So the indents were returned to the local authorities with a request to hold courts of enquiry; then they were returned to us again; and so a vicious circle was created.

The situation was daily deteriorating, and it looked as if the authorities deliberately wanted to paralyse our recruitment by withholding from us the bare necessities of daily life for an army. This assumption was substantiated by the fact that only the cadre divisions encountered difficulties, while the old ones, who did not need any recruits, had everything given to them.

Despite this unhappy situation, I did not lose faith. I knew the ingenuity and the power of endurance of our soldiers, and I was convinced that the divisions would somehow settle down by their own efforts, and would soon begin to recruit new soldiers: they would be stimulated by the ambitions of their commanding officers and the influx of volunteers. I had no illusions about the opinions of the "wronged" ones: we, in Yanghi Yul would be held responsible

222

for all shortcomings. They would be sure to blame us for being incapable of catering for all requirements, and for not knowing how to stand up to SAWO and insist on all that Sikorski had demanded and Stalin had promised.

Soon the situation became obvious, but it was quite the reverse of our expectations. We first became aware of this when trying to organise recruiting. During our conference relating to this question, two basic decisions were intimated to me. According to SAWO's representative, these decisions had been reached in Moscow and must be strictly adhered to.

The first one stated that new recruits must be enlisted only through Soviet Army offices—the *Voyenkomaty*—and not directly by the Polish Divisions.

The second one defined who might be recruited—*viz.* only Poles who before 1939 had lived to the west of the Ribbentrop-Molotov demarcation line. All Poles living to the east of this line could only join the Polish Army if they were undoubtedly of Polish origin. All Jews, from any part of Poland, were deprived of this right.

We had no doubts about the meaning of this decision. The sovereignty of our Army, which, according to the Agreement reached, had the right to incorporate into her ranks all Polish citizens able to bear arms, was thus put in jeopardy. Entrusting the enlistment of new recruits to Soviet military authorities meant that we should receive only as many new recruits as the Soviet authorities were willing to let us have, and they need only enlist those men they wished to. This would enable the Soviets to prevent the increase of our Army to 100,000, which was the figure agreed during the Kremlin talks.

The differentiation of Poles in accordance with the German-Soviet demarcation line before 1939, and the denial to Polish national minorities of the right to serve in the Polish Army and thus fulfil their duty towards the country, was a political act, disclosing the will of the U.S.S.R. to annex the Eastern Polish territories. A denial of the right of Jews to join the Polish Army was also calculated to exacerbate Polish-Jewish relations and cast a slur on our nation in the West, especially in the U.S.A.

I immediately lodged a protest against both these decisions. SAWO's representative then announced that he could not discuss these questions, they being outside the scope of his competence.

That being the case, I adjourned the conference and sent a report to General Anders by wireless, asking him for further instructions.

223

The General replied promptly, informing me that a protest had been lodged at highest level. Nevertheless, I must aim at a speedy settlement of the recruiting organisation, even under the conditions thrust upon us, because the growth of our Army was the most important matter; all other questions were comparatively minor.

I considered this decision to be the right one. We should leave the Governments to exchange diplomatic notes, meanwhile doing everything in our power to increase our Army to 100,000 men without delay. I thought this possible of achievement, in spite of the regulations about the *Voyenkomaty*, because it was obvious that, once volunteers heard that recruitment for the Polish Army had begun, they would join that Army by hook or by crook, disregarding orders to apply at the *Voyenkomaty* and ignoring the national minorities regulation. The Divisions would thus be forced to enlist them themselves.

I therefore resumed discussion with SAWO along these lines, and we very soon reached agreement. We settled the mixed recruitment commissions in each *Voyenkomat*. To each of those commissions we had to send a Polish doctor to work with a Soviet one, and an officer to verify the nationality of the volunteers.

There were some amusing incidents during the drafting of instructions for these commissions. For instance, the Soviets wanted to insert a clause giving the commissions the right to reject not only national minorities, but also Poles who might cause suspicion by professing "pro-Fascist tendencies". I asked them what they meant by "pro-Fascist tendencies". Did they mean that if a volunteer were asked which he preferred, a *Kolchoz* or an individually-owned farm, and declared himself in favour of private enterprise, he would be regarded as a Fascist and for this reason not enlisted in the sovereign Polish Army? I also asked what they meant by "Fascist": was it everybody who was not a Communist?

They were all ticklish questions, and I did not receive any answer to them. The restrictions were withdrawn from the official instruction, although I had no illusions but that they would be retained in an additional secret one sent only to the Soviet members of the commissions. Taking into account this possibility, I asked that tribunals might be referred to for hearing all appeals in doubtful cases, and this was agreed to.

There were other incidents, too. I regarded them from a strictly formal point of view, as I wanted to speed matters up and begin recruitment officially. I felt convinced that circumstances would

224

King George VI visiting the Polish Army on the Italian front
in 1944. He is shaking hands with General Rudnicki.

General Rudnicki and his staff with Brigadier-General Harry B. Sherman of the 34th Infantry Division on 21 April, 1945, after the liberation of Bologna by Polish troops

General Rudnicki greeted by the population of Bologna after the liberation of the town by his division, 21 April, 1945

overcome them and our side would know how to bypass them: I had no desire to waste my time on fruitless bargaining over matters of "principle". We therefore concluded our talks, and recruiting began officially.

As I had foreseen, men did not wait to be called by the *Voyenkomaty*, which took a long time; they streamed in large numbers to their nearest Polish Army centres, which had only just set foot in their new encampments. Very often they arrived completely exhausted by starvation or illness. There were many cases of death at the very threshold of the divisional recruiting commissions. They brought epidemics of typhus, which quickly spread and took a heavy toll in casualties, especially in Kermine and Guzar. Local C.O's asked for more doctors, male nurses, and medicines; and they finally demanded that a stop should be put to any further influx of volunteers, to avoid spreading the epidemic. Everything we could mobilise we sent to them, but halting the stream of volunteers was out of the question: the conditions in our encampments were much better than those in which they had previously existed.

At first the Soviet liaison officers protested against direct enlistment of volunteers by Polish units; but inexorable facts overcame their protests. The Divisions began to grow in strength, conditions of life were slowly improving, and food began to be available.

One fact was definite: the Army was growing. At the same time, Polish Army transports were arriving from the North.

In the latter part of February, General Anders came to Yanghi Yul with H.Q., to assume direct command of all the units.

CHAPTER 30

"Anyone Against?"

I WAS anxious to learn what impression Yanghi Yul would make on the newcomers, especially as I had heard there was gossip circulating in Buzuluk with malicious criticism of our activities. However, first impressions were favourable.

An enchanting spring, and the fragrant orchard which surrounded our H.Q. being in full bloom, certainly helped. This spring enchantment was somewhat dangerous to men who came from 75° F. below zero and who, as prisoners, were morally depressed and their spirit undermined; but this could not be helped, and the conditions of life for our H.Q. were really good.

SAWO met General Anders ostentatiously, and showed him due respect. A party was given by SAWO's C.O., which coincided with the 25th anniversary of the Red Army, so we were all invited to a solemn festivity in the Tashkent Opera-house. There we met Soviet dignitaries from Central Asia, and witnessed a unique scene, impossible anywhere outside the boundaries of the Soviet Union.

The opera-house was crowded to excess. A dozen persons sat at a table on the stage; all of them leading personalities of the Party, headed by the *Sovnarkom*, the President of the Uzbek S.S.R. In the corner was a platform for the speakers.

The festivity opened with a statement by the *Sovnarkom*, who said that as it was the 25th anniversary of the formation of the heroic Red Army, he moved that a solemn meeting be held if present comrades agreed.

"Anyone against?"

As nobody opposed the motion, he declared that in accordance with the unanimous will of all present he opened the "solemn session" and called upon the Secretary of the Communist Party of

226

the Bolsheviks in the Uzbek S.S.R. to be the chief speaker.

"Anyone against?"

Again there was no opposition, and the comrade secretary began to deliver his speech.

He was followed by others, until all who sat on the stage had spoken. This lasted about four hours.

Each spoke in the same vein, only using different words. How pleased and proud they were with the achievements of the Soviet Union, and how happy Soviet citizens were. Thanks to the Revolution, citizens had ceased being tools exploited by the capitalists: they now enjoyed freedom unknown to the Western world, and, guided by the Party, lived in well-being and prosperity. They had plenty of everything—as much as they liked of bread, meat, cigarettes and other commodities; they also had theatres, cinemas and schools.

Every speech finished with the same rhetorical question—"To whom are we indebted for all this?"—followed immediately by the answer—"To our dearest comrade Stalin, the Sun and Leader of the nations!"

Every speaker moved a resolution to send a telegram to Stalin, which he read out, and it was voted for in the usual way: "Anyone against?"

Speakers occupying lower ranks in the Communist hierarchy produced speeches even more stuffed with lies, and their proposed telegrams were even longer and more servile.

To us, although we had thought we were already fully accustomed to these exaggerated statements, it was all unbearably nauseating. Every word spoken from the platform was a lie, and the telegrams were full of Byzantine servility at its worst. Yet the speakers neither blushed nor stuttered, although they knew as well as their audience that everything they uttered was untrue. There was not a person in the house but had some near relative in a labour-camp or prison, detained there for no reason whatsoever; and not one who was not possessed by the hellish fear of succumbing to a similar fate. Nobody believed it possible to buy bread, meat, or cigarettes in a shop: they all knew they were living in dreadful misery. They were swollen by starvation, molested by lice, and often suffering from typhoid fever.

I watched this tragi-comedy, looking from audience to stage. Not one word or sign of hesitation, not a smile or a cough could I note; nothing at all. People in the Soviet Union were perfectly trained, hopelessly patient, tragically enduring, pathetically obsequious.

My suspicions of the reasons why we had been prevented from

visiting Yanghi Yul while the builders were still working soon proved to be correct. Our experts, alert after the incident in Buzuluk, arrived with our H.Q. and easily discovered the newly installed microphones. This time they were fitted in the ceilings, hardly perceptible, and were covered with a thin layer of plaster. All the wires led to the part occupied by Wolkowyski. It was easy to guess where the receiver was!

The new discovery aroused amusement rather than anger, and became a standing joke. It was impossible not to laugh at this childish, stubborn determination of our hosts to intercept all our private talks, in spite of the disgraceful outcome of the previous similar attempt.

We decided that any complaint was useless: it was simply not worth bothering about—though we were ashamed to have such Allies. The General simply ordered all the wires to be cut, but everything else to be left untouched, and nothing was said.

Nevertheless, the Soviets immediately reacted to this incident. Three days after the wires had been cut, Wolkowyski called on the General to take leave of him. He said that he had been given another appointment, and he left the same day. We never saw him again.

He was replaced by Col. Tishkov. The incident with the microphones was never mentioned.

At the same time, the General decided to make changes in H.Q. I had been appointed second-in-command to the Commander of the 6th Infantry Division in Shachrizyabs; and Okulicki Commander of the 7th Infantry Division in Kermine, replacing General Szyrzko Bohusz, who took up his post as Chief of Staff of the Army H.Q.

Before we left to take over our new appointments, important changes had occurred in the Army. On 10th March we were officially informed that Moscow had cut our food issues down to the strength of 26,000; at that time we had about 70,000 enlisted soldiers!

The game was too obvious. Despite recruitment through the *Voyenkomaty*, our Army was increasing like an avalanche. The Soviets thought to hit us hard by compelling us to disband three-quarters of it.

This decision angered us intensely. Forthwith, General Anders sent a telegram to Stalin asking for an immediate interview in the Kremlin. Stalin agreed to this request, so the General flew with Okulicki to Moscow.

On 18th March he had a decisive discussion with Stalin. The General asked that the Agreement reached in December should be honoured. Stalin categorically refused, alleging the cut was owing to an acute shortage of food, due to insufficient supplies coming from the U.S.A.—much less than had been promised. Instead, he put forward a proposal to disband all men in excess of 26,000 from the Army and to send them, as labourers, to *Kolchoz* farms. This solution was categorically rejected by the General: it would be inhuman to send people back to starvation and typhus.

The situation became tense and dramatic. The General then proposed another solution: to evacuate the surplus soldiers to Iran, where they would be supplied by Great Britain. Stalin agreed in principle to this suggestion, but put forward the following compromise. He would raise the supplies of food, to a sufficiency for 44,000—enough men for the upkeep of two divisions and the Army Depot, to remain in the U.S.S.R. for use in the front line; the rest would be evacuated to Iran without delay.

The General returned with this agreed decision to Yanghi Yul. It was the only possible way of drawing our Army out of this new *impasse*; but for how long? After our previous experiences we were exceedingly sceptical. We were more convinced than ever that the Soviets did not want us to have a really sovereign Polish Army.

H.Q. began at once to work on the evacuation scheme. There were about 40,000 soldiers and their families to be transported to Iran, and General Anders managed to secure special consent for the evacuation also of some of the civilians. This was to begin in March—by rail to Krasnovodsk, and then by boat over the Caspian Sea to Pahlevi.

After lengthy deliberation, the General had decided to retain the best men and the best units in Russia; all the physically debilitated and unclimatised ones were to be evacuated. This seemed to be the best solution, as all our future, under Soviet conditions, was unpredictable.

The following instructions were therefore issued.

The complete 5th and 6th Infantry Divisions had to remain in Russia, except for those who were debilitated and in bad health; their losses would be replaced by new recruitment, which was still going on.

The 7th Infantry Division were to remain as the Army Depot, with the primary function of recruiting new volunteers.

The Engineers and Artillery Centres would remain, and continue the training of men.

The 8th, 9th and 10th Infantry Divisions were to be completely evacuated.

An Evacuation Centre was established in Krasnovodsk to speed up evacuation; liaison officers were sent to Iran to establish contacts with British authorities; and General Zajac was made the Polish C.O. in the Middle-East.

Col. Z. Berling was appointed by the General as Commanding Officer of the Evacuation Centre in Krasnovodsk, for it was impossible to leave him any longer in the 5th Infantry Division: everyone there was very much against him because of his Red sympathies and his known activity as a Soviet agent. Things had finally come to the point where General Boruta Spiechowicz had suspended him for disobedience.

General Anders' situation was extremely onerous. It was against our interests to bring relations with the Soviets to a break while the evacuation—the only deliverance for many thousands of people from death and starvation, as we then saw things—was still in its preparatory stage.

When Berling reported to the General in Yanghi Yul, he was severely reprimanded by him, and then appointed C.O. of the Evacuation Centre. The General told us that he expected Berling to render us good service there, on account of his cordial standing with the N.K.V.D., and he would be enabled to carry out Stalin's order about the evacuation.

Meanwhile, General Boruta Spiechowicz relinquished command of the 5th Infantry Division at his own request, and was appointed C.O. of the evacuated troops. His nerves were strained almost to breaking-point as a result of his sojourn in Russia, and he desired as soon as possible to be outside her frontiers. He probably had other reasons, too.

There were signs that for some time the Soviets had singled him out to be General Anders' successor, as the latter refused to be used as a medium for Communist plans and had accordingly become unwelcome to our hosts. It appeared that they had tried to ensnare General Spiechowicz in various ways, spying out his weaknesses and playing on his ambition. For instance, he was presented by the N.K.V.D. with an artistic sword, engraved with an appropriate inscription. Boruta Spiechowicz concealed reception of this gift from General Anders, which looked rather suspicious, and when the incident was suddenly brought to light it caused some embarrassment. Then came the incident of the suspension of Berling from his duties, which appeared like a severance of Spiechowicz' ties with the Soviets and caused further embarrassment. In view of all these facts, we considered it most desirable that Boruta Spiechowicz should leave Russia.

Immediately after the first transports had left, General Anders flew to Teheran, and from there to London, to discuss the new situation with General Sikorski. At the same time, Okulicki and I left Yanghi Yul to take over our new appointments with the 6th Division.

CHAPTER 31

In Uzbeck Country

I REPORTED to General Tokarzewski in Schachrizyabs on the 1st April, 1942.

From this time onwards I began to see events from an entirely different angle—from the point of view of the soldiers. I left behind me the worries tormenting Army H.Q., exchanging them for their causes and their repercussions in units and among the soldiers.

The first impression after my arrival in Shachrizyabs was most odd. I was sure that once before I had viewed all the surroundings. From the window of my railway compartment I noticed in the fields huge stooks of cotton, looking like enormous heaps of old, curly cotton-wool. Some of them were cut through the centre—probably a part of them had already been sent away. They struck a chord of memory: their dirty whiteness was known to me so well—but where?

When I walked in the streets of Shachrizyabs and saw the huts made of mud, people in colourful long gowns and wearing Tibetan caps, our soldiers dressed in British uniforms walking among them, I recognised the picture I had visualised in my dreams in Dniepropietrovsk—dreams so prophetically interpreted by Heller. Nearly everything was identical with what I had seen then: the features of the Uzbek faces, the houses, trees, were all quite familiar to me—they looked as they had in my dream. How amazing!

However, after all my trying experiences nothing very much could surprise me again, even miracles.

I reported to Tokarzewski (who had also featured in the dream) and rapidly began to get acquainted with the Division, its disposition and its life.

The Division consisted of the 16th, 17th and 18th Infantry regiments, the 6th Field Artillery regiment, one battalion of Signals, one battalion of Engineers, the Provost Company, transport, stores, and a Field Hospital. The strength varied a lot, but never exceeded 14,000. When I arrived there were only 8,000 men; a big transport of convalescents had just left for Iran, thus making room for newcomers.

The Division was disposed in four garrisons:—

the Divisional H.Q. and the Services in Shachrizyabs;
the 16th Infantry Division in Kitab;
the 17th Infantry Regiment and the 6th Field Artillery Regiment in Yakobak; and
the 18th Infantry regiment in Tshirakshi.

I would like to describe these garrison towns briefly.

Shachrizyabs was a little town about fifty miles south-east from Samarkand, previously governed by the Emir of Bukhara; it was about three miles from the railway terminus in Kitab, and was mostly inhabited by Uzbeks. An English translation of the town's name would be "Carrot Town".

In olden times, Shachrizyabs was, after Samarkand, the largest metropolis of Tamerlaine. Now it is only a small Asiatic town, modelled on Russian-Soviet lines. It is partially destroyed, some parts of it being almost abandoned. The houses were built, as is usual in the East, of clay; the streets were narrow and winding. The whole town was surrounded by a defensive clay wall, reminiscent of bygone centuries. Vines climbed up it, mingling with the green of the mulberry and *uruk* trees.

Wandering along the streets, one came across charming spots— among them the ruins of a minute mosque, with open-work pillars and, high up, slender minarets. In the centre of the town were the ruins of the colossal castle of Tamerlaine, whose turret of imposing magnitude and beauty was covered with small tiles, glazed in blue enamel and scrolled with beautiful arabesques.

This charming sight was enhanced by the colourful, trailing clothes of men and women, walking about or riding on *ishaks* (small donkeys). These people belonged to a completely different world from ours—to Asia—and it was difficult for a European to see through the dividing screen. It took a long time to realise how much they knew about their glorious past and how proud they were of it. Later on they told us that the Emirate of Bukhara lost its independence only in 1922. Even as recently as 1932, the whole territory between Karashi and the Pass of Samarkand had been under the rule of the Bassmatshi, who, having their headquarters in inaccessible mountains, had come down to the valleys and killed all the alien population—mostly Russians—and occupied a territory equal in size to one-third of Poland. Budionnyj's army, however, bloodily suppressed this rising, destroyed all the monuments to Uzbek greatness, and strengthened Soviet rule.

At first we were regarded as Russian Bolsheviks. No wonder our reception was so cool! Later on, when the news spread that we were Poles, they became openhearted and Uzbek hamlets were open to us. Our soldiers became friendly with the *bayans* (men) in colourful gowns and the *marzias* (girls) in *carsafs*. A legend was largely responsible for these demonstrations of acceptance.

An old prophecy went that when, from the ancient tower of Tamerlaine, Polish trumpets sounded, the Uzbeks would recover their liberty. We were unaware of this prophecy, but it so happened that after our Division's arrival in Shachrizyabs our trumpeter twice daily climbed the 150 steps to the top of the tower, and from there sounded the Cracow fanfare to the four corners of the earth.* This was the same fanfare which, according to the legend, had once been interrupted, eight centuries ago, by an arrow, shot by one of Gengis Khan's cavalry, hitting the trumpeter.

In the beginning the Uzbeks were suspicious of us and watched us cautiously. When everything became clear to them, friendship was born. Later, probably some of them paid the price for it and for the hopes which had been aroused, by being deported to the banks of the Kolyma river.

Kitab was the terminus of a local railway-line siding from the main Tashkent-Ashkhabad-Krasnovodsk line. It was our nearest garrison: only about three miles away.

The 16th Infantry Regiment was under canvas on the borders of the river Kashka-Darya, about six miles from Kitab. Only the Regimental H.Q. and the Medical Inspection Room were billeted in the wooden building of a wine factory. There were very few trees and practically no shade, and the heat made life in the tents unbearable. The nearby river and the channels for irrigating the fields soon proved to be plague spots—breeding-grounds for malarial mosquitoes.

Yakobak was a station on the same railway-line, about twelve miles from Shachrizyabs, but completely in the desert, without water,

---

* From the top of the spire of St. Mary's Church in Cracow a fanfare was sounded every hour, in accordance with an old tradition dating from the Middle Ages. Before the war the fanfare was always broadcast in the Polish News Service, like Big Ben on the B.B.C. radio service.

trees or green shrubs. Water for drinking, cooking and washing, had to be carried in big barrels on wheels, drawn by mules, from an oasis a couple of miles distant. This was where the tents of the 17th Infantry Regiment and the 6th Field Artillery Regiment were erected —dirty, second-hand Soviet tents. Men made dugouts for themselves to secure a little coolness.

Tshirakshi, about ten miles beyond Yakobak, was the name of a small Uzbek town near which the 18th Infantry Regiment was encamped. As at Kitab, the river Kashka-Darya flowed by the tents, and again there were many irrigation channels. But here there was plenty of green and shade. Also, Tshirakshi was full of folklore, and provided entertainment for our soldiers which was completely missing in Yakobak. Here, on market days, one could watch the poor Asiatic people riding on their little donkeys to the town's bazaar, carrying baskets full of melons, grapes, or nuts. Sometimes they brought homespun silken handkerchiefs in beautiful pastel colours, *carsafs*, bracelets, earrings and other wonders. In the evenings one could listen to Uzbek tunes, played on pipes, which to European ears sounded monotonous, like a kind of lamentation or prayer.

When our first units reached this area they were shaken to the core by unexpectedly encountering large numbers of Poles, existing in appalling conditions of life—emaciated, in rags, barefooted, swollen by starvation, plagued by insects, decimated by typhoid fever and other illnesses, and resented by the native population.

In the neighbourhood of Shachrizyabs there were about 1,600 of these persons; in the Yakobak and Tshirakshi area about 1,000; in the Kitab area about 1,600. It was very difficult to find out what numbers were dispersed deeper in the country, what their situation was, or how many had died.

The troops were so impressed by this horrifying discovery that they went almost mad to try and help rescue these living skeletons of women, children and old people. Organisation for their welfare became the principal aim of the Division. Welfare Committees, organised in units, were set up by the Divisional Committee.

Squads were sent out to search the country, and they continually found fresh groups of deportees living in misery. Derelict families and orphans whose parents had died of starvation were brought to the encampments; the welfare of children, medical assistance, and feeding, had to be organised at the expense of the soldiers' food ration. They were genuinely filled with sympathy for the tragedy of

235

this innocent population deported from Poland. Listening to their experiences, they clenched their fists in rage against those responsible for this misery.

Mostly the exiles were persons deported from Poland in February and April, 1940. Some of them had been straightaway directed to the *Kolchoz* farms there, or to the labour-camps, to dig irrigation channels; others had come there from the North after the promulgation of the "amnesty" in 1941.

As daily wages for their labour, they received, according to the prevailing custom on the *Kolchoz* farms, anything from 2 oz. of *jugary* (a kind of millet) to 14 oz. meal made from various kinds of corn. In theory, they were also entitled to one pint of milk daily and some meat, but in fact they hardly ever received these. No cash wages were paid at all. When workers lived on such rations, they lost their strength: they were then simply driven away to small towns and left to the care of Providence. "No work, no food." And so they died.

The native population had little pity for them, for they feared that by feeding the deportees they themselves would be deprived of their share; already they were half-starved and lived in misery.

As more civilians were rescued, naturally the food problem grew more acute. More and more of these people, not only from the neighbourhood but also from faraway places, came under the protection of our units, and our soldiers, who were issued with scarcely sufficient rations for themselves, had to give up more than half for the needs of the civilians. Army officers stopped feeding in the *Voyentorg* (a kind of Russian N.A.A.F.I.) and were included in the strength of the units, thus increasing the amount of food issued to the Division for sharing with the deportees.

But it was like a drop in the ocean. The situation became terribly tense, getting almost unbearable. Men of the Division were starving, and so were exhausted by the training, which we tried to carry on; they became susceptible to illnesses, which spread rapidly, reaping a large harvest of dead men. Instead of becoming a unit fit to fight, the Division, hardly able to exist, was slowly changing into a big relief institution for over 10,000 civilians.

But could the Division have acted any differently? Could they have cut all their ties with civilians to prevent them from becoming a hindrance to their fighting preparedness? Surely not! It could not be done.

At the same time, in Divisional H.Q. we realised that the opportunity for transforming our regiments into completely able fighting units was dwindling away. And we were afraid to think what would happen to those people under our protection if our Divisions were ordered to the front. All of them would probably die. This had to be prevented.

The generosity and the strenuous efforts of the welfare organisers brought it about that the situation, so critical at first, began to improve slowly. Only those people, who, through their previous lack of nourishment were unable to digest fresh nutriments, were now quietly fading away in the hospital or in the units.

When the first rush had passed, I brought to the Division most of the families of the 9th Lancers. My own family, however, was among those we had been totally unable to trace.

The two little sons of Capt. Bielecki, whose mother had died in the Kazak S.S.R., we managed to attach to a transport going to India, that had been organised by our Consul in Bombay, Mr. Lisicki; and my wife's brother's two sons also left by that same transport. Their mother, completely exhausted, remained in Samarkand, parting with the boys in a voluntary attempt to save them.

Soon, from our regimental family group, the wife of brave Capt. Ksyk died: her debilitated body could not stand the onslaught of typhoid fever. She left a boy, two years old, and the other ladies looked after him.

To our great joy, Sister Lauretta was found to be among the surviving deportees—and we summoned her by telegram to come and join the Army! Donning the uniform of a sergeant of the Polish Women's Auxiliary Corps, she took up military duties in our Division—a nun *and* a soldier!

CHAPTER 32

Division of Lions

IT WAS quite understandable that our Division should have a special regard for Lwow: it was not only Tokarzewski and myself who were strongly tied up to this town; the majority of our officers and other ranks came from south-eastern Poland, and Lwow—with the old motto of the city, *Semper fidelis* (Ever Faithful—interpreted as faithful to the Polish Commonwealth) was dear to them.

A special unit had been organised, the "Battalion of Lwow's Children", consisting only of people coming from Lwow. They especially upheld the traditions of the Polish Lwow. This attitude, of course, was distasteful to our Soviet hosts.

In a sly way, first of all, they drew our attention to the fact that such manifestations of feeling were unsuitable: they understood regional patriotism and affection, but it would be much better if we could tender our affections to another undoubtedly Polish town, not to Lwow, which in any case, they said, had been incorporated into the Soviet Ukraine in 1939. When we protested that we had never heard of an Act signed by the Polish Government ceding Lwow to the Soviet Union, we were met with an indulgent smile and were told: "It's possible . . . but the people's will. . . . It's better now not to create dissonances. We have a common enemy, and common aims. . . . Later on we can definitely come to some agreement."

These comments were made by our Soviet liaison officers, Col. Anapshuk and Col. Golinskyj. It was enough to make our soldiers —even those who did not originate from Lwow—become fervent Lwow patriots, united together to defend their beloved city.

New occurrences, very vexing to the Bolsheviks but undoubtedly proving the Polish character of Lwow and the affection of its people for this city, began to multiply spontaneously. Only Lwow songs were sung, sometimes with new words; Lwow's coat-of-arms was traced in pebbles in front of the tents; maps of Poland were ostentatiously drawn, with Lwow marked on them; and there were various other such manifestations, proving to the Bolsheviks that "Lwow is Polish and we would never allow it to be taken away from us."

As our demonstrations grew in strength, Soviet reaction increased too, displaying in plain terms Russia's will to annex Lwow, where, strange to say, at that time the Germans were roaming about.

An obstinate, ideological struggle about the possession of Lwow originated between the soldiers of the 6th Infantry Division and officials of the Soviet Union: it was the Division's ambition to defend that city.

Divisional H.Q. joined this struggle, which greatly annoyed Anapshuk. On the 2nd May, 1942, General Tokarzewski published the following letter written to the C.O. of the Polish Army in U.S.S.R.:—

The soldiers of the 6th Infantry Division have given proof during their trying experiences of their uncompromising attitude, their strength of mind and their unyielding will to carry on the fight.

To uphold and symbolise these soldierly virtues, will you please, Sir, give to our 6th Infantry Division the name of *Dywizja lwow*" (Division of Lions)?

The name of the town had not been mentioned; the "l" was written with a small letter, thus meaning "lion", the king of animals, not the town of Lwow. The Soviet authorities could not challenge this letter, although they realised well enough what was behind it. At the same time it aroused violent enthusiasm among the soldiers, strengthened their faith and raised their morale, which was then so necessary to enable them to endure the ordeals which our Division was suffering.

The last act of the Soviet authorities was to send from Moscow a special fact-finding Court of Enquiry, under Col. Gortshakov—ostensibly to ascertain the fighting preparedness of the Division, but in reality to ascertain its attitudes.

During his stay, Gortshakov visited the divisional theatre. Of course, they sang a song about Lwow—and he protested vehemently about it. When General Tokarzewski coolly informed him that since the Polish Prime Minister, General Sikorski, had not yet communicated to the Polish Forces that Lwow had been ceded to the Soviet Union, he could not forbid the singing of Lwow songs, Gortshakov left the Division, angrily banging the door, and all dispute on this subject came to an end.

We remained the Lwow Division, but Soviet spying activities were increased among our soldiers.

Only now did we realise what large numbers of our men—and even officers—had heedlessly signed the declaration to become informers working for the N.K.V.D., without confessing it to us. Anapshuk and Golinskyj held these declarations, and now they began to make capital out of them. The poor blackmailed men began to impart this information in confidence to their colleagues, then to their officers: they began to take shelter, to change their names, to join other garrisons—briefly, to try and blot out their traces. Some of them disappeared completely, and we never discovered what had happened to them.

A silent but bitter struggle, concealed behind surface politeness, flared up: there were not many of us left with illusions that loyal co-operation was still possible.

Tinned food, which had arrived, together with our uniforms, from Great Britain, *via* Archangel, was kept by the Soviets in reserve "in case of emergency". The Division still fed on the official food rations allocated by SAWO. According to the current strength of the Division, orders were given to issue us with food one month in advance. These orders were addressed to Army Service Stores, or sometimes directly to *Kolchoz* farms, and we ourselves had to collect the foodstuffs shown in the list.

In theory, SAWO issued to us the whole ration of food; in fact, it worked out quite differently. When we came to the various stores or farms indicated to us by SAWO, we usually discovered that the allocated foodstuffs were entirely missing or would only be available at some indefinite future date—yet any rations allocated for the current rationing period and not drawn during the month were automatically lost to us, for we were not allowed to claim them during the next monthly rationing period.

Adding to these impediments all the difficulties of transport, the big distances to cover, the struggle to get railway trucks, etc., no more than 60–70 per cent of the rations due to us reached the Division; and very often many of the items were replaced by less valuable products.

In view of the fact that the Division also shared its rations with civilians, thus doubling the numbers to be fed, the food issued to our own soldiers was really insufficient. This made our underfed soldiers more prone to contract the epidemic diseases, which so weakened the Division that finally there seemed to be no possibility of our realising our fighting preparedness.

In the spring, diseases again began to decimate our Division; first typhus, then typhoid fever, brought to us by new recruits and civilians. Later on, when swarms of mosquitoes had bred, various kinds of malaria, jaundice, deadly coma, dysentery, etc., spread rapidly. The doctors were almost helpless; there were no medicines, the nurses were ill themselves and over-fatigued; there was no room for new patients in the Divisional hospital or in the units. For a long time, 10–20 people died each day. About 95 per cent of the Division's strength, including Tokarzewski and myself, were attacked by these diseases, and there were days when there were not enough healthy men to perform the most necessary administrative jobs to keep going the daily existence of the Division and the civilians.

Kitab, Tshirakshi and Shachrizyabs were the worst affected by disease, as they were next to the water, which provided good breeding grounds for mosquitoes.

Well do I remember how I inspected the 16th Infantry Regiment in Kitab when the epidemics were raging at their worst. What a macabre sight! I walked round the regimental encampment, which was unguarded, without duty officer or N.C.O. The offices and kitchens were deserted, and the quarters were strewn with half-conscious people lying one beside the other, feverishly delirious or in coma. It was one vast, silent death camp!

This situation lasted until the autumn—that is, until all the Divisions had left the Soviet Union. During this time, the epidemics gradually died down, only to flare up suddenly with renewed strength, often re-attacking those who had only just recovered from them. It was a nightmare for the healthy and the patients as well, underlining the hopelessness of the situation and strengthening our desire to leave this country of misery and be transferred to where we might become an army fit to fight.

In June, a visit from the Chief Chaplain to our Forces, Bishop J. Gawlina, comforted our soldiers greatly and brought them much joy. Soldiers left their beds and trudged to greet him. They put up decorations and festoons, and gave their Bishop a hearty welcome. Crowds went to be confirmed, and the procession on Corpus Christi Day in Tshirakshi developed into a spontaneous manifestation of

241

the universal desire to return to Polish traditions and customs, which might bring us—even for a short while—a vision of our kinsmen, our hamlets, and our country. Everything was carried out exactly as in Poland: a canopy was carried, flowers were spread on the road in front of the procession, and altars were erected in the streets. These manifestations indicated above everything how hateful were the Soviet surroundings to the soldiers.

By now we had realised that our continued existence in Russia was futile. Eleven months of attempted co-operation with the Soviets had stripped us of all illusions. No longer could it be concealed: the experiment had been a failure. There was no possibility of real co-operation with Soviet Russia. One could only fight against her, or surrender unconditionally—there was no alternative.

During these terrible eleven months both sides had mutually disclosed their doubts: we averred we would never surrender to them, and they declared they did not want us as we were. Both parties revealed their attitude.

Under these circumstances, there was no hope of our carrying out our own decisions. Fatalistically, we expected some drastic, final settlement.

When our Embassy's delegates were arrested on the pretext of spying, we prepared for the worst. We decided to offer stiff resistance if the Soviets attempted to take us by force, and to hack our way through to Afghanistan or Iran. We even began to prepare plans for such an emergency. Under the pretext of excursions, we reconnoitred the passes and roads to the Afghan frontier, and studied the possibility of taking over by force the trains running to Ashhabad *en route* to the Persian frontier. We reconnoitred the disposition of the nearest Soviet garrisons, and their stores where we could secure necessary equipment.

This secretly designed plan was quite fantastic, and could hardly have been carried out in practice—especially as many soldiers were at the time laid low by malaria.

It was also conceived only by ourselves, and entirely for our own Division in isolation. We feared that one day we might be cut off from Yanghi Yul and from Army H.Q. Events might happen there, including the liquidation of General Anders, and we wanted to be prepared for any eventuality. We were determined to sell our lives dearly and withstand any attempt to incarcerate us again.

Tension was rising throughout June, and one sensed in the air that something was approaching. We watched events carefully, our nerves on edge, and waited for news from our Army H.Q., where General Anders did everything possible to find a way out from the *impasse*. We knew as well as he that the only reasonable solution would be permission to allow us to leave the Soviet Union. But would Stalin agree to it? Would he allow such living witnesses to depart from this world of treachery?

In mid-June, news reached us from London that General Sikorski desired us to stay in Russia "for higher political reasons". This caused much bitter disappointment. Surely he knew that this was only feasible on condition that we would sell ourselves unconditionally to Stalin and to Soviet political aims, discarding our oath to be faithful to the Polish Commonwealth? Did he not realise that staying there without changing our convictions would mean we should be annihilated, without serving any useful purpose to Poland?

Wholeheartedly we supported our Army Commander's efforts to evacuate us, and the civilian families rescued by us, to Persia, under British protection. Finally, the solution arrived.

On the 7th July the Soviet Government informed General Anders by telegram that "they agreed to the evacuation of the Polish Army from the U.S.S.R. to the Middle East, and had no intention whatsoever of hindering its immediate implementation".

We sighed with relief. So Stalin did not dare touch us! He realised what the consequences would be if he did. At last the nightmarish life in the Soviet Union would come to an end; we would receive equipment and become useful members of the Western Allies; we could at last play an important role in our common struggle.

The strength of our Army in the U.S.S.R. was numerically far superior to all other Polish Army units dispersed outside Poland's frontiers. We might therefore expect to play a leading role, and assume the bulk of responsibility. This consciousness made us proud and strengthened our spirits, which had been so badly strained during the struggle against all our adversities of illnesses and treachery.

During our deliberations as to why Stalin had felt compelled to let us depart from Russia—which was not in accordance with usual Soviet behaviour—we were inclined to exaggerate our role in it. We thought that our resolute attitude and our preparedness to face dangers, based on our high morale, had brought it about: that Stalin would not have hesitated to have destroyed us mercilessly had we shown less resistance; but that knowing he would encounter desperate opposition from us, he bowed and yielded to the inevitable.

In actual fact, our appraisal was, I now think, grossly exaggerated:

we did not take into account the political and military difficulties of Russia at that time, which forced her to avoid, at all costs, misunderstandings with the Western Powers—then her Allies—with a view to obtaining more supplies.

In our opinion, we departed from Russia as a victorious, not a defeated, Army. It was our first victory of the War, and we were proud of it. This pride helped to strengthen our worn-out bodies.

CHAPTER 33

The Free World Ahead!

OUR TRANSPORTS left Russia unexpectedly quickly, almost immediately after the decision was reached. In record time, we received orders for our move, with time-tables for special trains, which were to carry us from our stations to Krasnovodsk. From there, we had to cross the Caspian Sea, to be disembarked in Pahlevi in Persia, where our camps would be under British administration.

The organisation and carrying out of this operation, being purely political, was entrusted to the N.K.V.D.

It was the last of a long chain of activities performed by the N.K.V.D. with regard to Polish former prisoners and deportees—now soldiers. But this time we greeted it with delight. It was carried out with skill and speed, as if the N.K.V.D. were excelling itself to carry out the theoretically severest sentence in the Soviet Penal Code: deportation from the Soviet Union.

As they saw it, the "incorrigible element", completely unsuitable to the role foreseen for them by the Kremlin, was to be removed. Probably they would have liked to have liquidated us in a different way, but luckily circumstances saved us from that.

Anyhow, the evacuation was also a political act, severing an enormous mass of Poles remaining in Russia from General Anders and his officers and men, who represented Polish interests and sovereignty. Without changing the Politbureau's previously adopted scheme, they would again attempt to find new persons to bribe, and persevere in their attempt to annex Poland as a prerequisite to the planned seizure of Europe.

Those who remained would be more manageable: they were the bribed and trained soldiers from the "Red Group", and thousands of ordinary Poles not knowing the facts, still kept away from our

Army and remaining in labour-camps, "Stroy-battalions", or in prisons.

They would now be released from their places of incarceration and handed over, not to Anders, who had inexplicably disappointed them, but to Wasilewska and Berling, under strict supervision by the N.K.V.D. Thus the harassed victims were to be subjected to yet another betrayal: they would have to pay for their lives by being used as enemies to their own country's cause.

Our 6th Division was to leave with the last Army transports and thus complete our exodus. Amongst ourselves we agreed that General Tokarzewski would leave with the first transport to organise the life of the Division after disembarkation, and I would leave with the last to see that every soldier from our Division and Army had left Russia.

I would therefore be the last embarked Polish soldier in Krasnovodsk to take leave of this inhuman country—so ending the historical attempt at Polish-Russian co-operation.

The first Divisional transport, with General Tokarzewski, left for the South in the middle of August. I remained in Shachrizyabs with a part of our H.Q., and we mobilised the next transports, entraining them at the railway stations nearest to their encampments.

The last transport, with which I was to leave, was due for mid-September, so that the evacuation of the Division was spread over about a month. It was a month of nightmarish worries, a struggle against odds and of ever-increasing tension, which, instead of diminishing as the troops were leaving, mounted ever higher till it tore at our very vitals. Our nerves, strained to the utmost and almost unable to keep our bodies alive, could hardly bear it. We were seriously ill with untreated malaria, attacks of which flared up with increasing vehemence, causing some kind of malarial dysentery. With high temperatures, exerting what will-power remained to us, we had to rise from our mattresses to see off each convoy, to check up and sign the nominal rolls of the entrained soldiers, and hand over one copy of these rolls to N.K.V.D. agents (which I had to do personally). Then we had to muster sufficient strength to struggle with the N.K.V.D. commissars in each contentious case of families, or some sick soldier, or equipment.

Our families came with us; to have left them behind would have been inhuman. General Anders had succeeded in securing their release from the Soviet authorities, and our London Government simply had to face a *fait accompli*. But we had to reject the families which had gathered round our encampments. When news spread that we were evacuating civilians as well as soldiers, many families and single people came to us from the neighbourhood, and even from remote parts. Many of our soldiers begged to be left for the last convoys, hoping that their dear ones would manage to reach the Division's area in time to go with them. But the nominal rolls had to be prepared a long time ahead, and were painstakingly checked by the N.K.V.D. Once they had been accepted, they refused to admit late-comers. What tragedies the situation produced! We struggled to rescue people who were otherwise doomed to death.

It was not too difficult to evacuate the families of the soldiers who were leaving, or even of the soldiers who had already left in March, or those who had relatives in Great Britain; but how many women, children and orphans came to us who had no relatives to provide them with the right to be evacuated. It was too tragic to tolerate, and in many cases we found ways of bypassing the instructions. Single soldiers, for instance, adopted strangers as their own families. They did it willingly; but it required a lot of preparatory work for our organisers, who were already overtired.

The situation of the dangerously ill was also very tragic. People with a high temperature, typhus, dysentery or some undiagnosed tropical disease, were obviously excluded from the evacuation. When they heard that the Army was leaving the U.S.S.R., they left their huts in a hurry, pretending to be healthy in order not to be left behind: all they wanted was to be evacuated and thus saved. Many of them were detained in Soviet hospitals in Kitab and Tshirakshi, and they, most of all, were tormented by the uncertainty of their fate, as it was most difficult to simulate good health there. We had less trouble with the patients kept in our hospitals: they grinned, their colleagues propped them inconspicuously under their arms, holding them up during the last parade before the entrainment; then they were pushed into the trucks, where they collapsed on the floors, but happy that they were going, and not being left behind. We knew what was happening, but we had not the heart to prevent it, and so they went.

We ourselves visited Soviet hospitals with our doctors, selecting people fit to travel. We walked round the wards, from one patient to another, meeting mute imploring from burning eyes, or had to listen to their barely audible petitions: "Take me with you! Death is better than being left behind. . . . Take me, *please*. . . ."

Most of them we could not take, because only the very serious cases were sent to those hospitals. We tried to comfort the remaining ones. We told them that they would follow us to Persia after their recovery: a Polish liaison mission would be left behind in Ashkhabad on the Soviet-Persian frontier for the purpose of receiving all convalescents sent there by the Soviet authorities, according to instructions issued.

They did not believe it. "They'll send us to labour-camps if we recover," they said.

Another difficulty that we encountered which enraged us, was the Jewish problem. The Soviet authorities forbade us most rigorously to include any Jewish families in our transports. If we attempted to bypass this order, the convoy would be stopped. After much bargaining, they agreed that the wives and children of Jewish soldiers on active service in our Division might be admitted in transports with their husbands or fathers. This was subject to a severe inspection of nominal rolls at the entrainment. Parents, or more remote relatives, were denied this opportunity, to which the families of non-Jewish soldiers were entitled. It was a new tragedy.

There were quite a few families of Polish Jews who had no relatives in the Division; they lived in Samarkand, or Bukhara, or other places in the vicinity. Many of them, having heard that the Division was evacuating civilians, came to Shachrizyabs and begged us to take them with us, adjuring us in the name of humanity to save them. When we refused to admit them to our transports, citing the orders received and the threat that were we to take them our transports might be stopped, they went to the N.K.V.D. There they met with a civil reception, and were told that the Soviet authorities had nothing against their evacuation, but that it was the Polish military authorities who refused them passage as they hated the Jews so intensely. The Jews came back, cursing us and ascribing their tragedy to us. Our denials had no effect: they believed the Soviets. This was one of the most cunning and treacherous of the Soviet tricks, intended to smear the Poles throughout the world with the indictment that Polish soldiers were "Fascist anti-Semites".

Finally, came the turn of our last military transport. My colleagues helped me to climb into the railway-carriage. For several days I had taken hardly any food, as I had a bad attack of malaria and trouble with my intestines.

Just before my departure I had to accompany my Siedlecki, whose "interior was somehow wrong" to the cemetery. Before he died, he became yellow as a lemon; he shook my hand for a long time, as if saying his final goodbye.

I have few recollections of our many days' journey in the jolting train across the steppes of the Turkmen S.S.R. to Ashkhabad, except a memory of the solicitous care with which my colleagues looked after me, helped by nurses and A.T.S. girls—and the story of Sinbad the Sailor, which one of them so beautifully told me.

Sinbad wandered about strange countries and sailed across the Coral Sea; he struggled and fought—I do not remember for what— he walked and yearned—he got involved in terrible, hair-raising adventures—but he always had a miraculous escape. . . .

The story did not matter. I was happy to lie in the jolting train and to listen without criticism to fairy-tales, not having to use my brains to discriminate reality from illusion, truth from deceit. It ceased to be necessary. No longer did I have to be forever watching; I could relax my overstrained nerves and listen to childish fairy-tales about Sinbad the Sailor.

Then we came to Krasnovodsk. For three days we lay on the sand of the beach, alongside each other, waiting for the boat—which, for some reason, was late.

At last, we embarked. Some of the soldiers were able to walk up the gangway; others had to be carried. Soon the boat was really over-loaded, like the barges on the Petsera or the Amur-Darya. I was the last to be embarked. Col. Berling, C.O. of the Polish Evacuation Centre, accompanied by N.K.V.D. officers, bade me farewell.

"When and how will you link up with us?" I asked Berling.

"By train *via* Ashkhabad. Now I have to go to Yanghi Yul to return to the Commission winding up the Polish Army in the U.S.S.R., to give them all the documents relating to this recent evacuation," he said. And so we parted.

The boat left the landing-stage slowly and steamed out of the port. Only then did we realise how much of our equipment was left behind: thousands of bales of English uniforms, blankets and underwear, tinned food, and all the Service and Ordnance Corps supplies which had come from Great Britain to Archangel for the 100,000 men of the Polish Army in the U.S.S.R. All the stores had come, with our convoys, to Krasnovodsk; there we were told it was impossible for us to take them with us; and everything was confiscated by the Red Army.

Our soldiers, watching the horizon and the disappearing nightmare of the Soviet coast, which had stolen from every one of them three years of life in the most inhuman conditions, said: "May they choke themselves with our goods!"

249

If anyone asked me what were my strongest impressions of this country, I would probably say the treacherous deceit which has grown into a system, deprived men of dignity, and ill-treated and degraded them. Everybody and everything had lied, from the very moment I passed the threshold of this *régime*, that Sunday night near Jaroslaw, till the moment when Berling told me his own lie when taking leave of me, knowing quite well that he would be taking over the stores left behind in the port of Krasnovodsk, and would try to build up a new Soviet-Polish Army, despicably usurping Kosciuszko's name as its patron.*

Delightedly we watched the disappearing shores of this country of lies and deceit, knowing that we were now sailing towards the free world, to which we wholeheartedly belonged.

---

* Berling became C.O. of a Division formed by the Soviets from Poles who were left in Russia, and it was called the "Kosciuszko Division", taking its name from the Polish hero who, in 1794, gallantly fought against the Russian invaders for Poland's freedom and independence.

CHAPTER 34

The Path Goes Winding On

FROM the moment our feet touched Persian soil at the sea-port of Pahlari we felt like people who had suddenly emerged from the darkness of the night into the sunlight of the day. Gone was the nightmare, the hell we had left behind; and, as if touched by the magic wand, we had above us a bright, inviting, warm sky. It was no longer just the hope, it was now the certainty of our future that acted like the best cure and quickly strengthened our sick bodies.

It was almost unbelievable how rapidly our people began to regain their health. The sight of the white tents alongside the beautiful beaches was a tonic. So were the wares of the Persian vendors, milling around everywhere—such wares as we had forgotten existed: cakes, breadrolls, candies of all descriptions, rice, roast chickens, and many other things. And being able to swim in the refreshing warm waters of the Caspian Sea was another tonic. We were now certain that we were in a different world—a world that for us seemed almost unreal. And we were ready to continue on our path of destiny.

A convoy of trucks took us across Kurdistan within a few days, on the same road that Darius led his legions to the East. In Kermanshah we passed a rock with an inscription which Darius himself had ordered to commemorate his triumphs of world conquest, thousands of years ago. How strange that our paths of destiny should follow the same route, at such a distance of time.

Before arriving at Kermanshah we passed by the tomb of Esther— the biblical heroine who ordered Haman, arch-persecutor of the Jews, to be beheaded, thereby freeing all the Jews in Persia.

Finally we arrived in the area of Kahnagin and Quizil-Ribad (near Baghdad in Iraq) which became a staging point for re-organisation and training of the newly formed Polish Army in the Middle East.

There we received arms and equipment, and were transformed into an army capable of undertaking military campaigns.

In the summer of 1943 we were moved to Palestine. Manoeuvres, military training in the mountainous terrain in Syria, and manoeuvre exercises at the battalion, brigade, and division levels, became routine activity, interwoven with the piety of pilgrimage to many places in the Holy Land.

In Palestine we were joined with the Carpathian Brigade under Lt.-General Kopanski, already famous from the recent battle of Tobruk. We conducted joint manoeuvres with them; we "conquered" Mount Tabor; we "defended" Nazareth; and we carried out manoeuvres on the shores of the Sea of Galilee and in Jericho Valley, while constantly learning what were to us new military arts— armoured transport operations, replacing cavalry; new tactics; new strategy—a far cry from our 1939 campaign on horseback. Finally we were moved to Egypt.

And now our dreams were to come true at last—we were to be sent to Europe, to enter battlefields on the southern front.

The 2nd Polish Corps under the command of General Anders landed in Italy during the winter of 1943–4 as part of the British Eighth Army, and fought battles at Monte Casino, Ancona, and Bologna.

In the Italian campaign I was a line commander. As Deputy Commander of the 5th Kresowa Infantry Division, I had the honour of leading the troops at Monte Casino during the victorious attack on Phantom Ridge and St. Angelo Hill. When General Sulik, the Division Commander, was injured in an automobile accident and had to be hospitalised for a while, I commanded the Division at the battle of Ancona, and subsequently led the troops through the defensive German line "Gota". Finally, near Bologna I commanded a group named "RUD", comprising two brigades, newly formed in the 2nd Polish Corps, and we were fortunate enough to be the first Allied troops to enter the city of Bologna.

Immediately after the battle of Bologna, in late April 1945, I departed by plane to the western front, to take command of the 1st Armoured Division, taking over from General Marczek, who became Commander of the 1st Polish Corps.

I saw the occupation by my Division of the sea-port Wilhelmshafen —the pride of the German Navy—where we accepted the surrender of the German forces. Later, we were visited by our Acting Commander-in-Chief, General Anders, while the town, on my orders, was decorated with thousands of Polish flags. This, obviously, was no small satisfaction for us, avenging the September of 1939 and the destruction of Warsaw.

The 1st Armoured Division occupied the German territories of Friesland and Oldenburg for two years. It was the first time in history that Polish forces had occupied a German territory. And there we witnessed the full impact of the Gehenna of the one-and-a-half million Poles who had been dragged from their homeland by the Nazis into concentration camps, prisoner-of-war camps, and slave-labour-camps in Germany.

Unfortunately, a deep conflict developed between our Division and the Allied Forces of Occupation Higher Command. As an Allied occupation division, we often received orders to follow policies that were contrary to our Polish interests. The Allied Occupation Command, not being at all willing to organise the lives of the thousands of so-called "displaced persons" from Poland, was deliberately trying to induce them to "voluntary" repatriation. But we understood perfectly well the reasons why these Polish people, forced by the events of the war to be in Germany, were extremely reluctant to return now to Poland, and we felt that it was our duty to defend these people and give them our help and support. So there was a conflict between our military loyalty, as an Allied occupation division, and our patriotic duties and natural obligations to our countrymen.

Thanks to the great discipline of our soldiers and our well established tradition, we were able to work out a solution to this conflict, establishing what almost amounted to a little sovereign state which provided a temporary shelter and allowed many of the Poles in Germany eventually to immigrate to countries in the Western world, rather than return to their homeland under the Soviet occupation. We received great help from many of the British commanders. The German town of Haren, now renamed Maczkow (after the Polish corps commander of that name), with many streets also given Polish names, became, for two years, a centre for Polish schools which provided the education of the Polish youth. For that I should like to express my most sincere thanks to Lt.-General Sir Brian Horrocks.

The most important moment during our stay in Germany was the political crisis when, in July of 1945, the Polish Government in Exile in London became no longer recognised by the Western Powers.

I shall never forget a conversation I had with Field-Marshal Montgomery, Commander of the Army of the Rhein. It took place in his headquarters, at his request, just a few days before the Polish

Government in London lost its recognition. During this conversation, the Corps Commander, Lt.-General Thomas, was present. Field-Marshal Montgomery, in his cool and matter-of-fact way, questioned me on this important issue.

"I believe you must already know that His Majesty's Government intends, in the next few days, to withdraw its recognition of the Polish Government in London and recognise the interim government in Warsaw. I would like to know—what are the reactions of your officers and men likely to be to this development?"

"I am going to be frank," I replied. "There are three things in the minds of the soldiers of my Division. The first is the strong feeling of injustice. When they fought the Germans at Chambois and Falaise, under your command, with great losses, it was certainly not in order to see Poland traded away to Stalin. . . . They feel betrayed."

"But there will be free elections," interrupted the Field-Marshal.

"You should not have any doubts as to the outcome of these elections," I replied.

"I understand," he said; and from the gesture he made I gathered that the Field-Marshal shared my qualms about the "free" elections. "Now," he asked, "What is the second thought?"

"It may, perhaps, sound funny," I continued, "but the soldiers nevertheless still have faith in our Western Allies."

"Why is that?" Montgomery inquired. "Because they look upon their Western Allies as their friends and protectors—if only for the future," I replied. Montgomery remained silent.

"The third thought," I continued, "is their feeling of brotherhood and comradeship with the British soldiers, with whom they have very close ties as the result of the many battles they have fought together, side by side."

"Thank you, General," he said. "But what reaction do you expect from the Division after the formal announcement of the withdrawal of recognition of the Polish Government in London? For you must understand that I am responsible for the behaviour of the occupation forces under my command in Germany."

"With regard to political matters," I replied, "we shall have to await instructions from our Polish Government in London. However, you may rest assured that the Division will conscientiously fulfil all its assigned duties as an occupation force. . . . We will not betray you." "I am satisfied," Montgomery replied; and our conversation came to an end.

As a consequence of this conversation with Field-Marshal Montgomery, when, a few days later, Britain's recognition of our Government was formally withdrawn, I despatched an order (6th July, 1945) to all soldiers of the 1st Division. I mentioned the injustice that had befallen us, the hopes destroyed and the bitter disappointment, but I went on to point to the responsibility of fulfilling our duties as soldiers, and emphasised that our soldiers' conscience was clear, equally regarding our friends and our enemies. We had no reason to be ashamed. I spoke of our constancy in obedience to our Oath and to our Colours, and declared that no injustice against us should break our determination to follow the path of righteousness. I concluded the order with the following words:—

"Our duty as the Polish occupation Division on German soil, under Allied command, will be accomplished with loyalty and honour.

"We will one day return to Poland, but only with arms in our hands —to the Poland whom we have dreamt about during the last five years of the war, Poland truly free and truly independent.

"We will return to wipe the tears of our women and children, and to ensure that law and justice, and not foreign domination, will reign in Poland.

"We will never give up our struggle to free Poland and all the other enslaved nations, and we will live up to our traditional motto, 'For your freedom and ours.' In this struggle we shall not be alone. Polish soldiers! This is our position, our will, and our decision."

I had written a similar order once before, at the end of September 1939 in Warsaw, when I ordered disbandment of my 9th Lancers Regiment. There, too, I talked about faith, honour, and duty. Anything may happen to a soldier; political activities may make his sacrifices fruitless; but these three things cannot be taken away from him.

After the war, my wife escaped from the Soviet-occupied Poland, and joined me in Germany. Later we settled in Britain.

But we are still on the path of destiny, and I am deeply convinced that this path will lead us expatriate Poles back to a free Poland. I dream of finding myself one day again in Jazlowiec.

It is my dearest wish to knock once more at the gate of the convent there, and present an *ex voto* at the altar of the Holy Mother of Jazlowiec. And perhaps the gate will be opened by Sister Lauretta— the nun who loved the loud bangs, and who, after going through all the campaigns with the Polish Army from 1942 to 1945, returned to her religious life once more.